"*A Multitude of All Peoples* rewrites the narrative of early Christian history. Rather than focusing on Christianity's growth in the classical Greek and Roman world, Bantu positions what have traditionally been considered the margins of ancient Christianity (Asia and Africa) at the center. A much-needed addition to the field."

Caroline Schroeder, professor of classics and letters at the University of Oklahoma

"There are very few books we can legitimately call game-changers in the publishing world, that can revolutionize a field of study and transform our ongoing engagement on a topic. Dr. Vince Bantu has written a game-changer of a book that will rework our engagement with church history, global Christianity, missiology, evangelism, and multicultural ministry. Thoroughly researched while comprehensive in scope, all future discussion on the history of the church and its implication for the future of the church must now go through this book."

Soong-Chan Rah, Milton B. Engebretson Professor of Church Growth and Evangelism at North Park Theological Seminary, author of *The Next Evangelicalism* and *Prophetic Lament*

A MULTITUDE OF ALL PEOPLES

Engaging Ancient Christianity's Global Identity

VINCE L. BANTU

Academic
An imprint of InterVarsity Press
Downers Grove, Illinois

InterVarsity Press
P.O. Box 1400, Downers Grove, IL 60515-1426
ivpress.com
email@ivpress.com

InterVarsity Press® is the book-publishing division of InterVarsity Christian Fellowship/USA®, a movement of
students and faculty active on campus at hundreds of universities, colleges, and schools of nursing in the United
States of America, and a member movement of the International Fellowship of Evangelical Students. For
information about local and regional activities, visit intervarsity.org.

All Scripture quotations, unless otherwise indicated, are taken from The Holy Bible, New International Version®,
NIV®. Copyright © 1973, 1978, 1984, 2011 by Biblica, Inc.™ Used by permission of Zondervan. All rights reserved
worldwide. www.zondervan.com. The "NIV" and "New International Version" are trademarks registered in the
United States Patent and Trademark Office by Biblica, Inc.™

Cover design: Cindy Kiple

Interior design: Beth McGill

Cover image: Vince Bantu

ISBN 978-0-8308-5107-2 (print)
ISBN 978-0-8308-2810-4 (digital)

Printed in the United States of America ∞

InterVarsity Press is committed to ecological stewardship and to the conservation of natural resources in all our
operations. This book was printed using sustainably sourced paper.

Library of Congress Cataloging-in-Publication Data

Names: Bantu, Vince L., 1982- author.
Title: A multitude of all peoples : engaging ancient Christianity's global identity / Vince L. Bantu.
Description: Downers Grove, Illinois : InterVarsity Academic, an imprint of InterVarsity Press, 2020. |
    Series: Missiological engagements series | Includes bibliographical references and index.
Identifiers: LCCN 2019052368 (print) | LCCN 2019052369 (ebook) | ISBN 9780830851072 (paperback) | ISBN
    9780830828104 (ebook)
Subjects: LCSH: Globalization—Religious aspects—Christianity. | Church history—Primitive and early church,
    ca. 30-600.
Classification: LCC BR115.G59 B36 2020 (print) | LCC BR115.G59 (ebook) | DDC 270.1—dc23
LC record available at https://lccn.loc.gov/2019052368
LC ebook record available at https://lccn.loc.gov/2019052369

P   25   24   23   22   21   20   19   18   17   16   15   14   13   12   11   10   9   8   7
Y   40   39   38   37   36   35   34   33   32   31   30   29   28   27   26   25   24   23   22   21

For my mami chula

Contents

Acknowledgments

There have been so many community members the Lord has placed in my life without whom this work would not have been completed. The editorial team at InterVarsity Press has been massively helpful throughout this process—Jon Boyd, Rebecca Carhart, Scott Sunquist, and Amos Yong, I thank you for your guidance and patience in the publication of this book. Several colleagues provided specialized feedback for which I am profoundly grateful—Janet Timbie, Artur Obłuski, Adam Ployd, Aaron Butts, Scott F. Johnson, Philip Forness, Nathan Gibson, Robert Hoyland, Stephen Rapp, Jack Tannous, Monica Blanchard, Chiara Barbati, Blake Hartung, Jeffrey Wickes, and Li Tang, thank you for the invaluable insight you provided; all remaining errors are mine.

There have been several spiritual mothers and fathers that have taught me invaluable lessons about how to follow Jesus the way he made me—Soong-Chan Rah, Dante Upshaw, Brian Howell, Terry LeBlanc, Bil and Paulea Mooney-McCoy, Allen Callahan, Dennis Edwards, and Alvin Padilla, thank you for helping me to understand more of the Creator's love for his people. My family is the foundation that supports all that I am and do—I thank my mother for raising me in the light of the gospel; I thank my daughters, Taína and Naniki, for the joy that they inspire; I thank my wife, Diana, for her love, support, and partnership. This book is dedicated to you.

Finally, I give all thanks, praise, honor, and glory to my Lord and Savior Jesus Christ, and I pray this work is an act of worship pleasing to you.

Abbreviations

AAE	*Arabian Archaeology and Epigraphy*
AHPA	*Arabic History of the Patriarchs of Alexandria*
BSOAS	*Bulletin of the School of Oriental and African Studies*
CCDATJ	*Christian Community Development Association Theological Journal*
CSCO	Corpus Scriptorum Christianorum Orientalium
DOP	*Dumbarton Oaks Papers*
JA	*Journal Asiatique*
JAOS	*Journal of the American Oriental Society*
JCSSS	*Journal of the Canadian Society for Syriac Studies*
JECS	*Journal of Early Christian Studies*
JRA	*Journal of Religion in Africa*
JSP	*Journal for the Study of the Pseudepigrapha*
JSS	*Journal of Semitic Studies*
JTS	*Journal of Theological Studies*
ME	*Medieval Encounters*
NPNF	A Select Library of the Nicene and Post-Nicene Fathers of the Church. Edited by Phillip Schaff et al. 14 vols. Buffalo, NY: Christian Literature, 1819–1893.
OC	*Oriens Christianus*
PG	Patrologia cursus completus. Series Graeca. Edited by J. P. Migne. 166 vols. Paris: Migne, 1857–1886.
PO	Patrologia Orientalis. Edited by René Graffin et al. 41 vols. Paris, 1894–1984.
ROC	*Revue de l'Orient Chrétien*
STAC	Studien und Texte zu Antike und Christentum
StPatr	*Studia Patristica*

Introduction

The Global Religion

Christianity is and always has been a global religion. For this reason, it is important never to think of Christianity as *becoming* global.

Following the valuable work of prominent missiologists, it has become commonplace among twenty-first-century Christians to highlight the significant demographic shifts in the global church. The fact that the majority of Christians now live in the Global South has led many to speak of the "coming of global Christianity."[1] Andrew Walls has challenged the contemporary church to respond to what he calls the "Ephesian moment":

> The Ephesian moment—the social coming together of people of two cultures to experience Christ—was quite brief. . . . But in our own day the Ephesian moment has come again, and come in a richer mode than has ever happened since the first century. Developments over several centuries, reaching a climax in the twentieth, mean that we no longer have two, but innumerable, major cultures in the church.[2]

Contemporary missiologists have drawn much-needed attention to the demographic shifts that have taken place in the twentieth and twenty-first centuries and have given helpful challenges to the "Western, white captivity of the church."[3] However, in drawing attention to such developments, there has been an implication that global diversity is exclusively a twentieth-century innovation of the Christian movement. Indeed, Walls's statement

---

[1]The subtitle of Philip Jenkins's seminal work *The Next Christendom: The Coming of Global Christianity* (New York: Oxford University Press, 2002).

[2]Andrew Walls, *The Cross-Cultural Process in Christian History* (Maryknoll, NY: Orbis, 2002), 77.

[3]Soong-Chan Rah, *The Next Evangelicalism: Freeing the Church from Western Cultural Captivity* (Downers Grove, IL: InterVarsity Press, 2009), 22.

presents Christian diversity as a phenomenon that disappeared after the
early church and has only become manifest again in the "Ephesian moment"
of the twentieth century. Too many people, both Christian and non-
Christian, still perceive Christianity as the white man's religion.

Contemporary missiology has often advanced the church's cultural self-
understanding by highlighting the unprecedented recorded numbers of
Christians in Africa, Asia, and Latin America. The "typical" Christian of
the twenty-first century is not a white man but an African woman. However,
the modern global church has often been presented as emerging from centuries of a Western majority church.[4] Lamin Sanneh provides another example of this westernized Christian narrative: "In time, Christianity expanded from Europe into Asia and Africa, among other places, and was
able to break out of its Western cultural confinement by repeating the
process by which the church's missionary center shifted from Jerusalem to
Antioch and beyond."[5] The dominant concept of Christian history is now
that Christianity went from its multicultural beginnings in first-century
Palestine across a Western trajectory of European and North American
captivity to only now reflect global diversity.[6] It is this common misconception that requires further conversation. Many contemporary missiologists and church historians would have us believe that Christianity came
into Africa and Asia from Europe when the reality is quite the opposite in
several significant respects. Christianity is not *becoming* a global religion;
it has always been a global religion.

---

[4]Scott Sunquist highlights the early history of African and Asian Christianity in *The Unexpected
Christian Century: The Reversal and Transformation of Global Christianity, 1900–2000* (Grand
Rapids: Baker Academic, 2015), 2.

[5]Lamin Sanneh, *Translating the Message: The Missionary Impact on Culture*, 2nd ed. (Maryknoll,
NY: Orbis, 2009), 94. Sanneh displays greater awareness of early Christianity outside of the
Greco-Latin Roman world in *Disciples of All Nations: Pillars of World Christianity* (New York:
Oxford University Press, 2008). Yet his historiography still places the Greek and Latin patristic
sources at the center of Christian mission with Asia and Africa as recipients of evangelization
(32). As the present project will outline, divergent strands of Christianity developed independently of Hellenistic Christian influence.

[6]This perception is cultivated primarily in Christian church history textbooks that tell the story
of Christianity developing in tandem with the Western world. A helpful corrective to this is Dale
T. Irvin and Scott W. Sunquist, *History of the World Christian Movement*, 2 vols. (Maryknoll, NY:
Orbis, 2007, 2012). While these volumes are among the best and most inclusive of world Christian history, the accompanying reader leaves one in want of a greater inclusion of non-Greek and
Latin texts from early and medieval Christianity; see John Coakley and Andrea Sterk, *Readings
in World Christian History*, vol. 1: *Earliest Christianity to 1453* (Maryknoll, NY: Orbis, 2004).

Egypt was home to many of the earliest biblical manuscripts and had an organized ecclesiastical hierarchy no later than the late second century.[7] Ethiopia became a predominately Christian nation in the fourth century and, along with Nubia, functioned under the ecclesiastical hierarchy of Egypt.[8] Syriac-speaking Christian merchants brought Christianity along the Silk Road to the Persian Empire in the early third century, to Central Asia in the mid-fourth century, and as far east as China in the mid-sixth century.[9] While it is possible that the apostle Thomas brought the gospel to India in the first century, Syriac-speaking Christians reported missionary activity to India no later than the late third century.[10] These traditions spread rapidly across the continents of Africa and Asia and took on indigenous forms at a time when the majority of Northern and Western Europe practiced pagan religion. Despite the persisting association of the Christian faith with Western culture/whiteness, Christianity has always been a global religion that spread from Jerusalem in every direction.

When I served as a pastor in the Anacostia neighborhood of southeast Washington, DC, I had the privilege of organizing an interfaith dialogue with African-American Christians and Muslims. African-American leaders in the neighborhood led a vibrant discussion from Protestant, Catholic, Sunni, and Nation of Islam backgrounds. One of the most interesting themes of the discussion was that many of the Muslims expressed that they knew more about the Christian faith than many Christians seem to know about Islam. They explained that their familiarity with Christianity was due to the fact that either they or their parents were themselves former Christians. Participants continued to share that they found Islam to be a much more empowering response to the racism and oppression that confronts African Americans in the United States. Christianity, however, represented the religion of the white oppressors and did not offer an accessible medium of expression for the black experience. I walked away from this event burdened that many people in the African-American community have walked away from Christianity because

---

[7]Stephen J. Davis, *The Early Coptic Papacy: The Egyptian Church and Its Leadership in Late Antiquity* (Cairo: American University in Cairo Press, 2004), 19.

[8]S. Kaplan, "Ezana's Conversion Reconsidered," *JRA* 13 (1982): 101.

[9]Wilhelm Baum and Dietmar W. Winkler, *The Church of the East: A Concise History* (New York: Routledge, 2003), 47.

[10]A. Mathias Mundadan, *History of Christianity in India*, vol. 1: *From the Beginning up to the Middle of the Sixteenth Century (up to 1542)* (Bangalore: Theological Publications in India, 1984), 19.

it is seen as a Eurocentric, oppressive religion.[11] This is a critique of the church that must be taken seriously and should not be dismissed.

It is understandable that some African Americans perceive Christianity as an oppressive religion given the role Christianity has played in white hegemony in United States history. In the diverse milieu of contemporary Christianity, this Eurocentric perception of Christianity is still validated in the white, Western packaging in which Christianity functions. From white depictions of biblical characters in church art to "most influential Christian leaders" lists full of white men, it is not without reason that Christianity is still perceived as the white man's religion.[12]

African-American Muslims are not the only people with this perception. Missiologist Randy Woodley comments on the effects of Western, white cultural captivity on the Native American Christian community:

> For Native Americans to become Christians has often required us to divest ourselves of most of our cultural distinctives, including language, hairstyle, values and devotional practices. It is assumed that there is nothing in Native American culture worth redeeming. This evangelistic philosophy, brought over to the New World from Europe, made the broad assumption that European culture was "Christian" and that Indians needed to conform to Euro-American culture in order for God to accept them.[13]

The work of Woodley and others associated with the North American Institute for Indigenous Theological Studies (NAIITS) and the World Christian Gathering of Indigenous People represent the necessary step for non-white Christians to disentangle the Gospel from its Eurocentric entrapments. Another example is Chan Kei Thong's book *Faith of Our Fathers*, which demonstrates the *preparatio evangelica* in ancient Chinese culture and the compatibility of Chinese philosophy and indigenous religious practice with the gospel.[14]

---

[11]This common critique is addressed through a short introduction to early African (Egyptian, Ethiopian) Christianity in Glenn Usry and Craig S. Keener, *Black Man's Religion: Can Christianity Be Afrocentric?* (Downers Grove, IL: InterVarsity Press, 1996), 21.

[12]See Rah's discussion of a front-page article in *Time* magazine on the "Top 25 Most Influential Evangelicals," with twenty-three of them being white males; Rah, *Next Evangelicalism*, xix.

[13]Randy Woodley, *Living in Color: Embracing God's Passion for Ethnic Diversity* (Downers Grove, IL: InterVarsity Press, 2004), 46.

[14]Chan Kei Thong, *Faith of Our Fathers: God in Ancient China* (Shanghai: China Publishing Group, 2006). While Thong's book is a helpful step in the contextualization of Chinese Christianity, there is a surprising lack of discussion of the medieval presence of the Church of the East in China.

Such laudable efforts at contextualization, however, do not represent the majority of communities of color. Movements for contextualization or enculturation among Christians of color have been met with resistance not only by white Christians but by other Christians of color! Contemporary movements advocating for "counter contextualization" are often motivated by the fear of the loss of political influence and frequently attract many Christian leaders of color equally committed to a vision of Christianity in the service of white supremacy. A Native American Christian community incorporating sweat lodges into its communal worship will likely receive greater backlash from fellow Native American Christians than anyone else.[15] Likewise, Christian hip-hop worship services are criticized most vehemently from African-American church leaders.[16]

Another extreme position that can occur within dominant and subdominant communities alike is the tendency to think of one cultural expression of Christianity as superior to all others: "Although American cultural values have dominated Christian faith, there are growing pockets of Christians who have been less influenced by American cultural values and more rooted in other cultural values. However, both groups believe that they are the gold standard and are convinced that their cultural perspective on faith should be adopted by the universal church."[17] Many ethnic-specific Christian communities attempt to monopolize culturally mediated expressions of Christianity. As Andrew Walls puts it: "All churches are culture churches— including our own."[18] Culture has been commonly understood as the "system of shared beliefs, values, customs, behaviors, and artifacts that the members of society use to cope with their world and with one another, and that are transmitted from generation to generation through learning."[19] The interrelated system of interpretation of symbols and meaning is a fundamental mode of human existence and shapes religious life and thought. This is a

[15]Richard Twiss, *Rescuing the Gospel from the Cowboys: A Native American Expression of the Jesus Way* (Downers Grove, IL: InterVarsity Press, 2015), 112.

[16]Efrem Smith and Phil Jackson, *The Hip-Hop Church: Connecting with the Movement Shaping Our Culture* (Downers Grove, IL: InterVarsity Press, 2005), 9.

[17]Christena Cleveland, *Disunity in Christ: Uncovering the Hidden Forces that Keep Us Apart* (Downers Grove, IL: InterVarsity Press, 2013), 145.

[18]Andrew F. Walls, *The Missionary Movement in Christian History: Studies in the Transmission of Faith* (Maryknoll, NY: Orbis, 2002), 8.

[19]Daniel G. Bates and Fred Plog, *Cultural Anthropology* (New York: McGraw-Hill, 1990), 7.

concept that is being accepted increasingly in the twenty-first-century church: every Christian exists within a cultural matrix that governs our understanding of the gospel and relativizes our expression of the Christian faith. It is time to push the conversation further.

The concern that motivates this book is fundamentally missiological. That is to say, the primary concern of this investigation is rooted in the dilemma of people rejecting Christianity because of the perception that it is a Western/white religion and therefore not appropriate for non-Western/white people. The Western/white captivity of the church is a profound stumbling block to the reception of the gospel. In the Western world, the growth of secularism, agnosticism, and atheism is due in large part to historical atrocities committed by Western Christians. In the non-Western world, non-Christians perceive Christianity as a white, Western, or American religion while seeing the gospel as antithetical to their cultural identity. Therefore, fellow members of a non-Western people group who convert to Christianity are often seen as becoming white, Western, or American.

The church has two interrelated and indispensable tasks going forward: (1) the deconstruction of the Western, white cultural captivity of the Christian tradition and (2) the elevation of non-Western expressions of Christianity. Inherent in these tasks is the rejection of the incomplete history that has been transmitted in Western Christian context as well as a post-colonial, "bottom-up" view of Christian tradition. The goal here is neither the cultural idolatry of one group nor a prescription for abhorrence of another. Rather, this shift in focus is motivated by the continued realization of the kingdom of God through embracing the image of Christ among every tribe, tongue, and nation.

The following chapters will investigate the historical roots of the Western cultural captivity of the church in the patristic period and the concurrent development of early non-Western expressions of Christianity. Many people who reject Christianity as a Western/white religion often do so because of a particular historical understanding of Christianity's emerging from the Western/white world. Since incomplete history has contributed to a missiological dilemma, this attempt at responding to such a dilemma will be through a historical study. Chapter one will present the roots of Westernized Christianity focusing on the Christianization of the Roman Empire, the christological schism between the church of Europe and the church of Africa and Asia, and the formation of Islamic and European Christian empires. Chapter two will shift to an investigation of early Christianity in non-Western contexts beginning with Africa—specifically North Africa and the Nile Valley kingdoms of Egypt, Nubia, and Ethiopia. Chapter three will focus on early Christianity in the Middle East. Beginning with Antioch and Palestine, special attention will be given to the Syriac-speaking Christian communities of Syria, Lebanon, and Arabia, as well as early Caucasian Christianity in Armenia and Georgia. Chapter four will continue to trace the development of Syriac-speaking Christianity as it spread throughout the Asian continent from Persia to various regions in India, Central Asia, and China. In this section, and throughout the book, I will be using modern geographical terminology (e.g., Africa, Asia, the Middle East, Europe, Western) to refer to regions that did not use these terms in Late Antiquity. To avoid an anachronistic understanding of history, it is important to acknowledge that the ancient world did not employ the same categories that we do.[20] However, it is still useful to use these modern terms as they have greater currency for a contemporary audience.

God has been at work among every nation since the beginning. From the moment God called Abram to be the progenitor of God's chosen people, the vision for this plan was intrinsically global: "All peoples on earth will be blessed through you" (Gen 12:3). Through the Lord Jesus Christ, the Holy Spirit has continued to draw people from every nation into the body of Christ. Along the way, Christianity has come to be perceived as the historical and cultural possession of a particular geocultural region of the world. It is therefore necessary to explore how this dynamic came about.

---

[20]Ancient Egyptians and Ethiopians, for example, would not have considered themselves "Africans." Egyptians considered themselves Egyptians first and then Roman citizens, while the nation now known as Ethiopia was called "Axum" in Late Antiquity and shared more cultural and social identity with people in southern Arabia than most of what was then known as "Africa," which was a small Roman province along the Mediterranean coast in modern Libya, Tunisia, and Algeria.

The Roots of Western
Christian Identity Politics

Beginning with the pouring out of the Holy Spirit at Pentecost in Acts 2, the Christian movement spread in every direction out of Jerusalem during the formative years of the movement. As the gospel spread, it took on local cultural expression, and by the second century there existed variegated forms of Christian theology and worship across the Roman and Persian empires. However, in time the Christian faith became associated with the Roman world. In medieval times, the formation of European nations and the very concept of "the West" was inextricably bound with the form of Christianity that was a product of and the impetus for the formation of the Western world. Before gaining an understanding of the breadth of early Christian expression in the non-Western world, it is necessary to understand the roots of Western Christian identity politics. If the church has been global from the beginning, then why have so many people seen Christianity as a Western, white religion? Rather than offering an exhaustive historical treatment of Western Christianity, this chapter will explore the roots of an idea: the perception of Christianity as a product of the Western world, or the Western cultural captivity of the church.

Christianity was deeply embedded in the Greco-Roman world from the beginning. While the earliest Christians were Palestinian Jews whose first language was Aramaic, the New Testament was written in Greek, the dominant language in the Eastern Roman Empire. The apostle Paul and other New Testament writers took great efforts to communicate the Christian message in terms and concepts that were accessible to Greek-speaking Romans outside the Jewish community. While Hellenistic Christianity existed from the beginning of the church, Christianity was not seen as a

Hellenistic/Roman religion until the fourth century. This was due in large part to the religious and political reforms of the emperor Constantine as well as his patronage in the Christian community by figures such as Eusebius of Caesarea.

LIFE OF CONSTANTINE

Constantine was born in 272 CE in Naissus (in modern Serbia) to the Greek-speaking Helena and the Latin-speaking Flavius Constantius who would become caesar (deputy emperor) of the Western Empire in 293. Diocletian divided the Roman Empire again to include two caesars who would be subordinate to their corresponding augustus (senior emperor), a system known as the tetrarchy ("four rulers"). After being educated and rising through the ranks of Diocletian's army, Constantine was promoted by his father Caesar Constantius to become augustus of the Western Empire, which was opposed by a rival caesar, Maxentius, who waged war against Constantine in 311 for control of the entire empire.

The forces of Maxentius were ultimately defeated by those of Constantine at the famous Battle of the Milvian Bridge. The church historian Eusebius of Caesarea wrote one of the most famous biographies of Constantine in which he describes Constantine's celestial vision that was allegedly the cause of his victory: "About the time of the midday sun, a cross-shaped trophy formed from light, and a text attached to it which said, "By this conquer."[1] The embellished tone of Eusebius comes forth clearly throughout his *Life of Constantine*, which has been commonly understood to fit the literary genre of hagiography, purposed to establish Constantine as God's chosen servant and guardian of the church, and thus less historically reliable.[2] Eusebius claims that Constantine then crafted a cross out of precious jewels and received instruction in the Scriptures by Christian leaders, whom he then appointed as his high counselors.[3] Maxentius, however, is depicted as a bloodthirsty tyrant who murdered countless Roman citizens and practiced sorcery:

---

[1]Eusebius of Caesarea, *Life of Constantine*, ed. and trans. Averil Cameron and Stuart G. Hall (Oxford: Clarendon, 1999), 1.28.

[2]Cameron and Hall make the argument for the *Life* as hagiographical literature in the introduction to their edition and translation (31).

[3]Eusebius, *Life of Constantine* 1.32.

Constantine meanwhile was moved to pity by all these things, and began making every armed preparation against the tyranny. So taking as his patron God who is over all, and invoking his Christ as savior and succor, and having set the victorious trophy the truly salutary sign, at the head of his escorting soldiers and guards, he led them in full force, claiming for the Romans their ancestral liberties.[4]

Constantine's forces defeated those of Maxentius at the Milvian Bridge over the Tiber River in Rome, after which Constantine ordered the decapitated head of Maxentius paraded through the city streets.[5] Constantine rededicated the buildings of Maxentius in his own name and initiated propaganda presenting him as the liberator of the tyrannical Maxentius. Eusebius's *Life of Constantine* is one of the best examples of such propaganda. In 313 Constantine and his Eastern coemperor Licinius issued the Edict of Milan ordering the end of persecution of Christians and the return of confiscated property. However, Licinius began persecuting Christians in fear that they would be more loyal to Constantine. The two caesars waged a war that was seen in religious terms—with Constantine as the Christian protector and Licinius as the Christian persecutor:

Licinius, who had previously respected the Christians, changed his opinion, and ill-treated many of the priests who lived under his government; he also persecuted a multitude of other persons, but especially the soldiers. He was deeply incensed against the Christians on account of his disagreement with Constantine, and thought to wound him by their sufferings for religion, and besides, he suspected that the churches were praying and zealous that Constantine alone should enjoy the sovereign rule.[6]

After a series of defeats in 324, Licinius surrendered to Constantine, who initially promised to spare Licinius's life. However, Constantine ordered Licinius to be executed a year later on suspicion of conspiracy. Constantine was now the sole emperor and united the West and East into one empire. In 330 Constantine established the city of Byzantium (modern Istanbul) as the center of the Roman Empire in the Greek-speaking East and named it Constantinople in his honor. Constantine enacted several administrative reforms and expanded the empire following the conquest of Germanic tribes

---

[4]Eusebius, *Life of Constantine* 1.37.
[5]Timothy D. Barnes, *Eusebius and Constantine* (Cambridge, MA: Harvard University Press, 1981), 44.
[6]Sozomen, *Ecclesiastical History*, ed. Chester D. Hartranft, NPNF 1:7.

to the north. While preparing for a military campaign against the Sassanian Persian Empire in 337, Constantine became fatally ill. Preparing for death, Constantine began training as a catechumen and set out for Constantinople to be baptized. Constantine made it as far as Nicomedia where he was baptized by the bishop Eusebius of Nicomedia, who followed the teachings of Arius.[7] Constantine died shortly thereafter and was buried in Constantinople at the Church of the Holy Apostles.

Constantine's Christian Faith

The Edict of Milan (313) was immediately preceded by the Edict of Toleration by the Eastern emperor Galerius in 311. Galerius's edict ordered the cessation of Christian persecution and the right of Christians to privately worship:

> We had earlier sought to set everything right in accordance with the ancient law and public discipline of the Romans and to ensure that the Christians too, who had abandoned the way of life of their ancestors, should return to a sound frame of mind; for in some way such self-will had come upon these same Christians, such folly had taken hold of them, that they no longer followed those usages of the ancients which their own ancestors perhaps had first instituted, but, simply following their own judgement and pleasure, they were making up for themselves the laws which they were to observe and were gathering various groups of people together in different places. When finally our order was published that they should betake themselves to the practices of the ancients, many were subjected to danger, many too were struck down. Very many, however, persisted in their determination and we saw that these same people were neither offering worship and due religious observance to the gods nor practicing the worship of the god of the Christians. Bearing in mind therefore our own most gentle clemency and our perpetual habit of showing indulgent pardon to all men, we have taken the view that in the case of these people too we should extend our speediest indulgence, so that once more they may be Christians and put together their meeting-places, provided they do nothing to disturb good order.[8]

---

[7] Arius was a Libyan priest in Alexandria who taught that Jesus was a created being and did not accept the Nicene definition of Jesus being of "same essence" (*homoousios*) as the Father. See Rowan Williams, *Arius: Heresy & Tradition* (Grand Rapids: Eerdmans, 2001), 68; Philip Rousseau, "Baptism," in *Late Antiquity: A Guide to the Post Classical World*, ed. G. W. Bowersock, Peter Brown, and Oleg Grabar (Cambridge, MA: Belknap, 1999).

[8] Lactantius, *De Mortibus Persecutorum*, ed. J. L. Creed (Oxford: Clarendon, 1984), 34.

While the Edict of Galerius allowed Roman Christians to worship privately, it did not return the property that had been confiscated during the Great Persecution under Diocletian. The Edict of Milan issued by Constantine and Licinius took this extra step:

> We wish those things that belong justly to others, should not only remain unmolested, but should also when necessary be restored, most esteemed Anulius. Whence it is our will, that when thou shalt receive this epistle, if any of those things belonging to the catholic church of the Christians in the several cities or other places, are now possessed either by the decurions, or any others, these thou shalt cause immediately to be restored to their churches. Since we have previously determined, that whatsoever, these same churches before possessed, shall be restored to their right.[9]

Whether Constantine's benevolence toward the Christians was the result of an authentic conversion to the Christian faith remains a prominent question in the history of early Christianity. Constantine's mother Helena is reported by Eusebius to have traveled to Palestine and erected various churches throughout Palestine, such as Church of the Nativity in Bethlehem, Saint Catherine's Monastery in Sinai, and the Church of the Holy Sepulchre.[10] In various ways, Constantine gives clear gestures of a sincere Christian conversion and provides support for his Christian constituency. Following his victory over Maxentius, Constantine did not offer the customary celebratory offering to the gods. Rather, he clearly attributes his military victories to the Christian God as well as denouncing pagan deities.[11] However, in true Roman tradition, Constantine erected a triumphal arch that still stands today outside the Colosseum—the Arch of Constantine—which contains no Christian symbolism or reference.[12]

---

[9]Eusebius of Caesarea, *Ecclesiastical History*, ed. C. F. Cruse (Grand Rapids: Hendrickson, 1998), 10.5.16.

[10]Eusebius, *Life of Constantine* 3.43. While the various building projects were jointly associated with Constantine and Helena, it appears that her direct involvement was centered in Bethlehem while evidence is lacking for her participation with the Jerusalem projects. E. D. Hunt, *Holy Land Pilgrimage in the Later Roman Empire, AD 312–460* (Oxford: Clarendon, 1982), 37.

[11]Eusebius, *Life of Constantine* 4.10.

[12]For a contemporary theological debate reflecting on Constantine's faith in the context of a conversation on passivism, Christianity, and empire, see Peter J. Leithart, *Defending Constantine: The Twilight of an Empire and the Dawn of Christendom* (Downers Grove, IL: IVP Academic, 2010); see also the edited volume in response to Leithart in John D. Roth, *Constantine Revisited: Leithart, Yoder, and the Constantinian Debate* (Eugene, OR: Wipf & Stock, 2013).

While a detailed treatment of the Constantinian debate is beyond the scope of the present project, an understanding of the origins of westernized Christianity necessitates some consideration of the political and cultural implications of Constantine's conversion. Constantine's vision of the Christian faith was to a significant degree an innovation. Peter Brown demonstrates the distinctly "Roman" nature of Constantine's appropriation of the Christian tradition as a new form of *religio*.[13] Brown explains the Roman concept of *religio* as the system of worship appropriate for each god, passed down through familial and communal identities, for the purpose of maintaining civilized life and promoting Roman identity. Constantine saw in Christianity the opportunity to unite his empire under a single *religio*, in contrast to the plurality of gods common to Roman cosmology.[14] This new process of religious consolidation is exemplified in Constantine's gathering the Christian bishops of his empire at the first ecumenical council at Nicaea in 325. Constantine's primary goal at these proceedings was imperial unity. The date of Easter, previously celebrated at different times, was universally agreed on. One of the central theological questions addressed at Nicaea was the divinity of Jesus. A bishop from Alexandria named Arius was associated with the belief that there was a time when God the Son did not exist.[15]

In contrast to Arius's teaching that the Son is of a "similar substance" (*homoiousias*) as the Father, the Nicene and later the Apostles' Creed declared that Jesus eternally exists with God the Father and the Holy Spirit.[16] The Nicene Creed explicitly pronounced anathemas, or condemnations, on anyone who espoused the teachings of Arius and demanded that all profess the same substance (*homoousias*) that exists between the three persons of

---

[13]Peter Brown, *The Rise of Western Christendom: Triumph and Diversity, AD 200–1000*, 10th ed. (Malden, MA: Wiley-Blackwell, 2013), 61. Elizabeth DePalma Digeser argues that while Constantine ultimately makes his preference for Christianity clear, he does not advocate the use of force to compel others to accept the Christian message and envisages a Roman society based on religious tolerance, not exclusively Christian practice. *The Making of a Christian Empire: Lactantius & Rome* (Ithaca, NY: Cornell University Press, 2000), 126.

[14]Lactantius is more critical of traditional Roman *religio* but offers similar praise of Constantine as the first truly good emperor and as the protector of true Christian *religio*. *Divine Institutes*, ed. Anthony Bowen and Peter Garnsey (Liverpool: Liverpool University Press, 2003), 50.

[15]Arius, *Arius' Letter to Alexander of Alexandria*, in *The Trinitarian Controversy*, ed. William G. Rusch (Philadelphia: Fortress, 1980), 31.

[16]This latter point would be reaffirmed and clarified at the second ecumenical council at Constantinople in 381.

the Trinity. Through this gathering of his imperial subjects, Constantine was able to demand and enforce a prescription for Christian doctrine that would serve to promote Roman unity. Eusebius promotes this Roman vision of Christianity as he frequently deploys an example taken from Roman culture: that of the imperial laureled image as the exemplar of the emperor it depicts representing the Son and the Father, a curiously un-Nicene way of describing the role of the Son.[17] Constantine's adoption of the gospel message came at a time when Christianity had an increasingly universal nature. While the church of the first two centuries maintained a generally low profile, the empire-wide persecution that characterized the later third century was in response to the increasing presence of an organized ecclesiastical hierarchy. Indeed, Constantine was depicted not only as a statesman but a bishop:

> Hence it is not surprising that on one occasion, when entertaining bishops to dinner, he let slip the remark that he was perhaps himself a bishop too, using some such words as these in our hearing: "You are bishops of those within the Church, but I am perhaps a bishop appointed by God over those outside." In accordance with this saying, he exercised a bishop's supervision over all his subjects, and pressed them all, as far as lay in his power, to lead the godly life.[18]

Roman persecution of Christians, most notably the Great Persecution under Diocletian, specifically targeted the emergent Christian leaders in an attempt to reassert Roman civil and religious authority.[19] The Christian assertion of a sacred text that holds greater authority than Roman *religio* was met, not surprisingly, with resistance motivated by the desire to retain traditional Roman identity. Rather than continue the persecutions that were giving rise to increasing social unrest, Constantine adopted the message of Christian salvation as the mechanism to unite his empire with himself as "bishop." One of the most appealing facets of Christianity was its universal appeal. Whereas Roman *religio* was so often class or gender specific, Christianity preached a universal message of redemption that had thoroughly

---

[17]Barnes, *Eusebius and Constantine*, 265n60.
[18]Eusebius, *Life of Constantine* 4.24.
[19]Brown, *Western Christendom*, 62.

penetrated both gentry and aristocracy.[20] Christianity's uniquely diverse constituency afforded Constantine a mechanism with which to unite the empire under a new *religio*. Roman Christian leaders adopted and expanded on the role of Christianity as a vehicle for imperial order. Lactantius does so in a manner that perceives of Christianity principally as a mechanism for establishing the Roman concept of civilized order:

> How blessed and how golden the state of humanity would be if all the world were civilized, pious, peaceful, innocent, self-controlled, fair and faithful! There would be no need for so many different laws for the government of mankind, because the one law of God would be enough for the accomplishment of innocence, nor would there be need for prisons and warders' swords, nor for the threat of punishment, since the wholesomeness of heavenly commandment would be working in human hearts, forming them freely to the practice of justice. As it is, people are bad from ignorance of what is right and good. That is what Cicero saw.[21]

A CHRISTIAN STATE

Roman Christians understood the dramatic shift from the time of Diocletian to Constantine as emerging from intense darkness into a marvelous new light. Christians now felt empowered to revisit the same violence and persecution against the pagans with whom they been spiritually embattled for centuries.[22] An example of this was a statue commemorating the victory of Octavian over Antony and Cleopatra called the Altar of Victory. Christians and pagans debated the removal of this statue from the Roman Senate House throughout the fourth century until it was finally taken away by the Christian emperor Theodosius I.[23]

Tensions between Christians and pagans in the fifth century turned increasingly violent. Significant examples of this include a mob of Christians

---

[20]Brown, *Western Christendom*, 64.

[21]Lactantius, *Divine Institutes* 5.8.8-10.

[22]Brown, *Western Christendom*, 73.

[23]Bertran Lançon, *Rome in Late Antiquity: Everyday life and Urban Change, AD 312–609* (New York: Routledge, 2000), 93. The rejection of the Altar of Victory was but one of various "Theodosian decrees" that suppressed paganism including closing temples, forbidding pagan worship, and destroying sacred images. Ramsay MacMullen, *Christianizing the Roman Empire AD 100–400* (New Haven, CT: Yale University Press, 1984), 90.

led by a monastic leader who attacked pagans and students of Hellenistic philosophy in Alexandria.[24] One of the most famous incidents of Christian violence against pagans was the murder of the Neoplatonist philosopher Hypatia in Alexandria in 415. This murder was initially criticized by Christian sources but was later seen as a "blameless" act on the part of Christians.[25] Indeed, the Egyptian monastic figure Shenoute of Atripe represents this attitude of Christian "holy violence" in defense of his own actions of leading monks in a raid and destruction of the pagan idols in the private home of a local pagan: "For in this way, there is no robbery for those who possess Christ truly, as you have said about me because I peacefully took your gods and made your disgrace and shame bound to the doorposts of your house."[26] Shenoute lived in a Christian empire that found theological justification for the use of violence in combatting sin and idolatry.[27] Indeed, on another occasion Shenoute even attributes his murdering of a monk during physical punishment as the will of God.[28] The sentiment that God uses Christian agents to carry out violent acts for divine purposes is one that is strongly rooted in the administration of Constantine and, more importantly, in the Christians who lauded his efforts.[29]

---

[24]For a summary and analysis of this event, see Edward J. Watts, *Riot in Alexandria: Tradition and Group Dynamics in Late Antique Pagan and Christian Communities* (Berkeley: University of California Press, 2010).

[25]Socrates Scholasticus, *Ecclesiastical History*, ed. A. C. Zenos, NPNF 7:15; John of Nikiû, *Chronicle*, ed. R. H. Charles (London: Williams & Norgate, 1916), 84.87-103.

[26]Johannes Leipoldt, in *Sinuthii Archimandritae: Vita et Opera Omnia* (Louvain: Secretariat du SCO, 1955), 3:79. See also Stephen Emmel, *Shenoute's Literary Corpus* (Louvain: Secretariat du SCO, 2004), 621. For an alternative translation in English see John W. B. Barns, "Shenoute as a Historical Source," *Actes du Xe congrés international de papyrologues: Varsovie-Cracovie 3-9 septembre 1961*, ed. Jósef Wolski (Wroclaw, Warsaw, and Krakow: Zaklad narodowy Imienia Ossolinskich Wydawnictwo Polskief Akademii Nauk, 1964), 156.

[27]Michael Gaddis, *There is No Crime for Those Who Have Christ: Religious Violence in the Christian Roman Empire* (Berkeley: University of California Press, 2005), 1. Peter Brown describes the rise and function of the holy man following the advent of Roman imperial Christianity as a religious figure that demonstrates supernatural gifts through dramatic, public confrontations with demons as well as imperial officials. *Power and Persuasion in Late Antiquity: Towards a Christian Empire* (Madison: University of Wisconsin Press, 1992), 143.

[28]Émile Amélineau, *Oeuvres de Schenoudi: Texte Copte et Traduction Française* (Paris: Ernest Leroux, 1907), 1:44. I follow the emendation of Amélineau in changing "more than us" to "more than him" (44n3). See also Rebecca Krawiec, *Shenoute & the Women of the White Monastery: Egyptian Monasticism in Late Antiquity* (New York: Oxford University Press, 2002), 44.

[29]Eusebius, *Life of Constantine* 2.45.

Eusebius represents the emerging Roman Christian perspective depicting Constantine as God's divine agent: "Observing these things, one might well say that a fresh, new-made way of life seemed to have appeared just then, as a strange light after thick darkness lit up the mortal race."[30] As Sebastian Brock puts it, Eusebius identifies the Roman Empire "as an *eikon* of the kingdom of God."[31] Decades after the death of Constantine, Ephrem the Syrian constructs the memory of the emperor in a similar fashion: "The truth-loving kings in the symbol of two bulls yoked together equally the two Testaments. With the yoke of harmony they worked and adorned the earth."[32] Ephrem here refers to Constantine together with his son and successor Constantius. It is interesting that Ephrem, for the sake of maintaining the contrast against the pagan emperor Julian, praises Constantius despite his association with Arianism—a heresy Ephrem denounced.[33]

The association of the Christian religion with Roman civilization adversely disassociated non-Roman kingdoms with Christianity. Christians outside of the Roman Empire were soon seen not only as followers of Jesus, but also of the Roman emperor. Despite the multiethnic and international presence of the universal church during the fourth century, Eusebius presents the Christian faith as "inextricably interwoven" with the Roman Empire as his construction of Christian identity became foundational for subsequent Western iterations of church history down to the present day.[34] Eusebius demonstrates how Constantine's self-perception as Christianity's global patron affected international relations with the Persian shah and the Christians under Persian rule:

> When the Persian emperor also saw fit to seek recognition by Constantine
> through an embassy, and he too dispatched tokens of friendly compact,
> the Emperor negotiated treaties to this end, outdoing in lavish munificence
> the initiator of honorific gesture by what he did in return. Certainly, when
> he learnt that the churches of God were multiplying among the Persians
> and that many thousands of people were being gathered into the flocks of

---

[30]Eusebius, *Life of Constantine* 3.1.8.
[31]Sebastian Brock, "Christians in the Sasanian Empire: A Case of Divided Loyalties," in *Religion and National Identity*, ed. Stuart Mews (Oxford: Blackwell, 1982), 1.
[32]Ephrem the Syrian, *Hymns*, trans. Kathleen E. McVey (New York: Paulist, 1989), 230.
[33]Ephrem, *Hymns*, 230n44.
[34]Brock, "Christians in the Sasanian Empire," 2.

Christ, he rejoiced at the report, and, as one who had general responsibility for them everywhere, there too he again took prudent measure on behalf of them all.[35]

Eusebius then provides the letter written by Constantine to Shapur in which he instructs the shah to provide safe and equitable treatment for Persian Christians:

I believe that I am not mistaken, my brother, in confessing this one God the Author and Father of all, whom many of those who have reigned here, seduced by insane errors, have attempted to deny. But such punishment finally engulfed them that all mankind since has regarded their fate as superseding all other examples to warn those who strive for the same ends. Among them I reckon that one, who was driven from these parts by divine wrath as by a thunderbolt and was left in yours, where he caused the victory on your side to become very famous because of the shame he suffered. Yet it would appear that it has turned out advantageous that even in your own day the punishment of such persons has become notorious. I have myself observed the end of those next to me, who with vicious decrees had harassed the people devoted to God. All thanks therefore are due to God, because by his perfect providence the entire humanity which reveres the divine Law, now that peace has been restored to them, exults triumphantly. Consequently I am convinced that for ourselves also everything is at its best and most secure when through their pure and excellent religion and as a result of their concord on matters divine he deigns to gather all men to himself. With this class of persons—I mean of course the Christians, my whole concern being for them—how pleasing it is for me to hear that the most important parts of Persia too are richly adorned! May the very best come to you therefore, and at the same time the best for them, since they also are yours. For so you will keep the sovereign Lord of the Universe kind, merciful and benevolent. These therefore, since you are so great, I entrust to you, putting their very persons in your hands, because you too are renowned for piety. Love them in accordance with your own humanity. For you will give enormous satisfaction both to yourself and to us by keeping faith.[36]

---

[35]Eusebius, *Life of Constantine* 4.8.

[36]Eusebius, *Life of Constantine* 4.11-13. The "one who was driven from these parts by divine wrath as by a thunderbolt" was the Roman emperor Valerian, who persecuted Christians in Rome and was defeated by the Persian shah Shapur I, Cameron and Hall, *Life of Constantine*, 315. The reference here, while presented as a compliment to Persian military success, should also be understood as a veiled threat against any emperor who stands against the people of God.

Eusebius's account of Constantine's letter to Shapur not only reveals the condescending attitude of Roman Christians toward their neighboring superpower but also veiled threats of retribution for any anti-Christian oppression at the hands of Persian authorities.[37] Nationalized religion can often lead to the rejection of the same religion by the nation's enemies. However, the international dynamics of the fourth century and their subsequent theological interpretations had undeniable consequences for the associating of *romanitas* with *Christianitas*. It is not surprising, then, that the Christianization of Rome under Constantine led to instances of institutionalized persecution of Christians in Persia. A decree of Shapur expressed the emergent anti-Christian climate in Persia:

> These Christians destroy our holy Teaching, and teach men to serve one God, and not honor the Sun or Fire. They defile Water by their ablutions, they refrain from marriage and the propagation of children, and refuse to go to war with the King of Kings. They have no rules about the slaughter and eating of animals; they bury the corpses of men in the earth. They attribute the origin of snakes and creeping things to a good God. They despise many servants of the King, and teach witchcraft.[38]

This account exemplifies typical Persian frustration with Christians: burying the dead, celibacy, and refusal to worship fire or eat meat ritually sacrificed. Despite the Persian suspicion of Christian loyalty, Persian Christian martyrs display respect and allegiance to the shah. One such martyr was Martha, the daughter of a Persian official who was a "daughter of the covenant" (*bat qyāmâ*), or Syrian female monk. Martha's martyrdom represents her allegiance to the gospel and respect of the Persian shah:

> May king Shapur live, may his graciousness never leave him, may his compassion continue; may his graciousness be preserved by his children and his compassion redound to himself and on the people who deserve it. May the life that he loves be accorded to all his brethren and friends, but let all who imitate my father meet the evil death you said my father died.[39]

---

[37]Kyle Smith, *Constantine and the Captive Christians of Persia: Martyrdom and Religious Identity in Late Antiquity* (Oakland: University of California Press, 2016), 9.

[38]Ian Gilman and Hans-Joachim Klimkeit, *Christians in Asia Before 1500* (New York: Routledge, 1999), 112. From the Roman side, Sozomen understands Christian persecution in Persia as being the result of Persian imperial suspicion of Christian loyalty (*Ecclesiastical History* 2.9).

[39]*Martyrdom of Martha*, in *Holy Women of the Syrian Orient*, ed. Sebastian P. Brock and Susan Ashbrook Harvey (Berkeley: University of California Press, 1987), 69.

Despite the repeated exclamations of Persian loyalty as evidenced in Syriac hagiography, Christians were charged a double tax payment to aid Persian military efforts against Rome as further evidence of their loyalty. War times acutely brought the distrust of Christians to the fore (especially during the time of Shapur II) and the greatest anti-Christian animosity came not from the shah but from the local Magian authorities.[40] One such example is from the Magian official Mihrshabur who brought accusations against a Christian named Peroz and Christians in general:

> My lord, all the Christians [naṣrāyē] have already rebelled against you: they do not do your will, they profane your ordinances, they do not worship your gods. If it pleases you to hear me, O King, command that the Christians break away from their religion that they might be converted, for they are of the same household of faith [bnai haimānuthā] as the Romans, and they are completely one with them. If a war should occur between (Rome and Persia), these Christians will be an adversary against you in the war; and, by means of their deceit, they will put an end to your power.[41]

The association of Christianity and Roman identity came not only from Roman sources like Eusebius but also from Persian Christian sources. As indicated above, Persian authorities saw their Christian compatriots as of the "household of faith as the Romans" and being "entirely one with them." The Syriac-speaking theologian Aphrahat, known as the Persian Sage, expressed disloyal hope in the new Christian Roman emperor:

> Prosperity has come to the people of God, and a blessing remains for the one through whom this prosperity has come [Constantine]. But disaster looms against the army gathered by the evil and proud one who boasts [Shapur], and misery waits there for the one through whom this disaster has been stirred up. Have no doubt that the kingdom [the Roman Empire] will not be conquered. For a mighty champion, whose name is Jesus, will come with power, carrying all the power of the kingdom as his armour.[42]

Here Aphrahat confirms the Persian suspicion of Christians as being loyal to Rome and demonstrates that Roman Christian identity politics had

---

[40]Brock, "Christians in the Sasanian Empire," 6.

[41]Martyrdom of Peroz, in Acta Martyrum et Sanctorum Syriace, ed. Paul Bedjan (Paris: Otto Harrassowitz, 1894), 4:258-59.

[42]Aphrahat, Demonstrations, ed. Adam Lehto (Piscataway, NJ: Gorgias, 2010), 5.1-24.

infiltrated Persian Christianity as well.[43] However, despite Aphrahat's significance as one of the earliest and most influential Syriac Christian writers, there were many Persian Christians who expressed a different sentiment. There were various attempts to accommodate certain aspects of Magian practice and Persian culture, such as the decision of the synod of 486 to allow marriage for clergy of all ranks, taking into account the Magian distaste for Christian celibacy.[44] Two years earlier at the synod of Beth Lapat, Barsauma, bishop of Nisibis, established a christological position in conflict with that of the majority of Roman Christians. His explanation to the shah Peroz is significant: "Unless the doctrine of Christians in your country is altered from that in the Greek country, their love and allegiance towards you will not be firmly established."[45] The last words of a Persian Christian named Gushtazad make plain the allegiance many Persian Christians had for their empire.

> I have been true and sincere to all your hidden secrets, and I have been sincere to you and your father—as you yourself said. Now grant me this one request that I make of you: let a herald go up and proclaim that Gushtazad, who is being killed, is dying not because he divulged the secrets of the kingdom, nor (because) he was found at fault in anything else, but because he is a Christian and does not deny God.[46]

Indeed, Christians had a significant presence in the Persian military including, in one case, a Christian Persian general.[47] Persian Christians understood the temporal kingdom to be subject to the rule of the shah while the eternal kingdom of the heavens was under the reign of Christ.

Christianity first entered Persia during its Parthian era in which there was a high degree of religious syncretism and toleration. However, after the Christianization of Rome, the national Zoroastrian religion was more

---

[43]Smith, *Captive Christians*, 7.

[44]Brock, "Christians in the Sasanian Empire," 9n37.

[45]Barhebraeus, *Chronicon Ecclesiasticum*, ed. Joannes B. Abbeloos and Thomas J. Lamy (Louvain: Peeters, 1877), 3:65.

[46]*The Martyrdom of Blessed Simeon bar Ṣabba'e*, in *The Martyrdom and History of Blessed bar Ṣabba'e*, ed. Kyle Smith (Piscataway, NJ: Gorgias Press, 2014), 43. A similar exclamation is recounted in Sozomen, *Ecclesiastical History* 2.9. Kyle Smith identifies the "going up" as a herald ascending the rampart or wall of the city (*Martyrdom of Blessed Simeon bar Ṣabba'e*, 42n31).

[47]*Acts of Grigor*, in *Histoire de Mar-Jabalaha, de trois autres patriarches, d'un pretre et de deux laiques, nestoriens*, ed. Paul Bedjan (Paris/Leipzig, 1895), 359-61.

strongly promoted while Christians were forced to choose between their heavenly identity and their earthly citizenship.[48] This is evident in the martyrdom of Pusai, the chief craftsman of Shapur:

> But the illustrious Pusai said, "God forbid a servant of the living God consider you to be despicable and contemptible, O mighty king. Rather, he holds you to be a mighty king, a renowned king, the king of kings." The king said to him, "How can you consider me in this way as you have said? For behold you have the audacity to swear in my presence by God, and not by the gods." And the illustrious Pusai said to him, "I swore by God because I am a Christian [krestyānā]; I did not swear by the gods because I am not a pagan." And the king said to him, "How can you consider me your king, king of kings, mighty and powerful, given all this impudence to say in my presence that you are a Christian?[49]

A reference to shah Chosroes I from the synod of 576 is further indication of Christian loyalists in Persia: "It is right that in all the churches of this exalted and glorious earthly kingdom that our lord the victorious Chosroes, king of kings, be proclaimed in the litanies during the liturgy. No metropolitan or bishop has the authority to neglect the implementation of this canon in any of the churches of his diocese and jurisdiction."[50]

HELLENIZED CHRISTIAN THEOLOGY

The emergent Christian state resulted in a universal standard of doctrine cemented in Hellenistic thought and language. The fourth century certainly did not witness the introduction of Christian theology framed by Hellenistic thought. Many of the earliest Christian apologists such as Justin Martyr, Origen, and Clement of Alexandria were deeply influenced by Greek culture and education, which was evidenced in their theological approach. Although Christian theology found expression in Hellenistic idiom from the very beginning, it wasn't until the time of Constantine that a universal doctrinal standard framed by Roman identity was established.

---

[48]Ehsan Yarshater, The Cambridge History of Iran: The Seleucid, Parthian, and Sasanian Periods (New York: Cambridge University Press, 1983), 879.

[49]Martyrdom of Pusai, in Acta Martyrum et Sanctorum, ed. Paul Bedjan (Paris: Otto Harrassowitz, 1891), 2:214.

[50]Synodicon Orientale ou Recueil de Synodes Nestoriens, ed. J. B. Chabot (Paris: Imprimerie Nationale, 1902), 121.

Before the fourth century, Christian and Roman identity were not synonymous. In the Persian Empire, Christians were differentiated along ethnic
lines and had separate churches: the Roman refugees were referred to in
Syriac as *krestyānē* (Christians) while the native Persian Christians were
called *naṣrāyē* (Nazarenes).[51] It is clear, therefore, that the category of
"Christian" did not equate with "Roman" until after the time of Constantine.
Yet the idea that the Christian faith—the line of thought that was accepted
as orthodox during the fourth century—developed principally in the heart
of the Roman Empire still persists.

A popular view is that the Christian orthodoxy that would become
standardized in the fourth century developed principally in Rome, while
the Eastern centers of Christianity (Alexandria, Antioch, Urhoy) were
characterized primarily by heresy.[52] The Bauer thesis was a helpful corrective to the dominant view of Christian origins during his time. Bauer
summarizes this dominant view as follows: "For the period of Christian
origins, ecclesiastical doctrine (of course, only as this pertains to a certain
stage in its development) already represents what is primary, while heresies, on the other hand, somehow are a deviation from the genuine."[53]
Before the era of Constantine, the boundaries of orthodoxy had not been
clearly delineated and the fabric of earliest Christianity is characterized
principally by heterogeneity.

The problematic aspect of the Bauer thesis is its positioning of Rome as
the source of orthodoxy that shines its light toward the "dangerous Orient."[54]
This is not to say that Bauer is uncritical of Roman ecclesiastical hierarchy.[55]
Yet the Roman church is, for Bauer, the source from which the lines of orthodoxy are "running from Rome to the East and from the main representa-
tives of orthodoxy back again to Rome."[56] Bauer is correct to point out that
the influence that heretics such as Marcion and Valentinus exercised in

---

[51]Wilhelm Baum and Dietmar W. Winkler, *The Church of the East: A Concise History* (New York:
Routledge, 2003), 165; Sebastian Brock, *Fire from Heaven: Studies in Syriac Theology and Liturgy*
(Burlington, VT: Ashgate, 2006), 71.

[52]Walter Bauer, *Orthodoxy and Heresy in Earliest Christianity*, 2nd ed. (Philadelphia: Fortress,
1971), 128.

[53]Bauer, *Orthodoxy and Heresy*, xxiv.

[54]Bauer, *Orthodoxy and Heresy*, 105.

[55]Bauer, *Orthodoxy and Heresy*, 97-98.

[56]Bauer, *Orthodoxy and Heresy*, 108.

Rome considerably restricted Rome's influence.[57] The life and career of Marcion, a heretic who experienced greater success in Rome than his native Syria, challenges Bauer's depiction of Rome as the bastion of Christian orthodoxy.[58] Conversely, Ignatius of Antioch functions as a pillar of orthodoxy in the East and suffers martyrdom in Rome. Ignatius was produced in Antioch—the alleged center of heterodoxy—while he was rejected and killed in Rome, the supposed center of orthodoxy. Despite the presence of some of the most influential heretics in Rome, Bauer still perceives of the city as "essentially unanimous in the faith and in the standards of Christian living, tightly organized and methodically governed by the monarchical bishop."[59] Bauer here is referring to the close of the second century when a more centralized ecclesiastical hierarchy existed to combat heresy. Such representations of orthodoxy were not unique to Rome. Also, in the late second century, the career of Demetrius, archbishop of Alexandria, represents the terminus ante quem for an orthodox ecclesiastical hierarchy in Egypt.

Bauer argued that before Demetrius, the theological landscape of Egypt was characterized primarily by Gnosticism, an unclear category that has been called into question.[60] Bauer's argument is supported by the early existence of Gnostic texts such as the *Gospel of the Egyptians* and the *Gospel of the Hebrews*. However, in a reassessment of second-century papyri, the majority of a selection of Greek papyri, such as the *Shepherd of Hermas* and Irenaeus's anti-Gnostic treatise *Against Heresies*, represented the orthodox view.[61] Egyptian Christianity in the first two centuries should be understood "as a 'fluid' one, in which various types of Christians coexisted in a community not yet differentiated sharply along theological lines."[62] Bauer is

---

[57]Bauer, *Orthodoxy and Heresy*, 106.

[58]Bauer (*Orthodoxy and Heresy*, 71) dismissed Marcion's departure from Asia Minor as simply a desire to expand his influence by operating in the center of the Roman Empire. This argument also explains the connection Bauer seeks to make between Rome and orthodoxy. Orthodox figures (such as Tertullian) have a connection to Rome insofar as they also journeyed there for education and teaching opportunities.

[59]Bauer, *Orthodoxy and Heresy*, 129.

[60]Bauer, *Orthodoxy and Heresy*, 53. Michael A. Williams, *Rethinking "Gnosticism": An Argument for Dismantling a Dubious Category* (Princeton, NJ: Princeton University Press, 1996); Karen L. King, *What is Gnosticism?* (Cambridge, MA: Belknap, 2003).

[61]C. H. Roberts, *Manuscript, Society, and Belief in the Early Christian Egypt* (New York: Oxford University Press, 1979), 13-14.

[62]Stephen J. Davis, *The Early Coptic Papacy: The Egyptian Church and Its Leadership in Antiquity* (Cairo: American University in Cairo Press, 2004), 17.

correct in claiming that earliest Christianity was theologically variegated and that there had not yet come into existence a dominant view. However, it is problematic to view the Roman (and later, Western) world as the seedbed for the Christian faith. Indeed, Christians experienced relatively peaceful minority status in third-century Persia while Roman Christians were suffering under emperors such as Decius and Diocletian. Before the fourth century, there was no cultural, regional, or political group that was perceived as the source or guardian of the Christian faith. Indeed, the Christian faith represented itself as a new "race" (*genos*) that transcended the existing categories of social organization.[63]

Just as the political association of Christianity with the Roman Empire resulted in negative consequences on the public life of Persian Christians, the boundedness of Christian doctrine in Greco-Roman terminology became problematic for Christians operating with different cultural categories. Perhaps the clearest example of this is in the writings of the poet-theologian Ephrem the Syrian.[64] Ephrem lived entirely during the fourth century and was a champion of Nicene orthodoxy as a deacon and teacher (*malphānā*) in the Syriac-speaking cities of Nisibs and Urhoy. It was in the latter that Ephrem composed the majority of the *madrāshe* that survive.[65] In Ephrem's *Madrāshe on Faith*, the father of Syriac Christianity lays out a clear defense of Nicene orthodoxy: "The voice of our Lord counted them out, and their dwellings were lifted up—the Aetians, and Arians; Sabellians and Cathars; Photinians and Audians—They who accepted ordination from our Church and some of whom signed onto the faith which was written down at that glorious synod. Memorable is the king who convened them."[66] It is widely acknowledged that

---

[63]Denise Kimber Buell, *Why This New Race: Ethnic Reasoning in Early Christianity* (New York: Columbia University Press, 2005), 141.

[64]Some content in this section previously appeared in Vince Bantu, "Orthodoxy in Global Perspective: The Reception of Nicene Theology in the Syriac World," *Faith and the Academy* 3.1 (2018): 20-22.

[65]*Madrāshe* is a literary genre unique to the Syriac language and culture: stanzaic poems written in various syllable patterns involving the text read by the primary reader and a chorus (*qālā*) to be recited by the congregation. *Madrāshe* were meant to be sung and although the names of the melodies survive, the original music is unknown. Though the term is often translated as "hymns" in English, I have retained the Syriac name as this poetic method of theological expression has no exact modern equivalent.

[66]Ephrem the Syrian, *Madrāshe Against the Heretics*, in *Des Heiligen Ephraem des Syrers Hymnen Contra Haereses*, ed. Edmund Beck, (Louvain: Secretariat du SCO, 1957), 22.20.

the "synod" Ephrem refers to here is Nicaea and the "king" is Constantine.[67] It is significant that this reference to Nicaea is questionable and that there is no other direct reference to the council in the writings of Ephrem.[68] While it is clear that Ephrem opposes Arianism and any other theological attempt to posit a subordinationist status for the Son to the Father, he does so without reference to the famous council or its doctrinal language.

Given the historical and theological significance of the Nicene council and its definition of orthodoxy, it is difficult to underestimate the significance of Ephrem's decision to omit direct reference to the council and the word *homoousias*. Not only does Ephrem avoid the term, in one instance he refers to it negatively: "Why would we introduce some other thing into that truth he declared to us? The names that we have added, these, brothers, have become a foundation for the presumptuous."[69] While not explicitly mentioned, it has been widely accepted that the "thing" that has been added to God's truth by the "presumptuous" is the term *homoousias*. Ephrem stands in the company of many fourth-century writers who saw the term as an unnecessary addition that is held in suspect chiefly for its absence in Scripture.[70] Ephrem can be thought of as a supporter of Nicene orthodoxy insofar as he condemns Arianism and any subordinationist understanding of the Trinity. Ephrem speaks of the Father and Son existing in "one essence" (*ḥda 'itutā*),[71] instead of terms closer to the Greek *homoousias* (*bar 'itutā* or *bar kyānā*).[72]

---

[67]Beck, *Contra Haereses*, 169-70. See also Sidney H. Grffith, "Setting Right the Church of Syria: Saint Ephraem's Hymns Against Heresies," in *The Limits of Ancient Christianity: Essays on Late Antique Thought and Culture in Honor of R. A. Markus*, ed. William E. Klingshirn and Mark Vessey (Ann Arbor: University of Michigan Press, 1999), 102. Jeffrey Wickes challenges the common assumption that Ephrem's statement refers to Nicaea and Constantine as the process by which Nicene theology became dominant in the Syriac-speaking world was indirect and somewhat unclear, in *St. Ephrem the Syrian: The Hymns on Faith* (Washington, DC: Catholic University of America Press, 2015), 21.

[68]Wickes, *Ephrem the Syrian*, 23.

[69]Ephrem the Syrian, *Madrāshe on Faith*, in *Des Heiligen Ephraem des Syrers Hymnen de Fide*, ed. Edmund Beck (Louvain: Secretariat du SCO, 1955), 52.14. The Syriac word *marāhe* can also mean "bold" or "audacious."

[70]Frances M. Young, *Biblical Exegesis and the Formation of Christian Culture* (New York: Cambridge University Press, 1997), 31.

[71]Ephrem the Syrian, *Madrāshe on Faith* 73.21. Beck translates more emphatically: "eine einzige Wesenheit" ("one *single* essence"); *Hymnen de Fide*, 194.

[72]*Bar kyānā* is used to translate *homoousias* in the earliest Syriac translation of the Nicene Creed; Arthur Vööbus, "New Sources for the Symbol in Early Syrian Christianity," *Vigililae Christianae* 26 (1972): 295.

Ephrem argues clearly for the equality of the Son and the Father but does so without the "presumptuous" language of Nicaea. The only known instance of Ephrem using homoousias (bar kyānā) with reference to the Godhead was in a smaller, academic context in contrast to the more public, liturgical setting in which the madrāshe would be sung.[73] This further indicates that Ephrem's concern was to a certain degree motivated by a desire to nurture the Syriac congregations with more culturally and theologically accessible language.

Another motivating factor is Ephrem's concern for "presumptuous" attempts at theological innovation. Ephrem often cautions against inappropriate "investigations" into divine mysteries: "A thousand thousands stand; ten thousand ten thousands hasten; thousands and ten thousands—to the One they cannot investigate."[74] Ephrem's concerns about attempts to "investigate" God are connected to his overall distrust of "Greek wisdom."[75] Like many fourth-century Christian writers, Ephrem was critical toward Hellenistic thought and was concerned over what he saw as an unhealthy influence of Greek philosophy on the formulation Christian doctrine.[76] This is not an indication that Ephrem was anti-intellectual. Ephrem was the head of the School of Edessa and was deeply influenced by Hellenistic thought—which was deployed in unique ways in the Syrian context.[77] Ephrem's goal was not to create some sort of anti-Greek, pro-Syrian sentiment. Rather, Ephrem selectively appropriated those helpful elements of Hellenism in Christian thought and liturgy while elevating indigenous forms of worship and concepts accessible to his Syriac community of Urhoy. Ephrem's efforts in contextualizing orthodoxy for the Syriac world serve as an early example

---

[73]Wickes, Ephrem the Syrian, 38n153.

[74]Ephrem, Madrāshe on Faith 4.1.

[75]Edmund Beck, Die Theologie des heiligen Ephraem in seinen Hymnen über den Glauben (Rome: Pontificum Institutum S. Anselmi, 1949), 63.

[76]Peter Bruns, "Aithallaha's Brief über den Glauben: Ein bedeutendes Dokument frühsyrischer Theologie," OC 76 (1992): 46-73.

[77]Sebastian Brock, The Luminous Eye: The Spiritual World Vision of Saint Ephrem the Syrian (Kalamazoo, MI: Cistercian Publications, 1985), 21. Ute Possekel argues that Ephrem was familiar with and influenced by Greek thought but that his primary theological method differed from mainstream Hellenistic Christianity and was more Semitic in nature. "Ephrem's Doctrine of God," in God in Early Christian Thought: Essays in Memory of Lloyd G. Patterson, ed. Andrew Brian McGowan, Brian Edward Daley, and Timothy J. Gaden (Leiden: Brill, 2009), 197; Scott F. Johnson, Languages and Cultures of Eastern Christianity: Greek (Burlington, VT: Ashgate, 2014), 4. Johnson demonstrates the vast fluidity and localized deployment of the Greek language in Near Eastern contexts while acknowledging the imperial associations of Greek Christianity.

of indigenous expressions of Christian doctrine alternative to the dominant Roman trajectory.

Likewise, the Church of the East centered in the Persian capital of Se-leucia-Ctesiphon did not adopt the Nicene Creed for almost a century. When the Synod of Isaac met at Seleucia-Ctesiphon in 410, the creed was modified to suit the theology of the East Syriac Christians, displaying the autonomy of the Persian church from that of Rome.[78] Despite such early examples of theological formation outside the confines of Romanized Chris-tianity, the Romanization of Christianity and the proclamation of a "uni-versal" Christian doctrine in Hellenistic language laid the foundation for a particular trajectory of Christian social formation. The creation of theo-logical dominance concurrent with subaltern expressions of Christianity laid the foundation for the inevitable clash and subjugation of ideologies that would occur in the century following the era of Constantine.

THE ROAD TO CHALCEDON

The establishment of orthodox Christian doctrine by Greco-Roman termi-nology during the fourth century led to significant ecclesiastical schism along geocultural lines during the fifth century. The theological contro-versies of the first four centuries did not result in any church schisms along social or cultural lines that persist to present-day Christian traditions. Both in Late Antiquity and in the present, most members of the Christian faith have accepted the idea that Jesus is equal in essence to God the Father.[79] However, the problematic nature of the Hellenistic terminology that Jesus exists in two natures (*physis*) and one person (*hypostasis*) resulted in the marginalization of ancient African and Asian Christian communities as "heretics" and their separation from the world of Western Christendom that persists into the present time.

---

[78]Baum and Winkler, *Church of the East*, 16.
[79]As will be explored further below, several Germanic nations rejected Nicene Christianity and were predominately Arian from the mid-fourth to the mid-seventh centuries. While the theo-logical controversy between the dominant Roman church and Germanic Arian Christians dem-onstrated many of the same political, cultural, and linguistic dynamics as the Chalcedonian schism, Germanic kings (Goth, Lombard, Vandal) began to adopt Nicene Christianity, which remained the dominant Christian faith of Europe to the present day. However, in the case of early African and Middle Eastern Christians, the dominant Christian faith birthed in these lands in antiquity has been at variance with Western Christianity since the fifth century.

During the fifth century, christological controversy engaged the attention of the Christian world and tension was high between leaders of Egypt, Syria, and Constantinople. Patriarch Cyril of Alexandria condemned as a heretic Patriarch Nestorius of Constantinople for his refusal to call Mary the *theotokos* ("bearer of God"), preferring instead the term *christotokos* ("bearer of Christ").[80] This caused ecclesiastical tension between the sees of Alexandria and Antioch, who also expressed different christological positions. When Dioscorus became patriarch after Cyril's death (444), a Constantinopolitan monk named Eutyches began emphasizing a particular interpretation of Cyril's "one nature" Christology. Although Cyril's use of the phrase *mia physis* had caused a degree of unrest,[81] it was still broadly accepted while Eutyches's emphasis on the "one nature" led to his excommunication by Bishop Flavian, patriarch of Constantinople. However, Dioscorus, sympathetic to the views of Eutyches, convened a council in Ephesus (449) with the support of Roman emperor Theodosius II (402–450) that exonerated Eutyches and deposed Flavian. Having alienated both Constantinople and Rome, Dioscorus found himself in a vulnerable position following the death of Theodosius II (450).

The new emperor, Marcian (450–457), sharing the Roman bishop Leo's view of Ephesus II as a *latrocinium* ("Council of Robbers"), called for a new council in Chalcedon (451). The *Tome* of Leo had been written in 449 as a response to Eutyches but was ignored at Ephesus II; however, it became the accepted formula on which "two nature" Christology was founded at Chalcedon. For the majority of the Egyptian delegation at Chalcedon, as well as the Egyptian church, the following decisions made at Chalcedon were unacceptable: (1) the favoring of a "two nature" Christology that seemed to resemble the theology of Nestorius; (2) the reinstatement of Theodoret, who was bishop of Cyrrhus (a city in modern Syria) and was condemned by Dioscorus in 449;[82] (3) the refusal to accept a document written by Cyril

---

[80]Nestorius, *The First Letter of Nestorius to Celestine*, in *Christology of the Later Fathers*, ed. Edward Hardy (Philadelphia: Westminster, 1954), 348; Socrates Scholasticus, *Ecclesiastical History* 7.32.

[81]John of Antioch expressed concern that language such as *mia physis* would fail to take into account Christ's humanity. Cyril clarified Christ as having "one *enfleshed* nature" (Davis, *Early Coptic Papacy*, 81).

[82]Theodoret was condemned by Dioscorus at the Second Council of Ephesus (449) because of his refusal to pronounce Nestorius a heretic.

called the *Twelve Anathemas* (or *Twelve Chapters*), which condemned the theology of Nestorius; and (4) the decision to depose and exile Dioscorus.[83] It was especially the language of Christ existing in two natures after the hypostatic union that would perpetually disturb those who believed that Christ's humanity and divinity existed in "one nature." Egyptian Christians followed the use of *mia physis* in Cyril's writing which provided the foundation for the contemporary name Miaphysite. The definition that was adopted at Chalcedon by the dominant Roman church articulated an alternative theology which taught two natures in Christ:

> Following therefore the holy Fathers, we confess one and the same our Lord Jesus Christ, and we all teach harmoniously [that he is] the same perfect in Godhead, the same perfect in manhood, truly God and truly man, the same of a reasonable soul and body; consubstantial with the Father in Godhead, and the same consubstantial with us in manhood, like us in all things except sin; begotten before ages of the Father in Godhead, the same in the last days for us; and for our salvation [born] of Mary the virgin *theotokos* in manhood, one and the same Christ, Son, lord, unique; acknowledged in two natures without confusion, without change, without division, without separation—the difference of the natures being by no means taken say because of the union, but rather the distinctive character of each nature being preserved, and [each] combining in one Person and hypostasis—not divided or separated into two Persons, but one and the same Son and only-begotten God, Word, Lord Jesus Christ.[84]

For the Miaphysites, what was at stake theologically was a betrayal of Cyril's articulation of the hypostatic union of Christ's natures just a few years before Chalcedon. In his letters to Nestorius, Cyril proclaimed his famous *Twelve Anathemas* to Nestorius and specifically warns against any dividing of Christ's natures:

> If anyone does not confess that the Word of God the Father was united by hypostasis to flesh and is one Christ with his own flesh, that is, the same both God and man together, let him be anathema. If anyone divides the hypostases in the one Christ after the union, joining them only by a conjunction in

---

[83]Richard Price and Michael Gaddis, *The Acts of the Council of Chalcedon* (Liverpool: Liverpool University Press, 2005), 52.

[84]"The Chalcedonian Decree," in *Christology of the Later Fathers*, ed. Edward Hardy (Philadelphia: Westminster, 1954), 373.

dignity, or authority or power, and not rather by a coming together in a union by nature, let him be anathema.[85]

Cyril was concerned that Nestorius divided the human and divine natures of Christ and thus undermined the unity that provides human access to salvation. In the same way, the Miaphysite writers that came a generation after Cyril felt that Chalcedonian theology was making the same mistake as Nestorius. For their part, the Chalcedonians felt that the Miaphysite insistence on Christ existing in one nature would inevitably cause Christ's human nature to be "swallowed up" by his divinity.[86] Leo indicates in his *Tome* his concern that the Miaphysite theology of Eutyches undermines the full humanity of Jesus: "And he (Eutyches) should not have spoken idly to the effect that the Word was in such a sense made flesh, that the Christ who was brought forth from the Virgin's womb had the form of a man, but had not a body really derived from his mother's body."[87]

While the schism that resulted after Chalcedon eventually led to the separation of most Christian communities in Africa and Asia from the majority Roman church,[88] the initial opposition against two-nature Christology came principally from Egypt.[89] Even though there was a significant Chalcedonian constituency in Egypt (and even a Nestorian church) before and after the Islamic Conquest,[90] the Miaphysite church has remained the

---

[85]Cyril of Alexandria, *The Third Letter of Cyril to Nestorius*, in Hardy, *Christology of the Later Fathers*, 353.

[86]Theodoret of Cyrrhus, *Eranistes*, PG 83 (1864), 111.

[87]*The Tome of Leo*, in Hardy, *Christology of the Later Fathers*, 362.

[88]Historians contemporary to the christological controversies juxtapose Leo, the emperor of "Europe," with the Miaphysite communities of "Egypt, in Alexandria, in Palestine, and everywhere else"; Pseudo-Zachariah Rhetor, *Chronicle*, ed. Geoffrey Greatrex, Robert R. Phenix, and Cornelia B. Horn (Liverpool: Liverpool University Press, 2011), 139.

[89]Aloys Grillmeier, *Christ in Christian Tradition*, vol. 2, part 1: *From the Council of Chalcedon (451) to Gregory the Great (590–604)* (Atlanta, GA: John Knox Press, 1996), 105. Grillmeier's point holds especially true in the late fifth century when Egypt produced such anti-Chalcedonian figures as Dioscorus, Timothy Aelurus, and Macarius of Tkōw. Syria, in contrast, did not become as staunchly anti-Chalcedonian as Egypt until the sixth century, during the time of Severus of Antioch and John of Ephesus.

[90]For examples of Nestorians in Egypt, see Ian Gillman and Hans-Joachim Klimkeit, *Christians in Asia Before 1500* (New York: Routledge, 1999), 150. See also Otto Meinardus, "The Nestorians in Egypt: A Note on the Nestorians in Jerusalem," OC 51 (1967): 112-29. Maged Mikhail demonstrates that the Melkite Egyptian community was the second major Christian confession after the anti-Chalcedonians. *From Byzantine to Islamic Egypt: Religion, Identity, and Politics after the Arab Conquest* (New York: Tauris, 2014), 15.

majority since the Fourth Ecumenical Council.[91] This should not indicate, however, that Egypt was the only source of opposition while the rest of the empire reacted "only in a positive way."[92] The events at Chalcedon began the process leading to the formal schism between the majority Miaphysite churches of Egypt, Syria, and Armenia and the Chalcedonian church that was backed by imperial authority. The decades following Chalcedon also saw the gradual dissolution of the Western Empire by Germanic invasions, culminating with the removal of Romulus Augustulus in 476 by the Ostrogothic leader Odoacer.[93] Constantinople and the Eastern Empire were now the center of power and authority for the Roman world.

Initial Response to Chalcedon

The two centuries between the Council of Chalcedon (451) and the Arab Muslim Conquest (ca. 640) were ones of constant tension between opponents and supporters of Chalcedon at the highest ecclesiastical level. Prior to the fifth century, doctrinal matters were the concern primarily of the educated class (e.g., Origen). However, the support for Miaphysite doctrine in the fifth century existed in all social classes and cultural regions of the Eastern Empire resulting in the popular dissent against Chalcedon.[94] This was visible most notably in the monastic communities that provided significant support for various theological positions.[95] After the exile of Dioscorus to Gangra,

---

[91]James Howard-Johnston, *Witnesses to a World Crisis: Historians and Histories of the Middle East in the Seventh Century* (New York: Oxford University Press, 2010), 157.

[92]Rhaban Haacke, "Die kaiserliche Politik in den Auseinandersetzungen um Chalkedon (451–553)," in *Das Konzil von Chalkedon: Geschichte und Gegenwart*, ed. Aloys Grillmeier and Heinrich Bacht (Würzburg: Echter-Verlag, 1953), 2:111.

[93]Timothy E. Gregory, *A History of Byzantium* (Malden, MA: Blackwell, 2005), 108. Although the Western Empire was transformed into various barbarian successor states, Constantinople still considered the lost territories as part of the Roman Empire; John Haldon, *Byzantium: A History* (Stroud: Tempus, 2000), 22.

[94]Heinrich Bacht, "Die Rolle des orientalischen Mönchtums in den kirchenpolitischen Auseinandersetzungen um Chalkedon (431–519)," in Gillmeier and Bact, *Das Konzil von Chalkedon*, 2:270. Bacht also points out that the popularizing capabilities of monastic circles transcend divisions of socioeconomic status (310). See also Price and Gaddis, *Acts of the Council*, 22; Gregory, *History of Byzantium*, 116; W. H. C. Frend, "Popular Religion and Christological Controversy in the Fifth Century," in *Studies in Church History*, vol. 8: *Popular Belief and Practice*, ed. G. J. Cuming and Derek Baker (New York: Cambridge University Press, 1972), 19.

[95]"The opponents of Chalcedon had their strongest support in monastic circles." Maria Cramer and Heinrich Bacht, "Der antichalkedonische Aspekt im historisch-geographischen Schrifttum der koptischen Monophysiten," in Gillmeier and Bact, *Das Konzil von Chalkedon*, 2:326.

Emperor Marcian appointed the Chalcedonian Proterius as patriarch of Alexandria, a decision with severe consequences for the Egyptian church. Riots immediately broke out and after a few years in office, Proterius was murdered by a mob and the anti-Chalcedonian Timothy Aelurus was ordained patriarch of Alexandria by anti-Chalcedonian clergy (457).[96] The counterordination of Timothy Aelurus angered supporters of Chalcedon, such as Leo, bishop of Rome, and eventually Emperor Leo I (457–474) sent Timothy Aelurus into exile in 459. Meanwhile, Leo the Archbishop of Rome (440–461; not to be confused with Leo the Roman emperor of the same period) sent letters to major sees in the empire comparing the faith of the Miaphysites to Valentinianism, Manichaeism, and Eutychianism in an effort to discredit the movement.[97]

A Chalcedonian monk from the Pachomian community named Timothy Salofaciolus received imperial support as patriarch of Egypt from 460 to 482. However, Timothy Aelurus retained the support of Egypt's anti-Chalcedonian community while in exile by sending letters and theological treatises refuting Chalcedonian theology.[98] One of the earliest and most comprehensive statements of Miaphysite theology was Timothy Aelurus's treatise *Against Chalcedon*:

> For what teaching from the divine scriptures of Old and New Testaments has this man [Leo] received who has not even got so far as the beginning of the faith? What is rehearsed by the voice of all the regenerated throughout the world is not accepted by the mind of this old man. Ignorant, therefore, of what view he ought to take on God the Word's incarnation and refusing to toil in the broad expanse of the divine scriptures so as to be able from thence to become worthy of the knowledge of light, he ought to have attended carefully

---

[96]The presence of violent resistance immediately following Chalcedon demonstrates the inaccuracy of the commonly held opinion that "pro- and anti-Chalcedonian factions commonly co-existed" in the pre-Justinian period. Garth Fowden, "Religious Communities," in *Late Antiquity: A Guide to the Postclassical World*, ed. Glen W. Bowersock, Peter Brown, and Oleg Grabar (Cambridge, MA: Belnap, 1999), 94.

[97]Leo's lack of understanding of the various movements at odds with Chalcedonianism is evident in his identifying Timothy Aelurus as a Eutychian (Grillmeier, *Christ in Christian Tradition*, 192).

[98]Mark Moussa, "The Anti-Chalcedonian Movement in Byzantine Egypt: An Evaluation of Past Scholarship and Current Interpretations," in *Ägypten und Nubien in spätantiker und christlicher Zeit, Akten des 6 internationalen Koptologenkongresses, Münster, 20-26 Juli 1996, Band 1: Materielle Kultur, Kunst und religiöses Leben*, ed. S. Emmel, M. Krause, S. G. Richter, and S. Schaten, Sprachen und Kulturen des christlichen Orients 6.1 (Wiesbaden: Reichert, 1999), 506.

to the common, unchanging profession which the whole assembly of the faithful makes, and to believe in God the Father Almighty and in Christ Jesus his only son our Lord who was born of the Holy Ghost and the Virgin Mary, through which three statements most schemes of heretics are refuted.[99]

Here Timothy makes an argument characteristic of anti-Chalcedonians: that a two-nature Christology introduces nonbiblical terminology that divides the unified Christ and is inconsistent with prior theological tradition. Opponents of the one-nature position in ancient and modern times have understood Miaphysite doctrine to deny the unity of Christ's humanity and divinity following the incarnation, which is called the "hypostatic union." However, Timothy clearly understands Jesus to be fully human and divine:

> For when God is believed to be Almighty and Father, the Son is shown to be co-eternal with him, differing in nothing from his Father because as God from God, almighty from almighty and from eternity has he been begotten as co-eternal, not temporally younger, not less in power, not different in glory or separate in substance but the eternal Only-begotten of the eternal Father has been born of the Holy Ghost and Mary the Virgin; and this temporal birth neither detracted from nor added to his divine, eternal nature, but he emptied it all out to save straying man in order that he might conquer death and cast down by his power the accuser who possessed death's sway. For we could not have conquered the chief of sin and death had he not taken our nature and made it his own, a nature which sin could not sully nor death get hold of.[100]

Ironically, while Miaphysites are often depicted as schismatic, this is precisely how they viewed Chalcedonians. Severus, bishop of Antioch, was exiled to Egypt by Emperor Justinian for his rejection of Chalcedon and warned his fellow Miaphysites both in Egypt and Syria to avoid taking communion with the Chalcedonian "heretics":

> Whereas you say that those who assembled at Chalcedon, and divided our one Lord and God and Saviour Jesus Christ by calling Him two natures after the union fell under the anathema laid down against abominable godless heresies, and that men coming from them are not to be received, but their

---

[99]Timothy Aelurus, *Against Chalcedon*, ed. R. Y. Ebied and L. R. Wickham, in *After Chalcedon: Studies in Theology and Church History Offered to Professor Albert van Roey*, ed. and trans. C. Laga, J. A. Munitiz, and L. Van Rompay (Leuven: Peeters, 1985), 143.
[100]Timothy Aelurus, *Against Chalcedon*, 143-44.

'end is to be burned,' because they are devoid of the grace of the Holy Spirit, know that you have missed the truth. That by denial of the faith they are stripped of every spiritual heavenly gift it is impossible for me to gainsay; but that when they repudiate and renounce the heresy and condemn it by anathema, and come over to the church, they are according to the ordinances of the fathers to be received.[101]

Because the imperial authorities in Constantinople were majority Chalcedonian, attempts were made throughout the fifth, sixth, and seventh centuries to bring the primarily Miaphysite eastern provinces (Egypt, Syria, Palestine, Arabia) into agreement through forceful tactics.[102] Indeed, Stephen Davis describes the period following Chalcedon as one of "ecclesiastical colonialism" of Byzantine authority over the Miaphysite communities which were predominant in Africa and the Middle East.[103] Davis's postcolonial assessment of fifth-century Egypt is reflected in Miaphysite sources of this period.[104] Roman emperors oppressed the Egyptian church by imposing Chalcedonian patriarchs such as Timothy Salofaciolus and John Talaia who were rejected by the Egyptian populace through the counterordination of leaders such as Timothy Aelurus and Peter Mongus. Miaphysite leaders were allowed to rule in Egypt undisturbed during a brief coup by the Roman general Basiliscus in 475, demonstrating the link between Chalcedonian theology and imperial authority. In his *Church History*, Timothy Aelurus deploys totalizing rhetoric as he supplies the "heresy" of Chalcedon as the reason for the defeat of the Romans by the Ostrogoths soon after Chalcedon: "And they were the cause of the schisms and divisions of kings for it was not long after the council of the oppressors that the destruction of Rome occurred. Up until those days there was strife, division, and schisms in the ecclesiastical ranks who were among the kings. Because of this, the Westerners have not reconciled with the Easterners to this day."[105] One of the most significant tactics in anti-Chalcedonian polemic was associating two-nature

---

[101]Severus of Antioch, *The Sixth Book of the Select Letters of Severus, Patriarch of Antioch: In the Syriac Version of Athanasius of Nisibus*, ed. E. W. Brooks (London: Williams & Norgate, 1904), 1:295.

[102]The Chalcedonian schism had little direct relevance for the Persian Church of the East which was located outside of the Roman Empire and developed a distinct theology that was neither Chalcedonian nor Miaphysite. This will be discussed further below.

[103]Davis, *Early Coptic Papacy*, 87.

[104]On postcolonialism, see Edward Said, *Culture and Imperialism* (New York: Vintage, 1993).

[105]Timothy Aelurus, "Extraits de Timothée Aelure," ed. François Nau, PO 13 (1919), 215-16.

theology with the oppressive Byzantine Empire while simultaneously engendering a sense of Egyptian, Syrian, Armenian, and Arabian pride defined primarily by adherence to orthodox (i.e., Miaphysite) confession.

Miaphysitism and anti-Chalcedonian sentiment prevailed in many areas of the Middle East and Africa. A Chalcedonian named Juvenal was appointed by the Roman emperor as patriarch of Jerusalem which resulted in violent revolts of the majority Miaphysite population.[106] The holy pilgrimage sites of Jerusalem made it a tense battle ground for the warring christological factions of the fifth century resulting in the defeat of the revolutionaries and the reinstallation of Juvenal over the majority Miaphysite community of Jerusalem.[107] The Jerusalem rebellion also represented the creation of a separate, anti-Chalcedonian hierarchy in Palestine that would give support to other anti-Chalcedonian leadership in Egypt and Syria. One of the most prominent early Miaphysite leaders was Peter the Iberian who became bishop of Maiuma in Gaza. When he was forced into exile by Juvenal, Peter went to Egypt, supported the Miaphysite Enaton monastery, and aided in the ordination of Timothy Aelurus.[108] The solidarity between Palestinian and Egyptian figures in the years following Chalcedon demonstrates the common ascetic sensibilities and ecumenical concerns shared by the two groups.[109] The common hatred of Byzantine imperial authority is another important factor uniting Miaphysites across international boundaries during the late fifth century. Like Timothy Aelurus, Palestinian Miaphysites such as John Rufus—the successor bishop of Maiuma following Peter the Iberian—understood the fall of Rome as the result of Chalcedonian theology.[110]

Roman emperor Zeno (476–491) relied on the support of Peter Mongus to establish unity between Egypt and the rest of the Byzantine church through a compromise formula, the *Henotikon*, which reaffirmed the condemnation of Nestorius and Eutyches, affirmed the *Twelve Anathemas* of

---

[106]For a review of the revolt against Juvenal, see E. Honigmann, "Juvenal of Jerusalem," *DOP* 5 (1950), 208-79.

[107]Brouria Bitton-Ashkelony, *Encountering the Sacred: The Debate on Christian Pilgrimage in Late Antiquity* (Berkeley: University of California Press, 2005), 142.

[108]Zachary of Mytliene, *Ecclesiastical History*, ed. Geoffrey Greatrex et al. (Liverpool: Liverpool University Press, 2011), 132-34.

[109]Watts, *Riot in Alexandria*, 134.

[110]John Rufus, *Plerophories*, ed. F. Nau, PO 8 (1912), 89; Brouria Bitton-Ashkelony and Aryeh Kofsky, *The Monastic School of Gaza* (Leiden: Brill, 2006), 56-57.

Cyril, but avoided any explicitly Chalcedonian language (e.g., two natures). This document was issued—without the approval of the bishop of Rome—in an attempt to appease all sides of the Chalcedonian controversy and to win back the Miaphysite communities of the empire.

The Egyptian patriarch Peter Mongus and the Syrian patriarch Severus accepted the *Henotikon* as a via media because of the aspects of the document that were agreeable to the anti-Chalcedonian party (especially its inclusion of Cyril's *Twelve Chapters*).[111] However, especially in monastic communities in Egypt, the *Henotikon* was still unacceptable due to its lack of any specific condemnation of the *Tome* of Leo.[112] Because the *Henotikon* was also unacceptable to the majority of Chalcedonians, it ultimately failed to bring reconciliation.[113]

The year 518 brought renewed oppression of African and Middle Eastern Christians by Byzantine emperor Justin I who began expelling Miaphysite clergy in an effort to improve relations with Rome.[114] One of the most prominent such clergy was Severus of Antioch who was exiled to Egypt and continued to work together with the Miaphysites there under the persecution of Justin and his successor Justinian.

Chalcedonian Hegemony Under Justinian

Justinian, the nephew and successor of Justin, advanced the pro-Chalcedonian policy of Justin during a nearly forty-year reign (527–565). Justinian is often credited as one of the most influential Byzantine emperors who restored the Roman Empire to political, social, and economic dominance in the Mediterranean world. Enforcing a religious uniformity was a crucial component of Justinian's reforms.[115] Roman emperors of this period were cast as defenders

---

[111]Davis, *Early Coptic Papacy*, 96; James A. S. Evans, "The Monophysite Persecution: The Eastern View," *The Ancient World* 27 (1996): 195; Grillmeier, *Christ in Christian Tradition*, 255.

[112]Severus of Antioch, *Sixth Book*, 255.

[113]Evans, "Monophysite Persecution," 192.

[114]The reign of Justin, and later Justinian, is often thought of as the end of the classical Greco-Roman world and the beginning of what is called the Byzantine period. James A. S. Evans, *The Age of Justinian: The Circumstances of Imperial Power* (New York: Routledge, 1996), 13. See also Michael Maas, "Roman Questions, Byzantine Answers: Contours of the Age of Justinian," in *The Cambridge Companion to the Age of Justinian*, ed. Michael Maas (New York: Cambridge University Press, 2005), 4.

[115]Sarris, "Manorial Economy," 1; see also John W. Barker, *Justinian and the Later Roman Empire* (Madison: The University of Wisconsin Press, 1966), 131. Maas argues that Justinian's reform

of orthodoxy; the strengthening of the connection between emperor and subject was more effectively done in a religious manner as opposed to a purely secular one.[116] Therefore, it was in the interest of restoring the empire to its former glory that Justinian enforced Chalcedonian doctrine in majority-Miaphysite communities.

One prominent example is the removal of the sixth-century Egyptian monastic leader Abraham of Farshut from his position as leader of the Pachomian monastic community, whereupon he spent some time in the anti-Chalcedonian community of the White Monastery before founding his own community at Farshut.[117] Soon after becoming the leader (*hegoumenos*) of the monastic community, Abraham was confronted with Emperor Justinian's enforcing of Chalcedonian doctrine:

> And at that time, the devil set the storm in motion and raised up a disturbance against the church of the Lord, while an emperor named Justinian was rising up. And his heart was corrupt and his mind went astray, raving in the madness of the heretics. And when he sat on the throne, he dedicated himself to the blasphemies of Arius and Nestorius and the *Tome* of the impious Leo. Then he wrote a letter to the whole land of Egypt, to the bishops in each diocese and the superiors of the monasteries so that they might come to him in the imperial city. He wrote to the saint, Apa Abraham, who was superior of Pbow at that time, so that he might come to the court and appear before him.[118]

In this biography of Abraham, the disdain for Byzantine imperial authority and Chalcedonian theology on the part of Egyptian Christians is evident. The imperial policy that sought to suppress anti-Chalcedonianism was largely motivated by a desire for theological unity in the empire in the face of the growing threat posed by Belisarius, including the possibility of the loss of Rome.[119] In an effort to force theological and social uniformity, Justinian

---

is most characterized by his making himself the object of both religious and political loyalty (Maas, "Roman Questions," 22).

[116]Sarris, "Manorial Economy," 206.

[117]Cramer and Bacht, "Der antichalkedonische Aspekt," 335.

[118]*Panegyric on Abraham of Farhut*, ed. James E. Goehring, in *Politics, Monasticism, and Miracles in Sixth Century Upper Egypt: A Critical Edition and Translation of the Coptic Texts on Abraham of Farshut*, STAC (Tübingen: Mohr Siebeck, 2012), 78.

[119]Edward R. Hardy, "The Egyptian Policy of Justinian," *DOP* 22 (1968): 33.

used military coercion to remove the locally supported Egyptian patriarch Gaianus and replaced him with Patriarch Theodosius, whom he in turn replaced with a Chalcedonian patriarch when Theodosius refused to accept Chalcedon.[120] Justinian attempted to reconcile Chalcedonians and anti-Chalcedonians at the Second Council of Constantinople (553) by condemning the "Three Chapters": the writings of Theodore of Mopsuestia, Theodoret of Cyrrhus, and Ibas of Edessa. But the attempt was unsuccessful. By the time of the fifth ecumenical council, anti-Chalcedonian doctrine was too deeply rooted in Egypt, Syria, Armenia, and the Arabian Peninsula, and reconciliation with Chalcedonians did not happen.[121]

While in exile Theodosius still functioned as a spiritual leader for anti-Chalcedonians in Egypt, Syria, and Arabia. Theodosius consecrated Jacob Baradaeus as metropolitan of Edessa and Theodore as metropolitan of Bostra. While the sixth century saw the end of the Byzantine system of ruling curiales, Christian bishops in major metropolitan areas filled this leadership vacuum. Bishops, therefore, held much influence as they became an extension of the curia system.[122] Immediately following the deaths of Justinian in 565 and Theodosius one year later, Justin II (565–578) successfully prevented any anti-Chalcedonian leadership from taking hold in the Near East during the following decade. Now that the greatest imperial ally for anti-Chalcedonians, Empress Theodora, had also passed away, the situation for the Miaphysites was very difficult.[123]

The period following the Justinianic oppression was characterized by tensions between marginalized communities as well as broader civic unrest.

---

[120]Imperial and ecclesiastical politics in the time of Justinian were complicated by the ongoing support of Miaphysite communities by Empress Theodora. John Julius Norwich, *Byzantium: The Early Centuries* (New York: Alfred A. Knopf, 1997), 194.

[121]Andrew Louth, "Justinian and His Legacy (500–600)," in *The Cambridge History of the Byzantine Empire c. 500–1492*, ed. Jonathan Shepard (New York: Cambridge University Press, 2008), 118.

[122]Mark Whittow, "Ruling the Late Roman and Early Byzantine City: A Continuous History," in *Late Antiquity on the Eve of Islam*, ed. Averil M. Cameron (Burlington, VT: Ashgate, 2013), 169. Bishops functioned as curiales principally as local agents for the estates of the church in a particular region. However, there is no evidence that bishops ever had formal civic duties on the order of the previous curia system. John F. Haldon, *Byzantium in the Seventh Century: The Transformation of a Culture* (New York: Cambridge University Press, 1990), 97.

[123]Alfred J. Butler, *Arab Conquest of Egypt and the Last Thirty Years of the Roman Dominion*, 2nd ed., ed. P. M. Fraser (Oxford: Clarendon, 1978), 3.

Egyptian and Syrian ecclesiastical officials interfered in one another's governance and patriarchs debated trinitarian theology with varying emphasis placed on the distinction and unity of the Trinity.[124] At the same time, local uprisings in Egypt—such as various attacks on Roman grain shipments, Egypt's most valued export—were influenced by Roman political factions such as the Greens and the Blues.[125] Indeed, the Roman Empire's dependence on taxes from the wealthy landowners of Egypt's massive grain supply was only exacerbated by Justinian's imperial expansion. Wealthy, landowning Egyptians, inspired by political factions in Constantinople, sometimes leveraged their importance through refusal to pay taxes and supply grain.[126] The "circus factions" of the Greens and Blues originated as business sponsors for Roman athletes but evolved into political entities that resisted imperial control over local affairs. Such social groups often initiated violent revolutions—such as the Nika Revolt of 532, which claimed thirty thousand

---

[124]Caspar D. G. Müller, "Damian, Papst und Patriarch von Alexandrien," *OC* 70 (1986): 134. See also Rifaat Y. Ebied, "Contra Damianum: Some Remarks on an Important Syriac Manuscript," *Parole de l'Orient* 20 (1995): 209-19; Rifaat Y. Ebied, "Peter of Antioch and Damian of Alexandria: The End of a Friendship," in *A Tribute to Arthur Vööbus: Studies in Early Christian Literature and Its Environment, Primarily in the Syrian East*, ed. Robert H. Fischer (Chicago: Lutheran School of Theology, 1977), 277-82.

[125]Alan Cameron, *Circus Factions: Blues and Greens at Rome and Byzantium* (Oxford: Clarendon, 1976), 53. While originally developed in the hippodrome of Constantinople, there is evidence for extensive circus activity in Oxyrhynchus in the sixth century (Evans, *Age of Justinian*, 37).

[126]Walter Kaegi, "Egypt on the Eve of the Muslim Conquest," in *Cambridge History of Egypt I: Islamic Egypt 640–1517*, ed. Carl F. Petry (New York: Cambridge University Press, 1998), 36; Friedhelm Winkelmann, "Die Stellung Ägyptens im oströmisch-byzantinischen Reich," in *Graeco-Coptica: Griechen und Kopten im byzantinischen Ägypten*, ed. P. Nagel, Wissenschaftliche Beiträge 48 (Halle: Martin-Luther-Universität, 1984), 12; Walter E. Kaegi, *Byzantium and the Early Islamic Conquests* (New York: Cambridge University Press, 1992), 19; Peter Sarris, "The Origins of the Manorial Economy: New Insights from Late Antiquity," in Cameron, *Late Antiquity*, 3. Fergus Millar shows how among Egypt's upper class reluctance to render tax revenue to the state was a dilemma since Egypt's initial incorporation as a Roman province. *The Roman Empire and Its Neighbours*, 2nd ed. (New York: Holmes & Meier, 1966), 186; Sarris, "Manorial Economy," 221. The land tax in late antique Byzantium was evenly levied regardless of the size of property. Chris Wickham, "The Other Transition: From the Ancient World to Feudalism," in Cameron, *Late Antiquity*, 32; Jane Rowlandson, *Landowners and Tenants in Roman Egypt: The Social Relations of Agriculture in the Oxyrhynchite Nome* (Oxford: Clarendon, 1996), 7. Large estate owners in the fifth and sixth centuries were increasingly managed by in-resident landlords as opposed to the more common practice of renting in the third century (Sarris, "Manorial Economy," 118). Egyptian landowners were unique in the empire as being the only social elites allowed to hire *bucellarii* as private guardians of their property, as opposed to most landowners who retained the security of state military. Michael Whitby, "Recruitment in Roman Armies from Justinian to Heraclius (ca. 565-615)," in Cameron, *Late Antiquity*, 333.

lives—in response to Justinian's policies.[127] The existence of these factions further illustrates the role of popularizing movements and their influence in movements of African and Middle-Eastern theological resistance in response to Justinian's colonial hegemony.

DIVERGENT THEOLOGICAL LANGUAGE

The language of Christ existing in two natures—and especially the theological implications that were projected onto this language—proved scandalous for the majority of Christians in Africa, the Middle East, and Asia. On the part of Leo and the majority of Greek and Latin-speaking Roman Christians, the *Tome* was an accurate document that carefully balanced the humanity and divinity of Jesus, "acknowledged in two natures [*physis*] without confusion, without change, without division, without separation . . . and [each] combining in one person [*prosōpon*] and subsistence [*hypostasis*]."[128] Indeed, the *Tome* does represent a wonderful example of the contextualization of the Christian message—specifically the mystery of the incarnation—in idiomatic language that deploys terminology and concepts operative in broader Hellenistic society. In Platonic and Greek philosophy, an individual person (*prosōpon*) or substance (*hypostasis*) can exist in multiple natures (*physis*) without betraying its essential unity.[129] However, the vision of Jesus put forth by the *Tome* was deeply problematic to the churches outside of the mainstream Roman society.

For many Miaphysites, the idea that the divinity and humanity of Christ can be distinctly described too closely resembled Nestorius: "And when he (Justinian) sat on the throne, he dedicated himself to the blasphemies of Arius and Nestorius and the *Tome* of the impious Leo."[130] This is not to suggest that the Christians of Egypt, Syria, Armenia, and Ethiopia were

---

[127]Evans, *Age of Justinian*, 39. The common oversimplified identification of Greens as Miaphysite and Blues as Chalcedonian is not supported by historical evidence. Cameron, *Circus Factions*, 126; see also Geoffrey Greatrex, "The Nika Riot: A Reappraisal," in Cameron, *Late Antiquity*, 79. The name Nika comes from the common faction chant "Nika!" ("win!") during the hippodrome competitions.

[128]"The Chalcedonian Decree," 373.

[129]Such is the understanding of *physis* and *prosōpon* in Theodoret of Cyrrhus; Vasilije Vranic, "The Christology of Theodoret of Cyrrhus: The Question of Its Development" (PhD diss., Marquette University, 2009), 196.

[130]*Panegyric on Abraham of Farshut*, 78.

unfamiliar with Hellenistic thought. Some of the most influential Miaphysites emerging from Egypt and Syria—Dioscorus of Alexandria, Timothy Aelurus, Severus of Antioch, Peter the Iberian, Zacharias of Mytilene—were primarily Greek speakers. Even the most renowned Coptic and Syriac Christian figures—Shenoute of Atripe and Ephrem the Syrian respectively—were deeply influenced by Hellenistic philosophy despite their frequent condemnations of pagan religious practice.[131] However, as has been noted, the eastern Christians regions expressed a significant priority on biblical authority and distrusted the elevation of extrabiblical language as equally authoritative. Coupled with the fact that it too closely resembled the greatest nemesis of the Miaphysites, Nestorius, this entailed the absolute rejection of two-nature language.

This is not to suggest that the disagreement between the Chalcedonians and Miaphysites can be reduced merely to a linguistic misunderstanding. As has been stated frequently in anti-Chalcedonian scholarship since the mid-twentieth century, a reduction of Miaphysite sentiment to expressions of nationalism devoid of any theological significance is overly simplistic.[132] Miaphysite resistance was a deeply theological conviction that the unity of Christ's humanity and divinity was being betrayed by the *Tome* that motivated the Miaphysites to assert the unity of the natures after the union. At the same time, cultural and social factors also played a role, for theological controversies do not develop in a vacuum.[133] The overall cultural value of biblical literalism in the eastern provinces, as well as the lack of currency experienced by the distinction of *physis* from *hypostasis* in the multilingual context of Roman Egypt and Syria, also contributed to the schism. Political factors were at play as the sees of Alexandria, Antioch, Constantinople, and Rome were constantly vying for control. The See of Rome was elevated at Chalcedon, which laid the foundation for conflict with Constantinople centuries later.

---

[131]David Brakke and Andrew Crislip, *Selected Discourses of Shenoute the Great: Community, Theology, and Social Conflict in Late Antique Egypt* (New York: Cambridge University Press, 2015), 10; Brock, *Luminous Eye*, 21.

[132]R. Y. Ebied and L. R. Wickham, "A Collection of Unpublished Syriac Letters of Timothy Aelurus," *JTS* 21 (1970): 328.

[133]Volker Menze, *Justinian and the Making of the Syrian Orthodox Church* (New York: Oxford University Press, 2008), 59.

Linguistic factors also played a role in several cases of christological controversy. In the case of Ethiopia, the Geʿez language did not support the
concept of Jesus existing in one *hypostasis* and multiple *physis*:

> The Ethiopian Orthodox Tewahido Church's suspicion that Chalcedonian
> theology is really veiled Nestorianism is exacerbated by the implicit meanings
> of the words for "nature" and "person" in Amharic and Geʿez. Because a *ba-*
> *heriy* (nature) is a concrete idea that always expresses itself in an *akal* (person),
> to speak of two natures in Christ implies two persons.[134]

Indeed, the Ethiopian Orthodox Church's name *Tewahido* ("united") comes
directly out of its belief in the essential unity of the person and nature of Christ.

On another extreme, the Church of the East in the Persian Empire emphasized an extreme two-nature Christology that was amenable to their
linguistic categories. Following the theology of the Greek-speaking bishop
Theodore of Mopsuestia, the foundational East Syriac theologian Narsai
(399–502) established a distinct Christology that emphasized the unity of
the two distinct natures of Christ.[135] In the early seventh century, East Syriac
Christology was further developed by the theologian and patriarch of the
Church of the East, Babai the Great (551–628). Babai advanced a two-nature
theology that would remain the standard doctrine of the Church of the East
until the present day and was acceptable neither to the Chalcedonians of the
Roman Empire nor to the Miaphysites of Egypt, Syria, and Armenia. He
argued that Jesus existed in one person (*parsopa*) and in two natures (*kyane*)
with their own respective *qnome*. At the insistence of the Persian shah
Chosroes II, an ecclesiastical synod was convened in 612 between the West
Syrian Miaphysites and the East Syrians. The outcome of the synod was that
the East Syrians formally accepted the theological definition of Babai and
rejected West Syrian Miaphysitism.

The misconception that the Church of the East believes in two persons
developed from the inaccurate association of *qnome* with *hypostasis*: "*Kyana*
refers to the general, abstract nature, that is, the human being and the God

---

[134]Craig Ott and Harold A. Netland, *Globalizing Theology: Belief and Practice in an Era of World
Christianity* (Grand Rapids: Baker Academic, 2006), 150.
[135]The relationship of Narsai's Christology and that of Theodore is reflected in Narsai's *memre*
celebrating the "three doctors" of the Persian Church: Theodore of Mopsuestia, Diodore of
Tarsus, and Nestorius; see Narsai, "Homélie de Narsai sur les trois docteurs nestoriens," ed.
Pauline Martin, *JA* 14 (1899): 446-92; *JA* 15 (1900): 469-525.

being, while *qnoma* describes the concretization and individualization of this nature. Babai thus usually employed the formulation "the two natures and their *qnome*" which are united from the moment of conception."[136] His treatise the *Book of Union* explains that each *kyana* needs a *qnoma* to concretely subsist. Babai, therefore, laid the groundwork for an orthodox and uniquely East Syrian approach to the mystery of the incarnation. Because of the function of *kyane* and *qnome* in East Syrian thought, the Chalcedonian language of one *hypostasis* in two natures (*physis*) was unintelligible.

THE FIRST MAJOR SCHISM OF THE CHURCH

The imperial policies enforcing Chalcedonian doctrine resulted in the vehement rejection of this theological position throughout the eastern regions of the Byzantine Empire in Africa and Asia and the subsequent association of Chalcedonianism with Roman imperial identity. Such rhetorical constructions of identity are evident in Severus of Antioch who contrasts the faithful orthodox (i.e., Miaphysite) of Egypt and Syria with the "heretical" Roman Chalcedonians:

> They saw that we ought to receive them upon their giving us satisfaction up to this point, I mean up to the point of confessing the orthodox faith and anathematizing the things done at Chalcedon and the impious Tome of Leo, who was head of the church of the Romans (would he had never been so!), and those who speak of two natures after the union and the energies and properties of these.[137]

Here Severus gives instructions to fellow Miaphysite Christians on receiving "heretics" (i.e., Chalcedonians) into communion after they renounce two-nature theology. It is clear in his writing that the Council of Chalcedon, the Tome of Leo, and Roman imperial authority are blended together as the perpetrators of heretical belief. While the Council of Chalcedon began the schism between the mainstream Byzantine Empire of Constantinople and Rome and its Asian and African constituents in the East, the imperial policies of Justinian a century after Chalcedon finalized this schism.[138]

---

[136]Baum and Winkler, *Church of the East*, 39.
[137]Severus, *Sixth Book*, 258.
[138]Menze, *Justinian*, 9.

While there was already anti-Chalcedonian sentiment coming from Syria—most notably in the writings of Jacob of Serug and Philoxenus of Mabbug—the period of Justinian witnessed a wide-scale development of Miaphysite ecclesiastical authority in the Syrian and Arabian regions. The Syrian bishop John of Ephesus witnessed the need for Miaphysite Christians to have access to sacraments in their doctrinal community: "When the period of persecution had lasted about ten years, the rest of the believers everywhere were in difficulties about ordinations; and they began to have recourse to the believing bishops."[139] In his *Lives of the Eastern Saints*, John of Ephesus tells in great detail the work of establishing anti-Chalcedonian churches and priests by the Syrian bishop John of Tella: "John who is of remembrance of holiness, and was bishop in Tella, absolved those who received the ordination from the heretics, repented and turned towards the truth, and fulfilled the canon; [he absolved them] not at all only after the time of two years, but some also after four years. Through his blessing he gave permission that they be deacons or indeed priests."[140]

Miaphysitism also became the official faith of the Armenian church in the early sixth century. In 506 the Armenian catholicos Babugen convened the Synod of Dvin, which declared one-nature Christology the official faith of the Armenian church.[141] Though not as directly affected by Chalcedon, the Church of the East in Persia would also become estranged both from mainstream Roman Christianity as well as the Miaphysite communities of Africa and Syria during the late fifth century. Because of its adoption of the teachings of Theodore of Mopsuestia, Diodore of Tarsus, and Nestorius, the Church of the East was considered heretical following the condemnation of Nestorius at the Council of Ephesus in 431. However, this had little effect on the life of the Church of the East as it had already declared its independence at the Council of Isaac in 410.[142] However, those belonging to the Church of the East—known in western Syria as "Persians"—were expelled from Edessa in 489 by the Byzantine emperor Zeno, and the theology of the their foundational figure, Theodore of Mopsuestia, was condemned by Justinian at the

---

[139]John of Ephesus, *Lives of the Eastern Saints* 24, PO 18 (1924), 515.
[140]Menze, *Justinian*, 183.
[141]Nina Garsoian, *L'Église arménienne et le grand schism d'Orient*, CSCO 574 (Louvain: Secretariat du SCO, 1998), 186.
[142]Baum and Winkler, *Church of the East*, 26.

Second Council of Constantinople in 553. These events exacerbated the chasm between the Church of the East and Christians of the Roman Empire.

In sixth-century Egypt, the intense rejection of Chalcedonian doctrine and its association with Byzantine imperial authority that was well underway immediately following the council was intensified under Justinian. Just like Abraham of Farshut, Apollo of Hnēs was pushed out of the Pachomian monastery at Pbow by the Chalcedonian forces of Justinian:

> This very pit of the abyss was opened again in the days of the Emperor Justinian. Again that soul-destroying madness, again the torrents of lawlessness flowed in their ravines to shake the house of the faithful. For after Marcian, the culprit of peril of the faith, perished, and after Basiliscus and Zeno and still others after these, the bad weed sprouted again in the kingdom of Justinian like a hidden fire in chaff which continues to produce smoke. Now the wretched bishops who had gathered together at Chalcedon became fodder for destruction and death and heresy, but their sins continue to be active. And their wickedness was unending and even their retribution was unceasing. For the fire of apostasy which those wretched bishops kindled everywhere drew to itself the laments and tears of the holy prophets until the end.[143]

The author of Apollo's biography here likens Justinian and the Byzantine Chalcedonians to the smoke rising from the pit in Revelation 9, while the Egyptian and Syrian Christians are the oppressed faithful.[144] The Egyptian and Syrian churches also maintained a Miaphysite solidarity with the African churches outside of Roman territory in Nubia and Ethiopia despite Justinian's attempts to bring these nations into Chalcedonian solidarity.[145] Despite Ethiopia's relative friendly relations with the Byzantine Empire, the predominantly Miaphysite confession created an ecumenical distance that has persisted since the sixth century. Following the Islamic Conquest, Ethiopia entered into centuries of social, political, and economic isolation, and the strongest connection to a foreign Christian community was the Coptic hierarchy in Alexandria under whose jurisdiction the Ethiopians remained until modern times. The social and ecumenical isolation contributed

---

[143]Stephen of Hnēs, *Panegyric on Apollo*, ed. K. H. Kuhn, CSCO 394-95 (Louvain: Secrétariat du Corpus SCO, 1978), 14.

[144]Stephen of Hnēs, *Panegyric on Apollo*, 31-32.

[145]Ephraim Isaac, *The Ethiopian Orthodox Täwahïdo Church* (Trenton, NJ: Red Sea, 2012), 22.

Egypt, Syria, Arabia, and Palestine, which became part of the Sasanian Empire for the following decade (619–629).[147] Chosroes had conquered much of the eastern Byzantine Empire over the past two decades, taking advantage of Phocas's military coup against Emperor Maurice in 602.[148] The Persian and later Arab conquests of eastern Byzantium were made easier by the weakening of the Byzantine military, which occurred largely due to measures taken by Justinian and Maurice to revitalize the economy by reducing the burden of financial benefits paid to those in military service.[149] While many Christian texts of these periods put the blame for the Persian conquest on the Egyptian Jewish population, depicting them as "advisers" of the Persians, there is no evidence of a significant Jewish faction in support of the Persian invasion.[150]

A few years after Benjamin was installed as patriarch of Alexandria (626–665), the Byzantine emperor Heraclius reconquered Egypt in 629. Heraclius used the Egyptian campaign as an opportunity to study Persian military tactics, a strategy that would aid him for the duration of his reign.[151] Heraclius enacted certain changes such as making Greek the official language of the empire—which was already dominant in the Eastern Empire—as well adopting Persian military tactics which aided in reclaiming much eastern territory.[152]

The brief, ten-year period of Persian occupation favored the anti-Chalcedonian community of Egypt as the Chalcedonians were suspect due to

---

[147]Ruth Altheim-Stiehl demonstrates through papyrological evidence that the Persian invasion has a terminus post quem of 618 and a terminus ante quem of 621. Ruth Altheim-Stiehl, "Wurde Alexandreia im Juni 619 n. Chr. durch die Perser erobert: Bermerkungen zur zeitlichen Bestimmung der sâsânidischen Besetzung Ägyptens unter Chosrau II. Parwêz," *Tyche* 6 (1991): 14.

[148]Davis, *Early Coptic Papacy*, 113.

[149]Michael Whitby, "Recruitment in Roman Armies from Justinian to Heraclius (ca. 565-615)," in Cameron, *Late Antiquity*, 303.

[150]Averil M. Cameron, "Blaming the Jews: The Seventh-Century Invasions of Palestine in Context," in *Mélanges Gilbert Dagron: Travaux et Mémoires* (Paris: Association des amis du Centre d'histoire et civilisation de Byzance, 2002), 60. Robert Hoyland indicates that while there are examples of Egyptian Jews providing aid both in the Persian and Arab Conquests, such examples represented a minority of the Jewish community. *Seeing Islam as Others Saw It: A Survey and Evaluation of Christian, Jewish, and Zoroastrian Writings on Early Islam* (Princeton, NJ: Darwin, 1997), 530.

[151]Walter E. Kaegi, *Heraclius: Emperor of Byzantium* (New York: Cambridge University Press, 2003), 102.

[152]Gregory, *History of Byzantium*, 160.

their connection to Byzantine imperial power.[153] When Egypt returned to Byzantine control, Heraclius, a staunch supporter of Chalcedon, appointed Cyrus (known as the "Caucasian") as patriarch in Alexandria. At first, Heraclius along with Constantinopolitan patriarch Sergius promoted Monotheletism (the doctrine of Christ having "one will") in an attempt to win over anti-Chalcedonians without compromising the doctrine of Christ's two natures.

Although this doctrine had a significant following, it was finally rejected both by Egyptian and Syrian Miaphysites, who were suspicious of any imperially supported doctrine,[154] as well as by Chalcedonians who, especially in Constantinople, viewed this position as conceding too much to so-called "Monophysite" doctrine. In the mid-seventh century, the Chalcedonian patriarch Cyrus began to use military and economic pressure to enforce Chalcedonian doctrine in the anti-Chalcedonian community. Leveraging wealthy landowners for the sake of theological and social coercion was made easier especially in Egypt due to its relatively unchanging economic system amidst massive political change.[155] The anti-Chalcedonian patriarch Benjamin went into exile in Upper Egypt and the monastic leader Samuel of Kalamun went into exile among the Tamazight ("Berbers") along the Mediterranean coast after being severely beaten twice at Cyrus's orders. During this brief period between victory over Persia and the Arab Conquest (629–633), Heraclius was able to increase Roman affluence through theological colonialism.[156]

However, Arab forces soon began conquering significant territory. The Arab Muslim forces ascended in an era of empires increasingly characterized

---

[153]Davis, *Early Coptic Papacy*, 115. John 'the Almsgiver' was forced to flee to his native Cyprus during Persian occupation.

[154]Davis, *Early Coptic Papacy*, 116.

[155]Todd M. Hickey, *Wine, Wealth, and the State in Late Antique Egypt: The House of Apion at Oxyrhynchus* (Ann Arbor: University of Michigan Press, 2012), 157. Egypt differed from many Roman provinces and retained ancient Pharaonic practices of settling private disputes without state involvement and, after the Christianization of Egypt, clergy often served as mediators. Schafik Allam, "Observations on Civil Jurisdiction in Late Byzantine and Early Arabic Egypt," in *Life in a Multi-Cultural Society: Egypt from Cambyses to Constantine and Beyond*, ed. Janet H. Johnson (Chicago: Oriental Institute, 1992), 4; Mikhail, *From Byzantine to Islamic Egypt*, 154-55. These practices continued after the Islamic conquest of Egypt. Alexander T. Schubert and Petra M. Sijpesteijn, *Documents and the History of the Early Islamic World* (Leiden: Brill, 2015), 2.

[156]Kaegi, *Heraclius*, 226.

by forced social cohesion and universalizing monotheism.[157] Beginning one year after the death of Muhammad in 633, Arab Muslim forces swiftly conquered much Persian and Roman territory due in large part to the distance of these outlying regions from each imperial capital city and poor military defense plans for these regions.[158]

The Arab armies swiftly conquered Alexandria and much of Egypt (640–642) "without effort"[159] and began incursions into Libya in 645; after the Byzantine loss of Syria and Palestine to Arab forces, defending Egypt became a military impossibility.[160] The underestimation of the Arab armies on the part of Heraclius played no small part in the swift defeat of Byzantium.[161] The *Chronicle* of John of Nikiu presents a detailed report of the Arab conquest in which he indicates that it was ʿAmr's capture of the port city of Babylon that ensured the conquest of Alexandria.[162] Contrary to many historical interpretations of the Arab conquest of Egypt, the Christian community of Egypt was not unanimously supportive of the Arab conquerors.[163]

The conquering Arab Muslim armies led by general ʿAmr ibn al-ʿAs gained victory with relatively little bloodshed. Chalcedonian Christians continued to have Roman imperial support while Miaphysite Christians had more authority on the ground in Africa and the Middle East—this dynamic was evident in Egypt in the withdrawal of Cyrus, the Chalcedonian patriarch, and the return of Benjamin, the Miaphysite patriarch. While Miaphysites such as Benjamin expressed joy at the renewed empowerment of indigenous Christians under Muslim rule as opposed to the oppression of

---

[157]Robert G. Hoyland, *In God's Path: The Arab Conquests and the Creation of an Islamic Empire* (New York: Oxford University Press, 2015), 12.

[158]Kaegi, "Egypt on the Eve," 87. Regarding military action from the West, it has been rumored (though without substantiation) that Maximus the Confessor advised the exarch of Africa not to send troops to support Egypt because of their Miaphysite beliefs (Howard-Johnston, *World Crisis*, 160, 468).

[159]John of Nikiou, *Chronicle*, ed. R. H. Charles (Merchantville, NJ: Evolution, 2007), 200.

[160]Kaegi, *Byzantium*, 18. The loss of Egypt to the Arabs was the most crucial loss for Byzantium (Haldon *Byzantium*, 29; Howard-Johnston, *World Crisis*, 135).

[161]Kaegi, *Heraclius*, 236.

[162]Howard-Johnston, *World Crisis*, 188.

[163]Mikhail utilizes documentary evidence to demonstrate that the majority of Egyptian support for the Arab Conquest came not from clergy but from secular elites (*From Byzantine to Islamic Egypt*, 25-29).

Roman Christians, the Christians living under Muslim rule expressed a diversity of positive and negative reactions to the Arab Muslim conquest.[164] Over time Christian life became more insular as public processions were not allowed and Christians only practiced their cult within the confines of church structures.[165] Christians, along with Jews, were classified as *dhimmīs*, or protected people, and were required to pay a tax (*jizîah*) of two dinârs per adult male.[166]

The Muslim conquest had significant social, political, and economic ramifications that are difficult to overestimate. The use of Greek in Egypt and Syria went into rapid decline and disappeared during the eighth century. The replacement of the municipal economies dominated by senatorial elites after the conquest introduced a governing body that included a wider variety of social backgrounds.[167] While Roman Christianity continued to develop its theology and structure through further ecumenical councils in the late seventh century, such proceedings had little effect on African and Middle Eastern Christians now under Islamic rule.[168] The Arab conquerors became more hostile toward Christians in Egypt at the end of the seventh century. The new Egyptian emir, 'Abd al-Aziz, ordered the destruction of

---

[164]Hugh Kennedy, "Islam," in *Late Antiquity: A Guide to the Postclassical World*, ed. Glen W. Bowersock, Peter Brown, and Oleg Grabar (Cambridge, MA: Belnap, 1999), 220. There was a Roman-supported revolt against the Muslims in 645 led by Manuel the Augustulis (Kaegi, "Egypt on the Eve," 59). Melkites and other groups increasingly gravitated toward the anti-Chalcedonian Coptic Church, consolidating its ecclesiastical hegemony in Christian Egypt (Mikhail, *From Byzantine to Islamic Egypt*, 60; see also Averil M. Cameron, "Introduction," in Cameron, *Late Antiquity*, xiii). The common assumption held in prior scholarship was that the "bitterly disaffected Monophysites seem to have aided the invaders willingly, welcoming their escape from the oppressive and Chalcedonian central government" (Barker, *Justinian*, 233; Kaegi, "Egypt on the Eve," 49). While this view has been effectively repudiated, it is noteworthy that "there does not appear to have been any great longing for a return to Byzantine rule among Egyptians" (Kaegi, "Egypt on the Eve," 60).

[165]Béatrice Caseau, "Sacred Landscapes," in *Late Antiquity: A Guide to the Postclassical World*, ed. Glen W. Bowersock, Peter Brown, and Oleg Grabar (Cambridge, MA: Belnap, 1999), 51.

[166]Butler, *Arab Conquest*, 454. Cyrus paid tribute to the Arabs for three years prior to the invasion in an attempt to buy them off (481).

[167]Kennedy, "Islam," 222, 428.

[168]Judith Herrin argues that the Quinisext Council (or Council in Trullo) in 692 continued the spirit of Chalcedon by attempting to establish universal Christian doctrine despite the fact that the sees of Jerusalem, Antioch, and Alexandria were now under Islamic authority. Judith Herrin, "The Quinisext Council (692) as a Continuation of Chalcedon," in *Chalcedon in Context: Church Councils 400–700*, ed. Richard Price and Mary Whitby (Liverpool: Liverpool University Press, 2009), 164.

crosses and placed anti-Christian expressions of Muslim faith over church doorways in the Delta region.[169]

SEEING ISLAM AS CHRISTIANS SAW IT

The Christians who had long occupied the territory that came under Arab Muslim control in the seventh century exhibited variegated responses to their new rulers. One such witness was Benjamin of Alexandria, who was the Egyptian pope before, during, and after the conquest. As a result of the administrative reforms of Heraclius, however, Benjamin was replaced by the Chalcedonian patriarch Cyrus "the Caucasian" (*kaukos*, i.e., "one from the Caucus region"). Cyrus began to persecute the Miaphysites of Egypt and Benjamin went into exile. After the Muslims conquered Egypt, Cyrus surrendered his control of Egypt and fled. Because of the previously disaffected relationship between the Miaphysites of Egypt and Byzantine imperial authority, Benjamin was allowed to return from exile as patriarch of Alexandria once again.

Benjamin traveled through Egypt, reconsolidated his authority, and reconsecrated many churches that had been damaged. One such example is when Benjamin came to the Wadi El Natrun and reconsecrated the Monastery of Macarius:

> I give you thanks my Lord Jesus Christ because you have made me worthy once more to witness the freedom of expression [†ΠΑΡΡΗϹΙΑ] of the orthodox faith and the fulfillment of the holy churches, the destruction and overthrow of the godless heretics [ΝΝΙϨΕΡΕΤΙΚⲰϹ ΝΑΤΝΟΥϯ]. The praise is yours, benevolent Savior, for the way in which you have allowed me to see the churches yet again in their glory and their good condition [ΤΟΥΚΑΤΑϹΤΑϹΙϹ]. I give you thanks my Lord Jesus Christ for you have saved my soul from the hands of the tyrant [ΜΠΙΤΥΡΑΝΝΟϹ], dragon [ΝΑΡΑΚⲰΝ], apostate [ΝΑΠΟϹΤΑΤΗϹ], the one who chased me on account of the orthodox faith. I give you thanks, my lord Christ, for you have allowed me to see my sons once more as they surround me in your honor, my Lord Jesus.[170]

---

[169]Howard-Johnston, *World Crisis*, 322. The shift in attitude represents the diversity of Muslim response toward Christian imagery and practice in the early centuries of Islam. Textual evidence emerging from the Syrian region presents varying Muslim perspectives toward the cross in particular. Jack Tannous, "Syria Between Byzantium and Islam: Making Incommensurables Speak" (PhD diss., Princeton University, 2010), 477.

[170]Benjamin of Alexandria, *Livre de la consécration du sanctuaire de Benjamin*, ed. René-Georges Coquin (Paris: IFAO, 1975), 106-8.

Figure 1.1. Church door in the Monastery of the Syrians in the Wadi El Natrun, Egypt

Benjamin spoke these words on entering the Monastery of Macarius and being received as the true patriarch by the Egyptian people who had rejected the "tyrant" Cyrus. Writing after Roman authority—and therefore Chalcedonian authority—had ended in Egypt, it is striking that Benjamin continues to display vehement anger toward the Chalcedonians even after their absence.

Similarly, the Copto-Arabic biography of the Egyptian patriarchs, the *Arabic History of the Patriarchs of Alexandria (AHPA)*, recounts Benjamin's return after the conquest as a deliverance from oppression:

> Therefore when the holy Benjamin heard this, he returned to Alexandria with great joy, clothed with the crown of patience and sore conflict which had befallen the orthodox people through their persecution by the heretics, after having been absent during thirteen years, ten of which were years of Heraclius, the misbelieving Roman, with the three years before the Muslims conquered Alexandria. When Benjamin appeared, the people and the whole city rejoiced, and made his arrival known to Sanutius, the duke who believed in Christ, who had settled with the commander 'Amr that the patriarch should return, and had received a safe-conduct from 'Amr for him.[171]

---

[171]B. Evetts, ed., *Arabic History of the Patriarchs of Alexandria (AHPA)*, PO 1, 105-211; 383-518 (1904): 496.

to the separation of Ethiopian Christianity and the Western Christian world until the beginning of European colonial missions.

Likewise in Nubia, a one-nature theology remained predominant, contributing to the separation of this ancient African church from the Christianity of Europe. Nubia's Christian roots began around the time of Chalcedon and developed significantly during the time of Justinian. Contemporary accounts indicate that Justinian sent missionaries to Nubia in an attempt to gain a Chalcedonian outpost south of his jurisdiction in the majority Miaphysite Egypt. However, Justinian's wife Theodora supported Miaphysite endeavors worldwide and had already sent counter missionaries to Nubia.[146] The success of Empress Theodora's Miaphysite missionaries coupled with Miaphysite neighbors to the north in Egypt and to the south in Ethiopia contributed to the triumph of Miaphysite doctrine in the kingdoms of Nubia.

The two-nature Christology developed at Chalcedon became a dividing point that caused the first major split in the history of Christianity, equal only to the East-West schism of the eleventh century and the Protestant Reformation. The Chalcedonian schism, however, represents the most significant ecclesiastical divide with regard to the perception of Christianity as a white man's religion. While all schisms in church history are at once theological as well as cultural in nature, this first major schism resulted in the marginalization of all the major non-Western Christian traditions of antiquity. With the major ecclesiastical centers of Africa, the Middle East, and Asia now condemned as heretical, the church of the Roman Empire would increasingly come to see itself as the sole heir and guardian of orthodox Christianity. Non-Western Christian groups were then ignored, oppressed, and colonized by the dominant Roman church until an unprecedented world superpower emerged that dramatically altered the fate of the non-Western Christian world.

AN OVERVIEW OF THE ARAB MUSLIM CONQUEST

Just after an ecclesiastical union took place between Egypt and Syria, the Persian shah Chosroes II achieved his long-awaited goal and conquered

---

[146]Salim Faraji, *The Roots of Nubian Christianity Uncovered: The Triumph of the Last Pharaoh* (Trenton, NJ: Africa World, 2012), 66.

Benjamin, and the Egyptian Christian community, should not be seen as supportive of the Muslim invaders of the seventh century. The *AHPA* perceives of the conquest of the eastern Roman provinces as a divine retribution for the "sin" of Chalcedonian theology: "The Lord abandoned the army of the Romans before him [Muhammad], as a punishment for their corrupt faith, and because of the anathemas uttered against them, on account of the council of Chalcedon, by the ancient fathers."[172] A similar interpretation of the conquest is provided by the Egyptian bishop John of Nikiou in his *Chronicle*:

> And Abba Benjamin, the patriarch of the Egyptians, returned to the city of Alexandria in the thirteenth year after his flight from the Romans, and he went to the Churches, and inspected all of them. And every one said: "This expulsion (of the Romans) and victory of the Moslem is due to the wickedness of the emperor Heraclius and his persecution of the Orthodox through the

Figure 1.2. Ceiling cross from the Monastery of Macarius in the Wadi El Natrun, Egypt, eighth century CE; the double-sided ends on the cross are meant to represent the one united nature (miaphysite) of Christ

---

[172]*AHPA*, 492-93. This is also the perspective of the *Apocalypse of Samuel of Kalamun*, written several centuries after the time of Benjamin, *L'Apocalypse de Samuel, Supérieur de Deir-el-Qalamoun*, ed. J. Ziadeh, *ROC* 10 (1915–1917): 397.

patriarch Cyrus. This was the cause of the ruin of the Romans and subjugation of Egypt by the Moslem."[173]

Because Chalcedonian (two-nature) theology was sinful in the eyes of the Miaphysites of Egypt, Syria, and Palestine, the Muslim conquest was God's divine retribution on the Roman Empire. This has led previous scholarship to argue that Near Eastern Christians not only favored Muslim rulers over Byzantine authority, but that they even aided the Muslims in conquering Roman authority.[174] While this outdated view lacks evidence, there is yet an anti-Roman/Chalcedonian tone in Near Eastern Christian texts that persists long after Roman authority ended there. This should be understood not as evidence for Christian complicity in the Arab Muslim Conquest but as part of a broader Christian polemic against heresy. From the perspective of African and Middle Eastern Christians now under Islamic rule, the Muslims were simply barbarians who had no knowledge of the truth. Roman Chalcedonians, however, were Christians who had, from the perspective of Near Eastern Miaphysites, distorted the teachings of Scripture in claiming that Christ existed in two natures. In the perspective of many early Christians, heresy was "supremely dangerous,"[175] while pagans or barbarians simply did not know any better.

Therefore, the fact that Near Eastern Christians expressed greater vehemence against Roman Christians than Muslims after the conquest should be understood as concern about orthodox Christian theology. Christians living under Muslim rule were not uncritical of their Muslim rulers. John of Nikiou claims that the Egyptian Miaphysites fled their homes for "fear of the Moslem" while the Chalcedonians ("Melkites") were supported by the Muslims:

> The Muslims took possession of all the land of Egypt, southern and northern, and trebled their taxes. . . . The yoke they laid on the Egyptians was heavier than the yoke which had been laid on Israel by Pharaoh. . . . When God's judgment lights upon these Ishmaelites may He do unto them as He did aforetime unto Pharaoh! . . . For 'Amr had no mercy on the Egyptians, and did not observe the covenant they had made with him, for he was of a barbaric race.[176]

---

[173]John of Nikiou, *Chronicle*, 200.
[174]Mikhail, *From Byzantine to Islamic Egypt*, 25-29.
[175]Michael Foat, "I Myself Have Seen: The Representation of Humanity in the Writings of Apa Shenoute of Atripe" (PhD diss., Brown University, 1996).
[176]John of Nikiou, *Chronicle*, 194-95.

A more positive description of Muslim rulers comes from the biography of the Coptic patriarch Isaac who, before becoming patriarch, already had a high-ranking office as an archivist for the Muslim prefect of Egypt. While Muslims retained political and military dominance in the Middle East and North Africa, they were still numerical minorities in many places and non-Muslims continued to serve at all levels of government. The *Life of Isaac* provides a positive account of the Muslim governor of Egypt, ʿAbd al-ʿAziz ibn Marwan, after Isaac became patriarch: "And God kept him [Isaac] safe before the king of the Saracens, for he was greatly honored by him as he [ʿAbd al-ʿAziz] also honored him. He [ʿAbd al-ʿAziz] summoned him many times and they sat together and they socialized for the king had seen many healings by his [Isaac's] hands."[177] Despite the praise for the Muslim governor, this excerpt demonstrates the looming threat of Muslim violence against Christians as the governor is presented as a patron of Christians against the "Saracens," who presumably seek to harm the Christians. Even the governor at one point almost kills Isaac for fear that his authority as patriarch rivaled his own.[178] However, due to his change of heart, the text remembers him as one who "built churches and monasteries for monks around his city, for he loved the Christians."[179]

In Western Mesopotamia, Christian writers such as John of Damascus and Theodore bar Konai represented a flourishing apologetic literary activity. Writing in Greek, John of Damascus wrote one of the first comprehensive summaries of the Christian faith, *The Fount of Knowledge*, with a particular focus on polemicizing Islamic theology.[180] From the perspective of the Church of the East, Theodore bar Konai wrote a summa theologica titled the *Scholion*, synthesizing the theology of the East Syriac church. While intended to provide comprehensive treatment of an array of biblical and theological issues, the tenth chapter of the *Scholion* provides a Christian response to Muslim arguments against Christ, the Bible, and Christianity.[181] The catholicos of the Church of the East, Timothy I, was a contemporary of

---

[177]Mena of Nikou, *Life of Isaac Patriarch of Alexandria*, ed. E. Porcher, PO 11 (1915), 363.
[178]Mena of Nikou, *Life of Isaac*, 384.
[179]Mena of Nikou, *Life of Isaac*, 368.
[180]Andrew Louth, *St. John Damascene: Tradition and Originality in Byzantine Theology* (New York: Oxford University Press, 2002), 37.
[181]Griffith, *Church in the Shadow of the Mosque*, 43.

Theodore bar Konai and provided some of the most fascinating examples of
Christian-Muslim dialogue in the early years of Muslim rule. Patriarch
Timothy engaged in extensive missionary activity, extending the presence
of the predominately Syriac-speaking Church of the East across the Middle
East as well as Central, East, and South Asia. Timothy relocated the see of
the Church of the East from the former Persian capital Seleucia-Ctesiphon
to the new Abbasid capital of Baghdad in order to be in the center of political, economic, and intellectual activity. Baghdad was one of the largest
and most cosmopolitan cities in the early medieval world and the Syriac-
speaking Christians in the Middle East served as linguistic, philosophical,
and theological intermediaries. Among many other Syriac-speaking Christians, Timothy was part of an extensive translation movement wherein
Syriac Christians translated many Greek philosophical texts into Syriac and
then into Arabic. A prominent example of this for Timothy was his commis-
sioning by the Abbasid Caliph to translate Aristotle's *Topics* into Arabic. One
of the most well-known texts from Timothy was his *Apology*—an interfaith
dialogue between Timothy and the Abbasid Muslim Caliph al-Mahdi at the
turn of the ninth century. The dialogue is in a question-answer format
typical of Arabic dialogues and the two figures address principal questions
of theological difference between Christians and Muslims:

> And our gracious and wise King said to me: "What do you say about Mu-
> hammad?" And I replied to his Majesty: "Muhammad is worthy of all praise,
> by all reasonable people, O my Sovereign. He walked in the path of the
> prophets, and trod in the track of the lovers of God. All the prophets taught
> the doctrine of one God and since Muhammad taught the doctrine of the
> unity of God, he walked, therefore, in the path of the prophets.[182]

The cordial nature of the exchange represents the attempt to prescribe an
amicable mode of communication for its Christian audience with respect to
how they engage their Muslim neighbors. Timothy seeks to build common
ground with Muslims and makes an effort to explain points of theological
discord in an amiable and relevant way: "And our victorious King said to

---

[182]Samir K. Samir, "The Prophet Muhammad as Seen by Timothy I and Some Other Arab Chris-
tian Authors," in *Syrian Christians Under Islam: The First Thousand Years*, ed. David Thomas
(Leiden: Brill, 2001), 93. See full translation in Alphonse Mingana, *Woodbrooke Studies*, vol. 2
(Cambridge: Heffer, 1928).

me: 'You believe in one God, as you said, but one in three.' And I answered his sentence: 'I do not deny that I believe in one God in three, and three in one, but not in three different Godheads, however, but in the persons of God's Word and His Spirit. I believe that these three constitute one God, not in their person but in their nature.'"[183] Timothy here engages what has remained the central critique of Islam on Christianity for over a millennium, the doctrine of the Trinity:

> People of the Book, do not go to excess in your religion, and do not say anything about God except the truth: the Messiah, Jesus, son of Mary, was nothing more than a messenger of God, His word, conveyed to Mary, a spirit from Him. So believe in God and His messengers and do not speak of a "Trinity"—stop [this], that is better for you—God is only one God, He is far above having a son, everything in the heavens and earth belongs to Him and He is sufficient protector. The Messiah would never disdain to be a servant of God, nor would the angels who are close to Him. He will gather before Him all those who disdain His worship and are arrogant: to those who believe and do good works He will give due rewards and more of His bounty; to those who are disdainful and arrogant He will give an agonizing torment, and they will find no one besides God to protect or help them.[184]

This passage from sūrat an-Nisā' in the Qur'an has continued to serve both as the principle Muslim invective against the Trinity as well as a source for Christians engaging Islam on this subject, as it calls Jesus "His Word" and "a spirit from Him," which has been used as a defense of trinitarian doctrine. One significant example comes from the earliest extant Christian text to be written in Arabic, the treatise commonly called *On the Triune Nature of God*: "We praise you, O God, and we adore you and we glorify you in your creative Word and your holy, life-giving Spirit, one God, and one Lord, and one Creator. We do not separate God from his Word and his Spirit. God showed his power and his light in the Law and the Prophets, and the Psalms and the Gospel, that God and his Word and his Spirit are one God and one Lord." Written in the mid-eighth century, the anonymous author of this text goes to great effort to defend the doctrine of the Trinity using concepts already

---

[183]Karen Louise Jolly, *Tradition and Diversity: Christianity in a World Context to 1500* (New York: Routledge, 1997), 299-300.
[184]*The Qur'an*, ed. M. A. S. Abdel Haleem (New York: Oxford University Press, 2004), 4:171-73.

operative in Islamic belief (e.g., God's Word and Spirit) and focusing on the essential oneness and undividedness of God. The first known Arabic-speaking Christian was a Melkite (i.e., Chalcedonian) Christian from Edessa in the early ninth century named Theodore Abū Qurrah. Theodore wrote extensively in Arabic and Syriac, although all his works survive in Arabic. Theodore lived during the iconoclast controversy where the practice of the veneration of icons was in sharp dispute in the Christian world. Although he lived in the Muslim world in which the practice of even artistically depicting a holy person was shunned, Theodore, like his mentor John of Damascus, vehemently defended the practice of venerating icons.[185]

The early centuries of Islamic rule can be thus characterized as a period when Christians and other religious groups lived relatively peacefully. During the centuries of the Crusades, however, the situation for Christians living under Muslim rule became more oppressive. It is not surprising, therefore, that it is from this period that we begin to find more decidedly negative depictions of Muslim authority. In some cases historical imagination was reconfigured in response to heightened levels of persecution beginning in the tenth century. It was during this time that Severus ibn al-Muqaffa contributed to the *AHPA*, providing a starkly different picture of ʿAbd al-ʿAziz than the contemporary account found in the *Life of Isaac*:

> Then he [ʿAbd al-ʿAziz] commanded to destroy all the crosses which were in the land of Egypt, even the crosses of gold and silver. So the Christians in the land of Egypt were troubled. Moreover he wrote certain inscriptions, and placed them on the doors of the churches at Miṣr and in the Delta, saying in them: "Muhammad is the great Apostle of God, and Jesus also is the Apostle of God. But verily God is not begotten and does not beget.[186]

As the situation for Christians became worse after the first few centuries of Muslim rule, Christian polemic against Muslims also intensified sometimes to the point of rejecting the Arabic language. A text that was likely written in the tenth-century purports to have been written by an Egyptian monk named Samuel of Kalamun who lived before, during, and after the

---

[185]Sidney Griffith, "Theodore Abū Qurrah's Arabic Tract on the Christian Practice of Venerating Images," *JAOS* 105 (1985): 53-73.
[186]*AHPA*, 25.

Arab Muslim conquest.[187] In the *Apocalypse of Samuel of Kalamun,* an Arabic-speaking Egyptian Christian writes in the voice of the seventh-century Coptic monastic leader pronouncing apocalyptic visions of the Arab Muslim conquest of Egypt and the subsequent Arabization of the Coptic people. Like Severus ibn al-Muqaffa in the *AHPA,* the author of the *Apocalypse* presents a decidedly negative perspective of Islamic rulers in Egypt in sharp contrast to the more positive images of Muslims in seventh-century Christian sources: "Would to God that you would not recall their name among us today, for it is a proud race that we must not name in the assemblies of the saints. Ah! This name! That of the Arabs and their domination (which is) contrary to our laws! These haughty kings who reign in their time!"[188] The *Apocalypse* confirms the assessment of a more positive Muslim-Christian interaction in the earliest years of Islamic rule in Egypt: "When the Arab migrants had seized Egypt, they were few, but they have increased their benefits to the Christian people."[189] While Muslims were in political power, they were still the numerical minority and therefore required cooperation with Christian and other minority communities in various areas of social and civic administration. As the Muslim population grew and indigenous Egyptian and Arab people became increasingly blended, the Arabic language became the dominant language and Coptic went into rapid decline. The *Apocalypse* and its insistence on Copts rejecting the Arabic language was likely in reaction to the increasing popularity of Copto-Arabic figures such as Severus ibn al-Muqaffa.[190] While the *Apocalypse* represents an increasingly anti-Islamic sentiment among Coptic Christians that criticized Muslims for governmental mismanagement, sexual licentiousness, and oppressing the poor, its primary invective is focused on the deployment of the Arabic language among Christians: "They still commit another action which, if I told you, would cause your hearts pain: namely, that they will abandon the beautiful Coptic language in which the Holy Spirit has often expressed through the mouth of our spiritual fathers. They teach their children from

---

[187]*Life of Samuel of Kalamun,* ed. Anthony Alcock (Warminster: Aris & Phillips, 1983), vii–ix; for the pseudonomity of authorship, see Mikhail, *From Byzantine to Islamic Egypt,* 99.

[188]*L'Apocalypse de Samuel,* 393.

[189]*L'Apocalypse de Samuel,* 392.

[190]Arietta Papaconstantinou, "'They Shall Speak the Arabic Language and Take Pride In It': Reconsidering the Fate of Coptic After the Arab Conquest," *Le Muséon* (2007): 292.

their youth to speak the language of the Hegira and they worship in it."[191] The "language of the Hegira"—or *hijra* pilgrimage to Mecca—serves as coded polemic against the Arabic language, which, for the author of the *Apocalypse*, is tantamount to the Islamic faith. The irony is that, despite its attempt to dissuade Copts from speaking Arabic, the text itself only survives in Arabic! While the text could have been originally composed in Coptic,[192] the message of the *Apocalypse* still represents the changing cultural and religious landscape for Christians living under Islamic hegemony. The author of the *Apocalypse* is principally concerned with the use of Arabic in liturgical contexts as cultural shifts toward Arabic are equated with losing Christian identity: "They abandon this language (Coptic) to speak the Arabic language and to worship in it, to the point that we can no longer recognize them as Christians; but rather, we will suppose them to be Berbers."[193]

MUHAMMAD AND CHARLEMAGNE

The Arab Muslim conquest contributed to the Western captivity of the church in two important ways: (1) the reduction of missional efforts in Africa and Asia, and (2) the impetus for the Western world to reinvent itself as a religious empire to rival the ascendant Islamic power to the East. The Roman world lost much of its maritime influence over the Mediterranean Sea: "There was no longer any traffic in the Mediterranean, except along the Byzantine coast. As Ibn-Khaldoun says (with the necessary reservation as regards Byzantium): 'the Christians could no longer float a plank upon the sea.' The Mediterranean was henceforth at the mercy of the Saracen pirates."[194]

---

[191] *L'Apocalypse de Samuel*, 394-95.

[192] Papaconstantinou, "They Shall Speak," 274.

[193] *L'Apocalypse de Samuel*, 395.

[194] Henri Pirenne, *Mohammed and Charlemagne* (Mineola, NY: Dover, 2001), 166. Central to Pirenne's thesis is the idea that Western Roman Mediterranean commercial unity was uninterrupted after the Germanic invasions of the fifth century. But this has been largely refuted. Indeed, the idea of a strong Western Roman stronghold on Mediterranean commerce has been rejected as "low-pressure states and sluggish economies were the order of the day" from the start of the fifth century, long before the Germanic invasions (Brown, *Western Christendom*, 13). Herwig Wolfram provides a more neutral review of the Pirenne thesis as he affirms the connection between religious growth and maritime commerce in *The Roman Empire and Its Germanic Peoples* (Berkeley: University of California Press, 1990), 312-13. While Pirenne's work has received significant and valid critique, his thesis is helpful in shifting the focus during the transition of Roman to European successor states "from military and political to economic and cultural developments." Walter Pohl, *Kingdoms of the Empire: The Integration of Barbarians in Late Antiquity* (Leiden: Brill, 1997), 1.

After the fall of Rome in the late fifth century, the Greek-speaking Eastern Roman Empire (called Byzantium in modern times) centered in Constantinople became the seat of Roman power. Byzantine emperors such as Justinian provided leadership and stability for the weakened Western Empire during the sixth century. After the Islamic conquest in the seventh century, however, the East began to weaken, providing the impetus for the West to exist as a Christian empire equal to the ascendant Islamic empire to the east. While Islamic powers controlled the Mediterranean on the south, east, and west, the northern side was still largely under Western Christian control.[195] The emergence of a new European Christian superpower occurred when the Frankish Empire, ruled by the Merovingian dynasty, was overthrown by the Carolingian dynasty. This political transference was significantly influenced by the shifting centralization of Western Christendom. From the earliest period of Merovingian rule, figures such as Gregory of Tours interpreted the social and historical events of Gaul to be intimately connected with the spiritual foundation of the Frankish people.[196] Thus in the early years of the life of Muhammad one of the earliest and most prominent Roman successor kingdoms was reestablishing its ethnic and religious identity in the manner of Eusebius centuries prior. Indeed, the ethnogenesis of early medieval European nations rested heavily on the memory of a Christianized Roman Empire.

After the Roman pope Zachary deposed the final Merovingian king, the next pope, Stephen II, supervised the ordination of Pepin the Short as the first Frankish king of the Carolingian dynasty. After the death of Pepin the Short in 768, his son Charles I became king of the Frankish Empire and maintained his father's support of the papacy and Western Christendom by continuing to expand the borders of the Carolingian Frankish kingdom. After the death of his brother and coregnant, Carloman I, Charles I (Charles

---

[195]Pirenne, *Mohammed and Charlemagne*, 184-85. The political, social, and economic significance of Mediterranean commerce and its role in redefining the social identity of the Western Roman world is one of the helpful remaining aspects of the Pirenne thesis as opposed to earlier scholarship, which leaned on a supposed spiritual unity provided by ecclesiastical leadership (Brown, *Western Christendom*, 11).

[196]Helmut Reimitz, *History, Frankish Identity, and the Framing of Western Ethnicity, 550-850* (New York: Cambridge University Press, 2015), 50. The connection between church and state in Merovingian Gaul is further evidenced by the earliest surviving document from a Merovingian king, Clovis, in the early sixth century in which Clovis petitions the support of the Frankish bishops for his kingship (98).

the Great or Charlemagne) assumed control of Italy and removed the
reigning Germanic Lombards who were reigning in northern Italy. Charlemagne also strengthened Frankish control of the border region Aquitania
and even ventured across the Pyrenees Mountains into Muslim-dominated
al-Andalus (Spain). Charlemagne's campaign was also directed north as he
conquered the neighboring Saxon kingdom after decades of warfare with
King Widukind. As his control of Saxony solidified, Charlemagne continued
supporting the missionary activity that had been underway under previous
figures such as Boniface. Charlemagne instituted harsh conversion laws in
Saxony, the most infamous of which were his *Capitulatio de partibus Sax-
oniae* ("Ordinances Concerning Saxony"), which issued the death of pagans
who refused to convert to Christianity. One of the most notorious incidents
of Charlemagne's missionary oppression of Saxony was the Massacre of
Verden in 782, where Charlemagne ordered the execution of 4,500 captive
Saxons who refused to convert to Christianity. Yet despite the religious persecution of the Carolingian dynasty, Christianity was characterized as a
peaceful religion by Charlemagne's contemporary Theodore Abū Qurrah
living under Islamic rule in Haran: "There is another reason why we have
come to the conclusion that the Christian religion is from God, namely that
the [Christian] nations have been led to [become] disciples of Christ and to
accept that religion by the power of God and not by the power of men, nor
by their coercion, nor their ruses nor their enticements, as is the case with
other religions."[197]

Charlemagne acted as patron and protector of Western Christendom.
While the Carolingians fashioned their empire with Rome as a symbolic
center, they nevertheless saw themselves as a vast improvement to their
"slothful forefathers."[198] The Carolingians engaged in a vast program of *correctio*, in which religious, cultural, educational, and linguistic restorations
of Western Christian society were undertaken. It is in this light that Charlemagne has been remembered frequently as the "restorer of the Western
empire."[199] The program of *correctio* was motivated by the Carolingians'

---

[197]Hoyland, *In God's Path*, 543.

[198]Rosamond McKitterick, *Charlemagne: The Formation of a European Identity* (New York: Cambridge University Press, 2008), 315.

[199]Edward Gibbon, *The Decline and Fall of the Roman Empire* (New York: Harcourt, Brace, and
Company, 1960), 644.

self-perception as the renovators of a "respected" Christian society which, from their perspective, had been long dormant and was their responsibility to rejuvenate.[200] Charlemagne's political and spiritual authority was effectively symbolized when he was crowned Imperator Romanorum ("Emperor of the Romans") by Pope Leo III on December 25, 800, in Saint Peter's Basilica in Rome. The Frankish scholar Einhard wrote a biography of Charlemagne that describes the king's coronation:

> Charles accordingly went to Rome, to set in order the affairs of the Church, which were in great confusion, and passed the whole winter there. It was then that he received the titles of Emperor and Augustus [Dec. 25, 800], to which he at first had such an aversion that he declared that he would not have set foot in Church that day that they were conferred, although it was a great feast-day, if he could have foreseen the design of the Pope.[201]

Einhard's hagiographical account of Charlemagne strategically presents Charlemagne as the reluctant hero with no aspirations for power. By contrast, the Roman "emperors" are envious antagonists who oppress the ecclesiastical leadership and confuse the "affairs of the church," which are both in need of Charlemagne's rescuing. Despite the bias of Einhard's account, it is clear that the memory of Charlemagne was constructed to cast him as a new Constantine who stands in a succession of Roman emperors who act as protectors of the church. Such religious and imperial exceptionalism is rooted in late antique Western Christendom and is mirrored by a similar dynamic among Muslim historians such as Ibn Qutayba of Baghdad (828–889): "God sent the Prophet among them [Berbers] . . . unified them . . . granted them dominion in the lands . . . and, at a time when there were yet no non-Arabs among them, addressed them, saying, 'You are the best nation ever brought forth to men.'"[202] As the Carolingian Empire experienced unprecedented dominance across Europe, writers from this period asserted the primacy of their Christendom more pointedly than their Merovingian

---

[200]Brown, *Western Christendom*, 440.

[201]Einhard, *The Life of Charlemagne*, ed. Samuel Epes Turner (New York: Harper & Brothers, 1880), 65-66.

[202]Ann Christys, "The History of Ibn Habib and Ethnogenesis in al-Andalus," in *The Construction of Communities in the Early Middle Ages: Texts, Resources, and Artefacts*, ed. Richard Corradini, Max Diesenberger, and Helmut Reimitz (Leiden: Brill, 2003), 344.

predecessors.[203] Western Christians such as the British historian Bede represent the view that Charlemagne emerged as the new Christian leader since the rest of the Christian world was seen as immobilized by Islam: "But that was long ago. Now, however, so much is his [Ishmael's] hand against all and the hand of all against him that they press the length and breadth of Africa under their sway, and also the greater part of Asia and, hating and inimical to all, they try for some of Europe."[204] Similarly, the greatest Muslim victory in Europe—the conquest of Hispania, or al-Andalus—was interpreted by Christian historians as the result of divine retribution for the prominence of the Arian heresy in Visigothic Spain. One example is the Spanish *Chronicle of 754*, which recounts the fall of Hispania through the lens of religious orthodoxy: "Who can recount such perils? Who can enumerate such grievous disaster? . . . All this and more Hispania, once so delightful and now rendered so miserable, endured as much to its honour as to its disgrace."[205]

For eighth-century Spanish historians, like Eusebius in the fourth century, the success of the empire and her successor states was coextensive with the kingdom of God. As the rise of Islam significantly weakened Christian communities considered heretical in Spain, Byzantium, North Africa, Mesopotamia, and Persia, the previously "barbarian" heirs to the empire shifted from periphery to the center of Christendom. The vacuum created in the seventh century for a Christian superpower was filled by Charlemagne and was able to flourish in Northern and Western Europe largely free from Islamic interference. While the West would not enter into large-scale conflict with Muslims until the Crusades, they adopted the hostile view of Muslims that was developing among their Byzantine Christian neighbors. The eighth-century historian Theophanes's account of the emperor Leo III's victory over the Umayyad fleet in 717 reported that God favored the "Christian Empire" and wrought calamities on the Muslims.[206]

Although the Carolingian Empire did not last much beyond the death of Charlemagne, his dynasty provided the political, social, and religious impetus

---

[203]Reimitz, *Frankish Identity*, 405.

[204]Hoyland, *In God's Path*, 227.

[205]Ann Christys, "The Transformation of Hispania After 711," in *Regna and Gentes: The Relationship Between Late Antique and Early Medieval Peoples and Kingdoms in the Transformation of the Roman World*, ed. Hans-Werner Goetz, Jörg Jarnut, and Walter Pohl (Leiden: Brill, 2003), 223.

[206]Brown, *Western Christendom*, 318.

for the creation of the Holy Roman Empire under Otto I in 962. Following the practice of Charlemagne, Otto I took up the title of "Emperor of the Romans" in a Western Christian empire that would last for a millennium founded on the memory of Christian rulers like Constantine and Charlemagne. Louis the Pious, Charlemagne's son and successor, provides an example of how Western Christendom presented itself as the rival religious empire to Islam: "Had this people (the Saracens) worshipped God, pleased Christ and received holy baptism, we should have made peace with them and kept that peace in order to bind them to God through religion. But this people remains detestable; it spurns the salvation we offer and follows the commandments of the demons."[207]

Such combative rhetoric is infrequent if not absent from Near Eastern Christian texts such as the *Chronicle* of John of Nikiou, the *Life of Isaac*, or the writings of Theodore Abū Qurrah. While Near Eastern Christians were certainly critical of the Muslim rulers, the Christian West went further in presenting itself as the only Christian empire that could stand as a rival to Islam. That this perception was operative among Muslims is evidenced in some of the earliest hadiths: "Persia is [only a matter of] one or two thrusts and no Persia will be after that. But the *Rûm* [the East Romans] . . . are people of sea and rock. . . . Alas, they are your enemies to the end of time."[208] Like Western Christians, Muslim conquerors also understood divine favor as demonstrated by imperial and religious dominance, as represented in the construction of the Great Mosque of Damascus under Calif al-Walid:

> For he beheld Syria to be a country that had long been occupied by Christians and he noted the beautiful churches still belonging to them, so enchantingly fair and so renowned for their splendor [such as the church of the Holy Sepulcher in Jerusalem]. . . . So he sought to build for the Muslims a mosque that should prevent them from looking with admiration at the Christian churches, and that should be unique and a wonder to the world.[209]

After the Muslim conquest of Spain, a failed attempt was made by the governor 'Abd al-Rahman to conquer territory in Gaul at Poitiers in 732. 'Abd

---

[207]Hoyland, *In God's Path*, 228. He goes on to point out that not until the time of the Crusades was there significant interest in the writings of Islam among Western European Christians.
[208]Brown, *Western Christendom*, 297.
[209]Brown, *Western Christendom*, 302.

al-Rahman's defeat at the hands of Frankish commander Charles Martel was celebrated by Bede: "The Saracens who had wrought miserable slaughter on Gaul . . . were punished for their faithlessness."[210] To be certain, the interests of Western Europe were taken to be synonymous with the will of God as the Frankish victory over the Muslims of al-Andalus was seen as the result of "Christ's help."[211] Despite the relative insignificance of this conflict to the overall development of al-Andalus and Merovingian Gaul, the event was remembered in medieval and even early modern times as God's divine protection of the West from becoming an Islamic stronghold. The eighteenth-century historian Edward Gibbon credited the Western victory at Poitiers with saving European Christianity from Islamicization as it was the closest conflict with Muslims to the center of the new Christian West.[212] The victors of Poitiers were called "European" in a manner that both transcended regional affiliation and was synonymous with Christianity.[213] Meanwhile, non-Western identity was associated with non-Christian identity as the battle at Poitiers has also been remembered as the point when the Franks saved Europe "from the Asiatics and the Africans."[214] The rise and conquest of Islam in many ways shaped the attempt of Western Christians to transform Europe into the imagined community of a Christian civitas.[215] It is of note that this process was largely at the initiation of Christian leaders such as Pope Leo III, who represented the Western church's view that the European empire should receive the seal of Christendom.

THE ENDURING LEGACY OF WESTERN CULTURAL CAPTIVITY

Proclaiming Charlemagne as "Emperor of the Romans" was understandably offensive to the Byzantine empress Irene, who occupied the office that represented the center of Roman Christendom for centuries prior.[216] The rise

---

[210]Hoyland, *In God's Path*, 178.

[211]David Levering Lewis, *God's Crucible: Islam and the Making of Europe, 570 to 1215* (New York: Norton, 2008), 170.

[212]Gibbon, *Decline and Fall*, 7:34.

[213]Lewis, *God's Crucible*, 173.

[214]Ernest Lavisse, *Histoire de France* (Paris: Hachette, 1903), 2:260.

[215]Walter Pohl, "The Construction of Communities and the Persistence of Paradox: An Introduction," in *The Construction of Communities in the Early Middle Ages: Texts, Resources and Artefacts*, ed. Richard Corradini, Max Diesenberger, and Helmut Reimitz (Leiden: Brill, 2003), 9.

[216]Unlike the schisms between Catholics, Miaphysites, and the Church of the East, the schism between the "Latins" of Rome and the "Greeks" of Constantinople cannot be identified with a

of Western European Christendom now centered at Aachen in Germany provided a rival to Eastern Byzantine Christendom that contributed to East-West tension that was epitomized by the mutual anathematization of Rome and Constantinople in 1054. Only decades later in 1096 the Roman pope Urban II called for the First Crusade in order to impose Christian rule in the Holy Land against the reigning Seljuk Empire. That the Crusades were instigated not by a king or emperor but a pope illustrates the function that the papal office—indeed, Western Christendom as a whole—understood itself to have as guardian of Christianized society. In the eighth century a forged document, the *Donation of Constantine*, claimed that before reestablishing Constantinople, Constantine transferred his authority over the Western Empire. While this document is inauthentic, it contributed to Western Christendom's self-imposed role as the "ultimate depository and guarantee of *romanitas* in the medieval world."[217] By the time of the Crusades, the power of Byzantium was diminishing under Islamic pressure to the east while Western Christian authority had risen to unprecedented heights.[218] The increased papal authority that enabled Urban II to command knights in a religious crusade in the late eleventh century came on the heels of the Investiture Controversy. Just a few years before the First Crusade, the ability to *invest* authority in, or ordain, bishops became contested between the emperor and the pope. Because the bishops also served as feudal lords in much of Western Europe, the emperor had significant interest in securing loyal bishops to administer various districts. Pope Gregory VII condemned Emperor Henry IV for attempting to invest bishops and excommunicated him. Henry IV was forced to walk to Canossa, where Gregory resided and was refused entry for three days as penance. The infamous walk to Canossa was but one of many examples of the growing church-state tension that significantly shaped the evolution of Western Europe. In the midst of a decidedly provincialized ancient world, Western-church authority provided a

---

singular event or even half-century, as the political, linguistic, religious, and cultural differences were exacerbated over the course of many centuries. Tia M. Kolbaba, *The Byzantine Lists: Errors of the Latins* (Urbana: University of Illinois Press, 2000), 9.

[217]Evangelos Chrysos, "The Empire in East and West," in *The Transformation of the Roman World, AD 400–900*, ed. Leslie Webster and Michelle Brown (Berkeley: University of California Press, 1997), 15.

[218]Kolbaba, *Byzantine Lists*, 166.

universalizing marker of identity that the earliest missionaries of Northern Europe drew on to unite the various peoples of Ireland, Saxony, and Britain as Roman Christians.[219] Indeed, the ethnogenesis, or the formation and development of ethnic identity, among many Northern European people groups was instigated by the reception of both Christianity and romanitas as equally formative factors in the development of Germanic, Irish, and British identity.[220] Likewise, the rise of Western Christendom beginning with the Carolingians effected the reception of Christianity in Viking and Scandinavian communities such as Iceland, Denmark, Greenland, and Norway beginning in the tenth century.[221] The introduction of Latin— known in Irish sources as "the blessed white language"—into the learned classes of Ireland was instrumental to the spread of Christianity and the development of Irish identity.[222]

The self-appointed role of world Christian patron assumed by Western Christendom in its early years would continue to shape the following centuries of Western cultural captivity. The Crusades represented a three-century long attempt at establishing Western Christian dominance whose propaganda centered principally on defending fellow Christians in the East. Legitimizing Western Christian military force in response to Islamic threats remained a central component to the rhetoric surrounding the beginning of Western colonialism and the trans-Atlantic slave trade at the end of the fifteenth century. The papal bull "Romanus Pontifex" issued by Pope Nicholas V in 1454, only a year after the fall of Constantinople to the Ottoman Empire, gave the Portuguese king Alfonso

> the full and free capacity to invade, conquer, take by storm, defeat, and subjugate any Saracens and together Pagans as well as whatever dominions,

---

[219]Brown demonstrates how Northern Europe, previously thought of as peripheral with reference to Rome, now understood itself as a new Rome (*Western Christendom*, 15).

[220]Walter Pohl, "The Barbarian Successor States," in *The Transformation of the Roman World, AD 400–900*, ed. Leslie Webster and Michelle Brown (Berkeley: University of California Press, 1997), 46. Pohl corrects the view advanced by Edward Gibbon that barbarian groups were completely absorbed into Roman society to the point of losing provincial and cultural distinctiveness. Rather Pohl demonstrates that part of Roman society was the incorporation of local identity and customs (33).

[221]Brown, *Western Christendom*, 468.

[222]Brown, *Western Christendom*, 337; Walter Pohl and Gerda Heydemann, *Post-Roman Transitions: Christian and Barbarian Identities in the Early Medieval West* (Turnhout: Brepols, 2013), 24.

possessions, movable and immovable property are detained or possessed by them: and to seize and appropriate for himself and for his successors their own persons in perpetual servitude, as well as their kingdoms, dukedoms, counties, principalities, dominions, possessions, and property, and to convert these to his own use and utility and to that of his successors.[223]

The Christian West saw itself as the last remaining bastion of Christendom and was motivated to compete with the Ottomans over colonial rule across Africa. Eight centuries after the advent of Islam, the reality that Europe "defined itself in opposition to Islam"[224] was as salient as ever. The "Romanus Pontifex" largely contributed to the age of imperialism and resulted in colonial practices including the *padroado* system in India, *encomiendas* in Latin America, the application of *terra nullius* against Aborigines of Australia, and the US Supreme Court's Doctrine of Discovery among Native Americans.

After the association of Christianity with the primary empire of the West, the Christian faith became seen as incongruous with non-Roman identities. During the fifth century, divergent christological positions resulted in the ostracization of the majority of Christians in Africa, Asia, and the Middle East and the imposition of the dominant Roman theological perspective. Finally, the rise of Islam resulted in the decline of Byzantine, Persian, and Near Eastern Christianity and the ascendance of a competing Western Christian power epitomized during the tenure of Charlemagne. Yet despite the embedded association of Christianity with the Western world that persists today, the gospel took firm root across Africa, the Middle East, and Asia, resulting in many indigenous Christian communities that also still persist in the present day.

---

[223]Valentin Y. Mudimbe, "Romanus Pontifex and the Expansion of Europe," in *Postcolonialisms: An Anthology of Cultural Theory and Criticism*, ed. Gaurav Desai and Supriya Nair (New Brunswick, NJ: Rutgers University Press, 2005), 54.
[224]Lewis, *God's Crucible*, xxiii.

2
. . . .

The First Christians of Africa

The preceding historical survey of the first millennium of Western Christianity has provided a basic understanding of the development of Eurocentric Christian identity politics. Attention will now be given to the development of Christianity in the non-Western world and the contextualized/enculturated theological expression that developed in precolonial Africa, the Middle East, and Asia.

Beginning in the fifteenth century, Christianity encountered new territories in Africa, Asia, and the Americas as a result of Western colonialism. Many people today think that Christianity began for people of color only five-hundred years ago through this colonial enterprise. It is for this reason that the following survey will focus on Christian history in the non-Western world preceding the fifteenth century. By focusing on precolonial Christianity in the non-Western world, the myth of a Eurocentric origin of the gospel message will become all the more untenable. Western Christian history will be discussed in its relationship to the African and Asian theological developments that both preceded and continued concurrently with Western Christianity. Specific attention will be given to how Western Christianity developed in conflict and contact with different African and Asian Christian communities. Various regions will be briefly introduced with attention to notable examples of how Christianity was enculturated in these cultural contexts.

EGYPT

Alexandria and Egypt represent the gateway for Christianity on the continent of Africa. To this day, the Egyptian, or Coptic,[1] Orthodox Church

---

[1]An anglicized version of the Greek word *aiguptos* meaning "Egypt." The Coptic word for Egypt is *khme* and for an Egyptian is *rmnkēme*.

understands the introduction of Christianity to Egypt to have taken place through the missionary efforts of the apostle Mark.[2] The *Acts of Mark* is the story written in the late fourth century that narrates the tradition of Mark traveling to Alexandria and establishing Egypt's earliest Christian church. According to this story, Mark went to Alexandria from Cyrene at the leading of God and converted a local cobbler named Anianus, whom Mark later anointed as Egypt's first bishop. Before ultimately being arrested and martyred by Egyptian pagans, Mark ordained many priests across Upper Egypt.[3]

Figure 2.1. Icon of Saint Mark at the Hanging Church in Cairo, Egypt

There are several Christian manuscripts found in Egypt that antedate 200 CE, including copies of Irenaeus's *Against Heresies*, the *Shepherd of Hermas*, a fragment of the *Gospel of Thomas*, and several biblical manuscripts.[4] Among the biblical fragments from second-century Egypt is a fragment of the Gospel of John, which is the earliest material evidence of a canonical New Testament text. Such Christian literature, which constituted the foundation of dominant, orthodox Christianity in subsequent

---

[2]C. Wilfred Griggs demonstrates the lack of evidence in arguing for 1 Peter 5:13 as a reference to Egyptian Babylon: C. Wilfred Griggs, *Early Egyptian Christianity from its Origins to 451 CE*, 2nd ed. (Leiden: Brill, 1991), 18. The earliest report of Mark in Egypt comes from Eusebius of Caesarea, *Ecclesiastical History*, ed. C. F. Cruse (Grand Rapids: Hendrickson, 1998), 2.16.1. It is noteworthy, however, that Eusebius's account of Mark in Egypt relies completely on the prevalence of this tradition before the time of Eusebius.

[3]For the full English text of the *Acts of Mark*, see Allen Dwight Callahan, "The Acts of Mark: Tradition, Transmission, and Translation of the Arabic Version," in *The Apocryphal Acts of the Apostles*, ed. F. Bovon, A. G. Brock, and C. R. Matthews (Cambridge, MA: Harvard University Center for the Study of World Religions, 1999), 62-85.

[4]C. H. Roberts, *Manuscript, Society, and Belief in Early Christian Egypt* (New York: Oxford University Press, 1979), 13-14.

centuries, proved useful for the early church in Egypt in its interaction with early Gnostic figures such as Basilides and Valentinus. Such heresies were combatted by Patriarch Demetrius who oversaw the Catechetical School of Alexandria during its administration by Clement of Alexandria and his successor Origen.

Clement and Origen are two of the earliest Christian apologists who were also prolific theologians, incorporating much Hellenistic philosophy into Christian theology and exegesis. Alexandria was one of the largest and most cosmopolitan cities of the Roman Empire in Late Antiquity—a meeting point of Hellenistic, Jewish, native Egyptian, and other influences. Although not an Egyptian, Clement came to Alexandria as a student of the catechetical school's first teacher, Pantaenus, and wrote the majority of his theological treatises during his tenure as head of the school.[5] At the beginning of the third century, Origen assumed control of the school and expanded its curriculum to include both elementary catechetical instruction and a more advanced level of theological education.[6] Origen eventually came into conflict with Patriarch Demetrius, who wanted to bring the school more closely under the jurisdiction of ecclesiastical authority. After Origen left Alexandria, Demetrius appointed a new head of school who would be closely supervised by the patriarch of Alexandria, a tradition that would continue for centuries to come.

During the mid-third century, severe persecutions systematically targeting Christians were enacted by Emperor Decius, in contrast to the more sporadic persecutions that preceded. In Egypt, Christian persecution resulted in the beginning of a pattern of Egyptian patriarchs being exiled from their office and produced an overall Egyptian Christian narrative of persecution and martyrdom. This began with Patriarch Dionysius, the first

---

[5]Clement's three central works—*Protrepticus*, *Paedagogus*, and *Stromata*—are the best examples of his philosophical and theological method and were all written during his time in Alexandria. For background on Clement, his theology, and its relationship to Platonism, see Salvatore R. C. Lilla, *Clement of Alexandria: A Study in Christian Platonism and Gnosticism* (New York: Oxford University Press, 1971).

[6]There is a question of how official the school was before this point and if the school of the time of Clement and Pantaenus was an unofficial study circle or simply the theological trends developing in Alexandria; see David Dawson, *Allegorical Readers and Cultural Revision in Ancient Alexandria* (Berkeley: University of California Press, 1992), 219.

Christian bishop to use the term *pope*,[7] who fled Alexandria due to persecution. Dionysius's flight brought home to Egypt a debate that raged across the third-century church: whether Christians ought to flee in the face of persecution. Much like Cyprian in Carthage, Dionysius defended his actions as necessary for the continuity of church leadership. And like the Novatian opposition to Cyprian in Carthage, an Egyptian bishop named Melitius would later give voice to a more radical perspective in Egypt that opposed the flight of the early fourth-century patriarch Peter I. Like the Donatists of North Africa, the followers of Meletius—the Meletians—held stricter views on the readmittance of Christians who apostatized under persecution (the *lapsi*, or "lapsed") while Peter of Alexandria exercised a more lenient attitude. While the issue of readmitting the *lapsi* was significantly diffused after the time of Constantine, the theme of martyrdom would continue to profoundly shape Egyptian Christian identity.[8] This is most evident in the orientation of the Coptic Orthodox calendar which to this day begins at 283 with the great persecution of Diocletian.

As a result of the Roman imperial support of Christianity, Christians across the world began following the example of Egyptian Christians who began withdrawing to the desert and living an ascetic lifestyle. Desiring to continue in the sufferings of the early Christians, fourth-century Egyptian Christians began living lifestyles of prayer, fasting, and studying Scripture in the Egyptian wilderness—most famously in the monastic community at Scetis in the Wadi-al-Natrun. The sayings and deeds of the Egyptian monks of Scetis, the most famous of whom is Anthony the Great (251–356), are recorded in the *Apophthegmata Patrum* (*Sayings of the Fathers*).[9] Anthony was "an Egyptian by race [*genos*]," born to wealthy parents.[10] He lived an ascetic lifestyle in the Egyptian desert in response to the call of Jesus as recorded in the Gospels:

> But once again as he [Anthony] entered the church, he heard the Lord saying in the Gospel: "Be not solicitous for the morrow." He could not bear to wait

---

[7]Dionysius refers to his predecessor Heraclas as "our blessed pope," decades before the first documented use of this title in Rome (Griggs, *Early Egyptian Christianity*, 69).

[8]Stephen J. Davis, *The Early Coptic Papacy: The Egyptian Church and Its Leadership in Late Antiquity* (Cairo: American University in Cairo Press, 2004), 42.

[9]*Apophthegmata Patrum*, ed. John Wortley (Trappist, KY: Cistercian Publications, 2012).

[10]Athanasius of Alexandria, *Life of Anthony*, ed. Robert T. Meyer (New York: Newman, 1950), 18.

longer, but went out and distributed those things also to the poor. His sister
he placed with known and trusted virgins, giving her to the nuns to be
brought up. Then he himself devoted all his time to ascetic living, intent on
himself and living a life of self-denial, near his own house. For there were not
yet so many monasteries in Egypt, and no monk even knew of the faraway
desert. Whoever wished to concern himself with his own destiny practiced
asceticism by himself not far from his own village.[11]

The Egyptian patriarch Athanasius wrote Anthony's biography, which increased the popularity of both men as central figures of Egyptian Christianity
and promoted the ascetic lifestyle as the ideal Christian expression of piety. An

Egyptian Christian identity
centered in martyrdom would
continue to develop during
the various exiles of Patriarch
Athanasius during the Arian
controversy of the mid-fourth
century. After Nicene theology was solidified at the
Council of Constantinople in
381, the Egyptian church continued to combat both he-
retical and pagan religious
practice. By the end of the
fourth century, orthodox
Christianity was dominant in
Egypt while paganism and
heterodox expressions of
Christianity became margin-

Figure 2.2. Traditional cave dwelling of Saint Anthony
the Great

alized. During the time of
Theophilus at the turn of the
fifth century, the Alexandrian patriarch destroyed the Serapeum, a pagan
temple, and garnered the support of the monastic communities. This was
achieved primarily by his decision to adopt the monks' view that humans were

---

[11]Athanasius, *Life of Anthony*, 20.

Figure 2.3. Monastery of Saint Anthony, the oldest monastery in the world, in the Red Sea Mountains of Egypt

created in the image of God—one of the central questions of the "anthropo-morphite controversy" that raged in Egypt during this time.[12] The strong veneration of Alexandrian patriarchs and the centralization of episcopal power in one see through the cultivation of monastic support remained one of the defining characteristics of the Egyptian church in the ancient Christian world.[13] Monasticism would become a defining feature of late antique Christianity that, while present in other places in the early fourth century, developed quite early in various forms in Egypt.[14] Desert hermits followed the patterns outlined in

---

[12]Paul A. Patterson, *Visions of Christ: The Anthropomorphite Controversy of 399 CE* (Tübingen: Mohr Siebeck, 2012), 5.

[13]Roger Bagnall, *Egypt in the Byzantine World, 300–700* (New York: Cambridge University Press, 2007), 13. The role of Egyptian episcopal authority came into sharp focus during the time of Athanasius; David Brakke, *Athanasius and Asceticism* (Baltimore: Johns Hopkins University Press, 1995), 2.

[14]This is demonstrated in that, although indigenous forms of asceticism began in Syria independently of Egyptian monasticism, later sources in Syriac falsely attribute the origins of Syrian monasticism to Egypt due to the renown of the Egyptian desert fathers. Sebastian Brock, *The Luminous Eye: The Spiritual World Vision of Saint Ephrem the Syrian* (Kalamzoo, MI: Cistercian Publications, 1985), 131-32. However, Anthony was not the first Christian ascetic hermit; there were many before him.

the *Life of Anthony* in great numbers in the Lower Egyptian desert, while monastic communities living under a monastic rule were developed in the model
of Pachomius the Great in Upper Egypt.

Perhaps the most significant monastic figure in the coenobitic—or communal—style pioneered by Pachomius was the late fourth/early fifth-century
archimandrite Shenoute of Atripe.[15] Shenoute led a federation of monasteries in Upper Egypt where he combatted pagan religion, administered the
monastic community, and engaged in an extensive writing campaign that
would earn him the status of the greatest Coptic writer in the history of the
language. A significant aspect of Shenoute's theology—as well as Egyptian
Christians as a whole—was critiquing native Egyptian religion:

> Accursed be he who worships or pours out (libations) or makes sacrifice to
> any creature whether in the sky or on the earth or under water! Woe upon
> those who will worship the sun and the moon and the whole army of heaven,
> putting their hearts in them as gods, when they are not gods! Woe upon those
> who will worship wood and stone or anything made by man's handiwork with
> wood and stone, or molded by putting clay inside them, and the rest of the
> kind, and (making from these materials) birds and crocodiles and beasts and
> livestock and diverse beings.[16]

In the modern world, many African and African-descended people are
attempting to revive ancient Egyptian religion, claiming this to be the
"original" religion of black people. It is significant, however, to note that the
most significant Egyptian author of Late Antiquity was a Christian and
voluntarily chose to reject pre-Christian, Egyptian religion. Shenoute participated in the Egyptian tradition of lending monastic support to the Alexandrian patriarch in the cause of orthodoxy. In 431 Shenoute attended
the Council of Ephesus with Cyril of Alexandria in support of the patriarch's fight against Nestorius of Constantinople.[17] Nestorius, patriarch of

---

[15]For background on Shenoute's life and literary career, see Bentley Layton, *The Canons of Our
Fathers: Monastic Rules of Shenoute* (New York: Oxford University Press, 2014); David Brakke
and Andrew Crislip, *Selected Discourses of Shenoute the Great: Community, Theology, and Social
Conflict in Late Antique Egypt* (New York: Cambridge University Press, 2015).

[16]Shenoute of Atripe, *The Lord Thundered*, in *Oeuvres de Schenoudi*, ed. Emile Amelineau (Paris:
Leroux, 1909), 1:381.

[17]For a more detailed account of the controversy involving Cyril and Nestorius, see Susan Wessel,
Cyril of Alexandria and the Nestorian Controversy: The Making of a Saint and of a Heretic (New
York: Oxford University Press, 2004).

Constantinople, refused to call Mary the "God-bearer" (*theotokos*), resulting in Cyril issuing anathemas of Nestorius's theology.[18] Cyril's anathemas of Nestorius were accepted at the Council of Ephesus resulting in the deposition and exile of Nestorius.

Cyril's emphasis on the significant role of Mary in the incarnation has been commonly understood as a response to the Egyptian religious worship of the goddess Isis and her son Horus. Because the worship of Isis and Horus was so prevalent in Egypt, Cyril desired to emphasize the real presence of the divine Christ in the human Mary.[19] However, the fact that Christians like Nestorius had divergent views on Mary demonstrates that it was primarily the Christians of Egypt that did theology in response to Egyptian religion. This is a significant fact given the prevalence of the conspiracy theory that the Christian doctrine of the incarnation was a copy of the Isis-Horus mythology. As noted by New Testament scholar Bart Ehrman—who makes clear that he is not a Christian nor does he believe the historic theological claims of Christianity—the "mystery religion" theory that the Christian claims about Jesus are copies of other ancient religions is ludicrous and historically unsubstantiated. Ancient religious stories about savior-figures such as Horus did not include a virgin birth, nor the claim of a fully human and fully divine savior, nor the belief in the savior-figure's death as an atonement for sin. Regarding the uniqueness of the Christian doctrine of the atonement, Ehrman states:

> So far as I know, there are no parallels to this central Christian claim. What has been invented here is not the Christian Jesus but the mythicist claims about Jesus. I am not saying that I think Jesus really did die to atone for the sins of the world. I am saying that the Christian claims about Jesus's atoning sacrifice were not lifted from pagan claims about divine men. Dying to atone for sin was not part of the ancient pagan mythology. Mythicists who claim that it was are simply imagining things. My main objection to this line of argumentation, however, is the one with which I began. There certainly are

---

[18]Opposing the idea that God could have a beginning in time, Nestorius spoke of the deity "passing through" the Virgin Mary (Wessel, *Cyril of Alexandria*, 229).

[19]Matthew R. Crawford, *Cyril of Alexandria's Trinitarian Theology of Scripture* (New York: Oxford University Press, 2014), 142. The role of the Isis cult in Cyril's theology has been explored further in John A. McGuckin, "The Influence of the Isis Cult on St. Cyril of Alexandria's Christology," *StPatr* 24 (1992): 191-99.

similarities between what pagans were saying about their divine men and what Christians were saying about Jesus, as we have seen in the case of Apollonius. But the parallels are not as close and as precise as most mythicists claim. Nowhere near as close.[20]

In addition to the unique claims of the New Testament in comparison to other ancient religions, the varied approaches to Mariology across Christian contexts further complicate the claim that the Jesus story is a copy of Horus. The theology of the Egyptian pope Cyril demonstrates the degree to which Egyptian Christians both rejected indigenous Egyptian mythology yet contextualized the gospel according to their Egyptian culture.

As discussed above, the patriarch of Alexandria experienced deposition and exile following the Council of Chalcedon in 451. Following Cyril of Alexandria's teaching that Christ existed in one nature (*physis*), Patriarch Dioscorus of Alexandria excommunicated the bishop of Rome at the Second Council of Ephesus in 449 for teaching that the humanity and divinity of Christ persisted in two distinct natures (*physis*) united in one person (*hypostasis*).[21] Dioscorus of Alexandria was exiled, and Chalcedonian—or "two nature"—theology was imposed on Egypt by the ecclesiastical authorities of Rome and Constantinople.

Figure 2.4. Christian cross in the style of an Egyptian Ankh from the Monastery of Apollo at Bawit, Egypt, sixth century

The persecution enacted by Chalcedonian Byzantine emperors such as Justinian I intensified the resistance of Egypt's anti-Chalcedonian majority and also caused a rupture between the authorities in Constantinople and the anti-Chalcedonian communities of Nubia, Armenia, Syria, and Arabia. In these areas, and especially in Egypt, monastic communities continued to shape much of Christian life and served

---

[20]Bart D. Ehrman, *Did Jesus Exist? The Historical Argument for Jesus of Nazareth* (New York: HarperOne, 2012), 215.

[21]For a discussion on Miaphysite doctrine as it developed in Egypt, see Aloys Grillmeier, *Christ in Christian Tradition*, vol. 2: *From the Council of Chalcedon (451) to Gregory the Great (590–604)*, part 4: *The Church of Alexandria with Nubia and Ethiopia After 451* (Louisville: Westminster John Knox, 1996).

as bulwarks of anti-Chalcedonian resistance. One of the reasons that the monastic leader Shenoute has occupied a more significant space in Coptic memory than his predecessor Pachomius, despite the greater renown of the latter in Late Antiquity, is because of the allegiance to Miaphysite doctrine articulated by Cyril that persisted in the White Monastery after the time of Shenoute.[22] However, the Pachomian community at Pbow came under Chalcedonian leadership while its previous Miaphysite leader, Abraham of Farshut, was exiled by Justinian and found refuge at the White Monastery before founding his own monastic community at Farshut. At the beginning of the seventh century, Egypt experienced renewed Chalcedonian oppression under Byzantine Roman Emperor Heraclius who was concerned with uniting the Roman Empire during times of intense war with Persia.[23] Heraclius promoted a conciliatory doctrine known as Monothelitism—the teaching that Christ had "one will"—in an attempt to unite the Chalcedonians and Miaphysites, but this was ultimately disagreeable to both sides.

The Persian shah Chosroes II occupied much of the Eastern Roman Empire, including Egypt, in the year 617. A decade later, Heraclius reclaimed the Eastern Roman Empire only to lose it again in the 630s during the Arab Muslim Conquest. As was the case in all of North Africa, Egypt came under Muslim rule quickly in the mid-seventh century but remained a Christian majority for the first several centuries of Muslim rule. Benjamin of Alexandria (ca. 590–662) was the first patriarch of Alexandria from whom writings in Coptic survive. This exemplifies how after the Islamic conquest, Greek began to decline in Egypt and Coptic became the dominant literary language for several centuries. Benjamin, supported by the Egyptian populace, was sent into exile by Emperor Heraclius, who replaced Benjamin with Cyrus. Benjamin's treatment continued the Egyptian theme of persecution, with the leader suffering in the likeness of Athanasius and Timothy Aelurus. The Chalcedonian colonial replacement, Cyrus, is frequently referred to in Egyptian Christian sources by his ethnic origin ("the Caucasian"). Egyptian Miaphysites highlighted the foreign

---

[22]See James E. Goehring, *Ascetics, Society, and the Desert: Studies in Early Egyptian Monasticism* (Harrisburg, PA: Trinity Press International, 1999), 261.

[23]For background on Heraclius and his imperial career, see Walter E. Kaegi, *Heraclius: Emperor of Byzantium* (New York: Cambridge University Press, 2003).

nature of Chalcedonian theology in contrast to the Egyptian people who were faithful to Miaphysite doctrine.

After the Islamic conquest, Miaphysite Christians enjoyed greater favor by Muslim rulers than Chalcedonian Christians because of the Chalcedonian association with the Roman church centered in Constantinople. Because of this, Benjamin was allowed to resume his position as pope and began consecrating churches and unifying the Egyptian church after the Islamic conquest:

> I give you thanks my Lord Jesus Christ because you have made me worthy
> once more to witness the freedom of expression of the orthodox faith [*pinahti*
> *etcoutown*] and the fulfillment of the holy churches, the destruction and over-
> throw of the godless [*natnoute*] heretics. The praise is yours, benevolent
> Savior, for the way in which you have allowed me to see the churches yet again
> in their glory and their good condition. I give you thanks my Lord Jesus
> Christ for you have saved my soul from the hands of the tyrant, dragon,
> apostate, the one who chased me on account of the orthodox faith. I give you
> thanks, my Lord Christ, for you have allowed me to see my sons once more
> as they surround me in your honor, my Lord Jesus.[24]

Benjamin critiques the Roman Chalcedonian theology as "godless" (*natnoute*) while fighting for the Miaphysite faith of Egypt as "orthodox" (*etcoutown*, literally "straight"). Many people in the modern world understand the concept of "orthodoxy"—especially Christian orthodoxy rooted in Scripture—as a facet of white supremacy and Western hegemony. However, as evidenced in the theology of Benjamin, the practice of contending for orthodox belief based on the authority of Scripture is a long-held tradition among African Christians and is by no means an innovation of Western Christians.

Christians continued to occupy significant positions in the Islamic government, a notable example being the late seventh-century patriarch Isaac.[25] While Egyptian Christians coexisted with their Muslim rulers relatively peacefully in the initial stages of Islamic hegemony, anti-Islamic polemic

---

[24]Benjamin of Alexandria, *Livre de la consécration du sanctuaire de Benjamin*, ed. René-Georges Coquin (Paris: IFAO, 1975), 106-8.

[25]For an introduction on Isaac and the biographical *Life of Isaac*, see Maged S. A. Mikhail, *From Byzantine to Islamic Egypt: Religion, Identity, and Politics After the Arab Conquest* (New York: Tauris, 2014), 40-43.

Figure 2.5. Entrance to the Hanging Church in Cairo, Egypt

began to appear in Christian texts in the tenth century. This development occurred around the same time that the Coptic language began to decline as a spoken language and Arabic became the dominant language of all Egyptians. The *Apocalypse of Samuel of Kalamun* was written during this time of linguistic and cultural transition in tenth-century Egypt.[26] It called on Coptic Christians to reject speaking the "language of the Hegira" (Arabic) out of fear that this would lead to conversion to Islam. The text implores Egyptian Christians to speak the "beautiful Coptic language," which is the language of the Scriptures and the Egyptian ancestors.[27] The *Apocalypse*

---

[26] An edition of the Arabic text with French translation is provided by J. Ziadeh in *L'Apocalypse de Samuel, supérieur de deir-el-Qalamoun, ROC* 20 (1915–1917): 374-404. For further discussion on the provenance of the *Apocalypse*, see Jos van Lent, "The Nineteen Muslim Kings in Coptic Apocalypses," *Parole de l'Orient* 25 (2000): 664; Mikhail, *From Byzantine to Islamic Egypt*, 99; Arietta Papaconstantinou, "'They Shall Speak the Arabic Language and Take Pride in It': Reconsidering the Fate of Coptic After the Arab Conquest," *Le Muséon* 120 (2007): 292; John Iskander, "Islamization in Medieval Egypt: The Copto-Arabic 'Apocalypse of Samuel' as a Source for the Social and Religious History of Medieval Copts," *ME* 4 (1998): 221.

[27] *L'Apocalypse de Samuel*, 394-95. Given the insistence on speaking Coptic instead of Arabic, the *Apocalypse* was likely written originally in Coptic, although it only survives in Arabic (Papaconstantinou "They Shall Speak," 274; *L'Apocalypse de Samuel*, 406). However some argue that it

demonstrates the degree to which language, religion, and ethnicity overlap in the construction of Egyptian Christian identity during this period.

The construction of Coptic identity against the backdrop of Islamic hegemony persists in the modern Coptic community. Despite the extinction of the Coptic language, Egyptian Christians claim an alternative genetic ancestry as the true "sons of the Pharaohs" in contrast to their Arab Muslim neighbors.[28] Despite the ethnic blending that has taken place

Figure 2.6. The Hanging Church in Cairo, Egypt

for over a millennium among Muslim and Christian Egyptians, many Copts to this day insist on an ethnic distinctiveness from Egyptian Muslims. This process of oppositional identity construction is evidence of the assertion of a distinct Coptic identity that is simultaneously ethnic and religious.

NUBIA

One of the principal sources for the introduction of Christianity in Nubia is the *Ecclesiastical History* of the Syriac-speaking bishop John of Ephesus.[29]

---

was originally in Arabic; see Jason Zaborowski, "From Coptic to Arabic in Medieval Egypt," *ME* 14, 15-40 (2008), 17.

[28]This process of identity formation in its modern form has been called "Pharaonism" and "Egyptianity." Jacques van der Vliet, "The Copts: 'Modern Sons of the Pharaohs?' in *Religious Origins of Nations? The Christian Communities of the Middle East*, ed. Bas ter Haar Romeny (Leiden: Brill, 2010), 279-80.

[29]Originally a three-part work, only the third part of the *Ecclesiastical History* survives in almost complete form. The first two parts describe the first four centuries of Christianity and focus on much the same material to be found in Eusebius's *Ecclesiastical History*. The third part is especially interesting in that it provides a contemporary account of late sixth-century ecumenical developments from a staunchly Miaphysite perspective. For an English translation of the third

A vehement Miaphysite, John was instrumental in establishing anti-Chalcedonian churches throughout Mesopotamia. It is therefore not surprising that the version of Christianity that John introduced into Nubia was intricately bound to the christological controversies that raged across the Roman Empire in the sixth century.[30] John of Ephesus says that an Egyptian presbyter named Julianus was passionate about converting the "wandering" people south of the Egyptian border.[31] Julianus requested the aid of Byzantine empress Theodora—queen of the Chalcedonian emperor Justinian—in evangelizing Nubia.

Theodora was remembered across the Syriac literary tradition—and especially in John of Ephesus—as the patron of Near Eastern Miaphysite communities. Often in competition with her husband the emperor, Theodora supported the Miaphysite cause across the eastern Roman Empire not out of confessional conviction but a desire for the imperial couple to rule over the fractious Chalcedonian and Miaphysite constituencies of the empire.[32] After Bishop Julianus appealed to Theodora for aid in his missionary efforts, Justinian attempted to thwart this endeavor by appealing to the Chalcedonian bishops of Upper Egypt to send a Chalcedonian envoy to Nubia. John of Ephesus reported that Justinian bribed the Egyptian Chalcedonians with gifts of gold. This was typical as Miaphysites from Egypt and Syria often saw their Chalcedonian neighbors as imperial sycophants.[33]

---

part, see Robert Payne Smith, *The Third Part of the Ecclesiastical History of John Bishop of Ephesus* (New York: Oxford University Press, 1860).

[30]Because the Miaphysite agenda is the principal focus of John of Ephesus's *Ecclesiastical History*, the historicity of its Nubian portion is questionable as it is a mere afterthought to John's primary anti-Chalcedonian focus. Salim Faraji, *The Roots of Nubian Christianity Uncovered: The Triumph of the Last Pharaoh* (Trenton, NJ: Africa World Press, 2012), 66.

[31]The Syriac word used to describe the Nubians here may likely have a double meaning: *tāʿeyā* can mean literally "to wander" but is also often used in a religious or spiritual sense (i.e., idolatry). This could have been a reference both to the nomadic nature of the Blemmyes tribe, who lived immediately southeast of Egypt (as opposed to the organized kingdoms of Makouria, Nobatia, and Alodia), and the polytheistic religious practices associated with them.

[32]John refers to her as "fervent with zeal for God" (John of Ephesus, *Ecclesiastical History*, 251). See also Volker Menze, *Justinian and the Making of the Syrian Orthodox Church* (New York: Oxford University Press, 2008), 227. It is also during this mid-sixth-century period that the earliest epigraphic evidence indicating the construction of a church in Nubia built within the remains of an ancient Kushite temple emerges; Derek A. Welsby, *The Medieval Kingdoms of Nubia: Pagans, Christians and Muslims Along the Middle Nile* (London: British Museum Press, 2002), 37.

[33]Timothy Aelurus was patriarch of Alexandria immediately following the schism of 451. In his treatise *Against Chalcedon*, Timothy accuses Chalcedonians of being motivated not by a sense of theological orthodoxy or spiritual piety but a desire to receive the favor of the emperor.

Before Justinian's Chalcedonian envoys reached Nubia, Theodora had Egyptian authorities stall the Chalcedonian dispatch at the Nubian border while she sent ahead her own Miaphysite missionaries led by Julianus. Emperor Justinian was enraged when he realized his envoys were too late, as the Miaphysite Egyptians had already established the Miaphysite faith in Nubia.[34] "And immediately, while rejoicing, they offered their souls, and they renounced in every way the error of their ancestors, and believed in the God of the Christians, saying, 'that He is the one true God, and there is no other beside Him.'"[35] Immediately after recounting how the Nubian court embraced Christianity, the text brings the christological controversies regarding the Council of Chalcedon into acute focus.

Julianus relates the recent events in Egypt wherein Patriarch Theodosius was removed from the patriarchate by Justinian but was supported by Empress Theodora. After receiving instruction on how to receive the Chalcedonian ambassadors of Justinian, the Nubian officials welcomed the imperial emissaries but affirmed their allegiance to Miaphysite doctrine:

> The gift which the king of the Romans has sent us we accept, and we will also send him a gift. But his faith we will not accept: for if we agree to become Christians, we will follow pope Theodosius who, because he was not willing to accept the evil faith of the king, he [Justinian] excommunicated and cast him [Theodosius] from his church. If, therefore, we abandon our heathenism and straying, we will not agree to fall into the evil faith.[36]

According to John of Ephesus, Julianus then remained among the Nubians for two years, establishing them in the Miaphysite faith of Egypt. Julianus left the "populous people" of Nubia to report on the mission effort and an Egyptian priest named Longinus to serve as bishop of Nubia due to his "perfect competence" in missionary work among the Nubians.[37] Emperor

---

Against Chalcedon, ed. R. Y. Ebied and L. R. Wickham, in *After Chalcedon: Studies in Theology and Church History Offered to Professor Albert van Roey*, ed. and trans. C. Laga, J. A. Munitiz, and L. Van Rompay (Leuven: Peeters, 1985), 141.

[34]The Syriac *Nobadis* is likely a reference to the northern region of Nobatia as "Nubia" was not a unified kingdom during this period. As the northernmost point in the late antique Sudan nearest to Egypt, this would also likely be the entry point into "Nubian" territory for an Egyptian missionary.

[35]John of Ephesus, *Ecclesiastical History*, 223.

[36]John of Ephesus, *Ecclesiastical History*, 224.

[37]John of Ephesus, *Ecclesiastical History*, 225.

Justinian feared that the Egyptian Christian alliance with Nubia would result in revolution against the Roman Empire, so he sought to arrest Longinus. However, the Nubian king supported the Egyptian missionary and Justinian backed down. Longinus later departed to attend to matters in Egypt with whom the Nubian Christians displayed strong solidarity: "'Once again, as before your stay, we shall be left like orphans without a father.' And thus, with much sorrow and bitter mourning, they let him go and supplied him for the journey."[38]

In contrast to this depiction of Nubian Christians, Salim Faraji has argued that a fifth-century inscription containing a monotheistic reference indicates the progressive introduction of Christianity into Nubia a century earlier than the account of John of Ephesus. The northern kingdom of the Nubian region of the Nile Valley, called Nobatia, provides the only Nubian monarchs mentioned in Greek literature during this period. This occurred soon after the rise of the kingdom of Nobatia, after the fall of the preceding Meroitic kingdom during the fourth century.[39] King Silko of Nobatia is mentioned in an inscription along the temple wall at Kalabsha celebrating his victory over the neighboring Blemmyes tribe. In this "Silko Inscription," one of the earliest monotheistic references is made by the king:

> I, Silko King of the Noubades and all the Aithiopians, came to Talmis [Ka-labsha] and Taphis [Tafa]. On two occasions I fought with the Blemmyes and God [*theos*] gave me the victory. On the third occasion I was again victorious and took control of their cities. I occupied them with my troops. On the first occasion I conquered them, and they sued for terms. I made peace with them, and they swore to me by their images [*eidola*] and I trusted their oath in the belief that they were honest people. I withdrew to my upper regions.[40]

Faraji points out that the use of the monotheistic term for "God" (*theos*) is likely juxtaposed intentionally with the "images" or "idols" (*eidola*) of the

---

[38]John of Ephesus, *Ecclesiastical History*, 228.

[39]It is likely that the fall of Meroë was due to the pauperization of Egypt resulting in declining trade with their Meroitic neighbors and the ascendant power of the neighboring nomadic tribes. Arthur Obłuski, *The Rise of Nobadia: Social Changes in Northern Nubia in Late Antiquity* (Warsaw: Journal of Juristic Papyrology, 2014), 21.

[40]"Greek Triumphal Inscription of King Silko at Kalabsha," in *Fontes Historiae Nubiorum: Textual Sources for the History of the Middle Nile Region Between the Eighth Century BC and the Sixth Century AD*, vol. 3: *From the First to the Sixth Century AD*, ed. Tormod Eide et al. (Bergen: University of Bergen Press, 1998), 1150.

Blemmyes.[41] While this inscription lacks any specific Christian reference, the reference to a single monotheistic God is quite rare as Nubian kings often rendered praise to their own divinity or other Nile Valley gods.[42] Much like Emperor Constantine, Silko's monotheistic/Christian identity was likely a gradual development that initially incorporated indigenous religious practice.[43] The inscription was previously thought to have originated in the sixth century precisely because Silko was thought to be a Christian; however, it is now clear that Silko reigned in the fifth century.[44] Although William Adams accepts the testimony given by John of Ephesus, he affirms the plausible root of Nubian Christianity in the Egyptian church.[45]

While it is ultimately not known exactly when Christianity entered Nubian territory, it may well have been before the time of Justinian in the sixth century or Silko in the fifth century. If the eunuch mentioned in Acts 8 is not actually from Axum (Ethiopia) but from the Kushite kingdom centered in Meroë, then the first Nubian Christian convert already appeared in the New Testament—and one who would have had access to the imperial court no less![46] One of the earliest Nubian Christians mentioned by name was the fourth century Moses the Black, who appears in the *Apophthegmata Patrum*. While the Greek text refers to him as an Ethiopian (*Aithiopos*), this is a common ethnic identifier in classical Greek literature for any black African south of Egypt. During the fifth century, Shenoute of Atripe provided shelter to Nubians seeking refuge in his monastery:

> How blessed is the whole flock and all the flocks of Christ in that they follow
> after Him, for they know him to be the God of truth; would that these friends

---

[41]Faraji, *Nubian Christianity*, 91.

[42]Faraji, *Nubian Christianity*, 70; monotheism was absent from Nubia prior to the introduction of Christianity (Obłuski, *Rise of Nobadia*, 172).

[43]Faraji further demonstrates this point by pointing out the combination of Christian and pagan paraphernalia found in the royal Ballana tombs in Nobadia (*Nubian Christianity*, 97).

[44]"Greek Triumphal Inscription," 1148.

[45]William Y. Adams, *Nubia: Corridor to Africa* (Princeton, NJ: Princeton University Press, 1977), 444. Likewise, Peter Shinnie argues that Egyptian missional efforts in Nubia were far more effective than imperial Byzantine attempts. *Ancient Nubia* (New York: Routledge, 1996), 121. Welsby holds this as a possibility that may be further substantiated with more archeological evidence (*Medieval Kingdoms*, 38).

[46]Edwin Yamauchi, "Acts 8:26-40: Why the Ethiopian Eunuch Was Not from Ethiopia," in *Interpreting the New Testament Text: Introduction to the Art and Science of Exegesis*, ed. Darrell L. Bock and Buist M. Fanning (Wheaton, IL: Crossway, 2006), 352.

sitting here, that belong unto the Blemmyes and the Nouba too, would mingle with us and follow after Him. That is, would know him to be God. For we have suffered them to mix with us and to come into God's house, that perchance they might come to reason. Can they, then, not know what the Psalmist writes, 'The idols of the heathen are silver and gold'?[47]

It is likely that through the missionary efforts of Egyptian monks such as Shenoute significant conversions took place among Nubians before the time of Justinian and Theodora. This theory again raises the question as to how Coptic monks—ardently devoted to the theology of Athanasius, Cyril, and Dioscorus—would have made contact in Nubia without establishing a Christian presence cognizant of such theological groundwork. Faraji follows David Frankfurter who understands the monks of Upper Egypt to have been much more syncretistic in their appropriation of indigenous religion than the hagiographical sources indicate.[48] Therefore, the Christianity introduced by the Coptic monks would have been one that was not as theologically advanced as the one in Alexandria; the Silko inscription is an example of such neophyte Christianity. It is likely that the scribe of the inscription was an Egyptian Christian who knew Greek and Coptic.[49] If Silko had been an orthodox Christian (by late antique Egyptian standards), he would not have inscribed his image on a temple of a Nubian pagan deity. The gradual Christianization of Nubia that began around the time of Silko represents a process of "symbolic and structural continuity"[50] in which traditional Nubian religious thought adapted to and merged with the Christian ideology introduced through contact with Byzantine Egypt. This is further demonstrated in that the inscription indicating the increasingly theistic nature of Nubian civil religion was written in Greek. For Faraji, the inscription's Greek composition does not indicate a colonial relationship between Nubia and Byzantium, for Nubia was an independent kingdom that existed outside the borders of the Roman Empire. Rather, King Silko's claim of monotheism

---

[47]Faraji, *Nubian Christianity*, 243-44.
[48]David Frankfurter, *Religion in Roman Egypt: Assimilation and Resistance* (Princeton, NJ: Princeton University Press, 1998), 267.
[49]"Greek Triumphal Inscription," 1151.
[50]This interpretive framework featured prominently in Adrian Hastings's analysis of modern Christianity in Africa and is helpful in understanding the cultural and religious transformation of late antique Nubia. *The Church in Africa 1450-1950* (New York: Oxford University Press, 1994).

inscribed in Greek stood in a long tradition of Graeco-African literary points of contact and represented the linguistic versatility of late antique Nubians.[51] It is likely also, given the text's claim that Silko's authority extended over Ethiopia as well, that the deployment of the lingua franca of the Nile Valley served to assert a more broad sense of Nubian dominion.

The dominant faith of the Nubian church was Miaphysite. While there is evidence of Chalcedonian (two-nature) Christianity in the middle kingdom of Makouria in the earliest centuries of Nubian Christianity, Miaphysitism quickly became the dominant expression in all Nubian kingdoms.[52] Not long after Miaphysite Christianity was firmly established as the faith of Nubia, the Arab Muslim conquest complicated matters further. After swiftly conquering Egypt, the Muslim commander 'Amr ibn al-'As unsuccessfully attempted to conquer Nubia. One of the most historically significant aspects of Christian Nubia is its unique achievement of successfully defeating Arab Muslim conquerors during the seventh century. While Muslim invaders during the seventh century successfully conquered North Africa, Egypt, Palestine, Syria, and Persia, the Nubians were reported to have been able to fight off Muslim conquerors by the strength of their archers. The ninth-century Arab historian Al-Baladhuri describes the Nubian archers thus: "I saw one of them [i.e., Nubians] saying to a Muslim, 'Where would you like me to place my arrow in you,' and when the Muslim replied, 'In such a place,' he would not miss. . . . One day they came out against us and formed a line; we wanted to use swords, but we were not able to, and they shot us and put out eyes to the number of one hundred and fifty."[53]

The failure of Muslim dominance in seventh-century Nubia resulted in the institution of a peace treaty that lasted between Christian Nubia and Muslim-ruled Egypt for over six centuries. The treaty stipulated that Egypt would remain under Muslim control while Nubia would remain neither an enemy of the Muslim world nor a member of it—a status unique to Nubia in that time:

---

[51] Faraji, *Nubian Christianity*, 206.

[52] Adams, *Nubia*, 445.

[53] Shinnie, *Ancient Nubia*, 123. Shinnie points out that the Nubians' reputation as skilled archers goes back to pharaonic times when one of the nicknames for Nubia was the "Land of the Bow." Other nicknames for Nubians were "pupil-smiters" and "archers of the eyes" (Welsby, *Medieval Kingdoms*, 69).

Verily, you are communities of Nubia enjoying the guarantee of Allah and that of His Messenger Mohammad, the Prophet; with the condition that we shall not wage war against you, nor declare war against you, nor raid you, as long as you abide by the stipulations which are in effect between us and you. [Namely] that you may enter our territories, passing through but not taking up residence in them, and we may enter yours through but not taking up residence in them. You are to look after the safety of any Moslem or ally [of the Moslems] who lodges in your territories or travels in them, until he departs from you.[54]

Part of this treaty was an agreement to exchange goods between the two empires—commonly called the *baqt* (the Arabicization of the Greek *pacton*, or "pact"). The account provided by the fifteenth-century Egyptian Muslim historian Al-Maqrizi goes on to stipulate that the Nubians must care for the only mosque in Nubian territory in the Makourian capital of Dongola and to deliver 360 slaves annually to the Muslim Egyptian rulers. While Al-Maqrizi's account is biased in that it presents the terms of the treaty as privileging the Muslims, other ancient historians note that the treaty required the Muslim rulers of Egypt to deliver shipments of wheat, barley, and wine in exchange for the Nubian slaves.[55] These terms are likely given the significant role that Egypt's wheat production and viticulture played in the late antique and early medieval world. It has been suggested that the terms of the *baqt* was a reinstitution of similar arrangements in previous centuries between the Roman Empire and Meroitic Kush.[56] However, the imbalanced representation in many Muslim sources is not surprising given that historians such as Al-Maqrizi, writing several centuries after the institution of the *baqt*, would depict its terms as more favorable to the Muslims.

Although much of early Nubian Christianity resembled that of Egypt, distinctive expressions began to occur as time went on. The peace and autonomy provided by the *baqt* as well as the consolidation of the Nubian kingdoms of Nobatia and Makouria in the late seventh century initiated a

---

[54]Adams, *Nubia*, 451-52. Al-Maqrizi, the Muslim historian who recorded the *baqt* treaty, has a view of the treaty that is likely more reflective of the situation in the fifteenth century rather than the seventh.

[55]John Lewis Burckhardt, *Travels in Nubia* (London: John Murray/Albemarle Street, 1819), 512. Ruffini points out that a ninth-century Persian historian describes the exchange of goods being of equal value. Giovanni R. Ruffini, *Medieval Nubia: A Social and Economic History* (New York: Oxford University Press, 2012), 7.

[56]Shinnie, *Ancient Nubia*, 124.

Nubian Christian golden age allowing for the development of distinctive Nubian culture.[57] Nubian homes, for example, had a characteristic arch while churches added a unique passageway running behind the apse connecting two corner rooms. While the purpose of these passageways is unclear, they are not attested in church architecture outside of Nubia.[58] Some of the earliest extant churches were converted temples, such as that of Ramesses II, which provide some of the earliest Old Nubian inscriptions.[59] One of the most architecturally significant structures was a church built in cruciform shape during the mid-ninth century.[60] Ancient Egyptian and Kushite underground, rectangular structures with vertical sides—or mastaba—also were appropriated by Nubian Christians and were even sometimes decorated with crosses.[61] The fact that the overwhelming majority of extant Old Nubian literature is religious (i.e., Christian) in nature attests to the associative overlap between Nubian and Christian identity.[62]

Nubian Christianity entailed a high degree of cultural fusion with Byzantine, Egyptian, and native Nubian features. This is evident in the social and economic practices of medieval Nubia as presented in the documentary texts emerging from the Nobatian fortress city of Qasr Ibrim. The small collection of land sales found at Qasr Ibrim exhibit broader Byzantine trends of public purchasing in the presence of witnesses. However, the Nubian land sales

---

[57]It has been suggested that the consolidation of Nobatia and Makouria during the seventh century was influenced significantly by the new threat of Islamic rulers to the north who conquered Egypt during the same time period. Stefan Jakobielski and Jacques Van Der Vliet, "From Aswan to Dongola: The Epitaph of Bishop Joseph (Died AD 668)," in *Nubian Voices: Studies in Christian Nubian Culture*, ed. Adam Łajtar and Jacques Van Der Vliet (Warsaw: Journal of Juristic Papyrology, 2011), 32n35. This confederation of united Nubian kingdoms came to be called Dotawo in the late medieval period. Giovanni R. Ruffini, *The Bishop, the Eparch, and the King: Old Nubian Texts from Qasr Ibrim (P. QI IV)* (Warsaw: Journal of Juristic Papyrology, 2014), 38.

[58]Adams, *Nubia*, 476.

[59]Shinnie, *Ancient Nubia*, 126.

[60]Wlodzimierz Godlewski, "The Birth of Nubian Art: Some Remarks," in *Egypt and Africa: Nubia from Prehistory to Islam*, ed. W. V. Davies (London: British Museum Press, 1991), 254.

[61]Welsby, *Medieval Kingdoms*, 57. Ancient Kushite burial practices, such as protecting the face and head of corpses from evil spirits entering the orifices of the body, were also maintained by the Christians. In some cases, a hole would be made in the mastaba above the head of the corpse for pouring ointments on the deceased body (66).

[62]While it is unfortunately the case that almost all Old Nubian religious texts are not original Nubian literature but translations from the Bible and early Christian literature in Greek, there is a fragment discovered at Qasr Ibrim that contains a small portion of a religious text relating a Nubian priest's desire for the establishment of a new king (Ruffini, *Medieval Nubia*, 221). For the full Nubian text with translation, see Gerald M. Browne, "Old Nubian Studies: Past, Present and Future," in Davies, *Egypt and Africa*, 291.

exhibit unique features not found in other Byzantine or medieval African contexts. Most notable among these unique features were ceremonial practices during land sales involving large feasts in which buyers and sellers would competitively feed their witnesses in order to display and reinforce social positioning in Nubian society.[63]

Nubian Christian culture is best demonstrated by architectural remains and the iconography found therein. One such site is the seventh- and early-eighth-century cathedral remains at the Nobatian capital of Faras.

Figure 2.7. Bishop Kyros, the earliest firmly identified bishop of the Faras Cathedral in the northern Nubian kingdom of Nobatia, late ninth century

Nubian icons provide insight into this community's approach to racialization. Biblical and non-Nubian saints are consistently depicted with lighter skin, while native Nubian kings and bishops are depicted with dark skin. While this may simply reflect the racialized imagination of medieval Nubians, it could also indicate a degree of internalized racism and deference to the broader Byzantine world to the north. Such perceived superiority is evident in the fact that Nubian religious texts employed Greek words at a higher rate than Coptic or Ethiopic, likely rooted in the perception that significant liturgical words retain greater spiritual potency when recited in Greek instead of Nubian.[64]

---

[63]Ruffini, *Medieval Nubia*, 90. It is possible that these land sale ceremonies involved indigenous forms of Nubian dance in addition to feasting (102).

[64]Ruffini, *Medieval Nubia*, 228. Coptic hagiographical traditions were also incorporated alongside Greek and Old Nubian inscriptions—as in the case of the earliest known inscription from Dongola, an epitaph for a foreign bishop named Joseph—indicating the high degree of multilingualism and crosscultural contact in Christian Nubia (Jakobielski and Van Der Vliet, "From Aswan to Dongola," 21-23).

One of the most distinctive ecclesiastical and political roles in Christian Nubia was that of the eparch of Nobatia.[65] When the Nubian kingdoms of Makouria and Nobatia merged in the seventh century, the latter retained a degree of political distinction as it was administered by the eparch. The

eparch served a political and religious role as the primary ambassador representing Christian Nubia to Muslim rulers in Egypt. The eparch of Nobatia had very close ties with the affairs of the church.[66] Church paintings found at the cathedral of Faras display various eparchs wearing a distinctive horned headpiece thought to be borrowed from Sassanian Persia as well as robes with Byzantine double eagles.[67] Such cultural appropriation demonstrates the social contact involved in negotiating Nubian Christian identity.

Figure 2.8. Unnamed Queen Mother of Nobatia from the Faras Cathedral, tenth century

An interesting contrast between the Christians of Nubia and their Egyptian neighbors to the north is the starkly low numbers of monastic communities in Nubia and how briefly monasticism took root.[68] This is surprising given the heavy Coptic influence on Nubian Christianity. Inscriptions and texts

---

[65]It has been suggested that the Greek title *eparch* finds its Nubian equivalent in the Old Nubian title *Migin sonoj* which appears frequently in Old Nubian documentary texts. J. M. Plumley, "New Light on the Kingdom of Dotawo," in *Études nubiennes. Colloque de Chantilly, 2-6 juillet 1975, Bibliothèque d'étude* 77 (1978): 241.

[66]At the Nobatian town of Qasr Ibrim, the majority of texts discovered in the home of the eparch were ecclesiastical in nature, primarily dealing with sales of church property (Ruffini, *Medieval Nubia*, 37).

[67]Shinnie, *Ancient Nubia*, 124.

[68]Adams, *Nubia*, 480.

emerging from medieval Nubia are primarily in the Coptic language, with many others in Greek and Old Nubian.[69]

Medieval Nubian culture was essentially Christian in nature.[70] Even the documentary papyri that highlight the social, legal, and economic nature of medieval Nubia provide examples of contracts and receipts that consistently begin with an invocation of the Father, Son, and Holy Spirit.[71] Perhaps the most intriguing example of contextualization in early Nubian Christianity is a painting in the monastery at the capital of Dongola from the late tenth century. This nativity painting contained typical images including Mary and child, shepherds, and angels. However, to the right of Mary and the baby Jesus is a unique painting of Africans worshiping the birth of the Savior wearing animal crest masks and loin cloths and holding percussive instruments.[72] It is believed that these Africans may have belonged to the Bambara tribe which later occupied much of modern Mali, Burkina Faso, and Senegal. This painting represents early evangelization efforts from the Nile Valley Christians of Nubia to cultures further south and west in the African continent. The gospel had already been spreading along the Nile River from Egypt to Nubia and then Ethiopia. This painting represents the continued spread of the gospel from Africans to neighboring Africans. If the Western church had not condemned, oppressed, and isolated the early African church, leaving it open to Islamic domination, the gospel may have continued to spread to the extremities of the African continent at an early period. Yet this painting raises the intriguing potential of Western and Central African Christians before the advent of Western colonialism.

---

[69]An example of Nubian appropriation of foreign culture is the exclusively funerary use of the *phōs-zōē* ("light-life") inscription on crosses in Christian Nubia as opposed to their broader use across Byzantium. Alexandros Tsakos, "Sepulchral Crosses from Nubia with the ΦΩΣ-ΖΩΗ Acclamation," in *Nubian Voices: Studies in Christian Nubian Culture*, ed. Adam Łajtar and Jacques Van Der Vliet (Warsaw: Journal of Juristic Papyrology, 2011), 165.

[70]The appearance and deployment of the Nubian language—and literacy in general in Nubia—directly correlates to the presence of Christianity. In other words, where the gospel spread in Nubia, so too did Nubian literature. Jacques Van Der Vliet, "What is Man?: The Nubian Tradition of Coptic Funerary Inscriptions," in Łajtar and Van Der Vliet, *Nubian Voices*, 175.

[71]Ruffini, *Bishop, the Eparch, and the King*, 150 (and throughout).

[72]Włodzimierz Godlewski, *Dongola—Ancient Tungul: Archeological Guide* (Warsaw: Polish Centre of Mediterranean Archaeology, 2013), 94.

ETHIOPIA

The Ethiopian people speak various Semitic languages (Amharic, Tigrena, Gurage, to name a few) whose ancient predecessor was called Geʿez. Many Ethiopians consider themselves part of the Hebrew people. The ethnic memory that has been constructed by a majority of contemporary Ethiopian Christians brings to the fore the question of the linguistic and cultural relationship between Ethiopia and the Near East. The inhabitants of Ethiopia during the millennium preceding Christian times had a complicated connection to a South Arabian ethnic group called the Sabeans. It was long accepted that the ancient Ethiopians were descended from an Arabian ethnic group called Habesha (later Abyssinia) who migrated across the Red Sea from southern Arabia.[73] In contemporary scholarship, this one-sided theory has been largely rejected. Scholars such as Ephraim Isaac have helpfully pointed out the racist, Eurocentric foundations of such views that sought to attribute the accomplishments of ancient Ethiopian civilization to the "superior" Arabian races while distancing Ethiopian civilization from the "negroid" races of the Horn of Africa.[74]

While the classical form of the Ethiopian branch, Geʿez, is a Semitic language, it is not of the same Semitic family as Sabean, as was originally thought.[75] Semitic languages are part of a larger Afro-Asiatic language family that likely traces to a specific homeland (or *Urheimat*), and later spread throughout the Levant, the Arabian Peninsula, and Northern Africa as far west as modern Chad. As part of this larger philological matrix, Geʿez likely developed independently in the Horn of Africa in the mid-first millennium BCE. Also, there are no Sabean inscriptions that mention an alleged mass migration of Sabeans across the Red Sea into Ethiopia, which would be expected given the magnitude of such a migration.[76] Many modern linguists understand Geʿez to belong to a Western branch of Semitic

---

[73]This view was promoted by the majority of nineteenth- and early twentieth-century Ethiopianists; chief among them was Carlo Conti Russini, *Storia d'Etiopia* (Bergamo: Istituto italiano d'arti grafiche, 1928), 110.

[74]Ephraim Isaac, *The Ethiopian Orthodox Täwahïdo Church* (Trenton, NJ: Red Sea, 2012), 2. For an example of earlier racist depictions of Ethiopia imposing a dichotomy between Arabian-descended "Habeshas" and black indigenous Africans, see Edward Ullendorff, *The Ethiopians: An Introduction to Country and People*, 2nd ed. (New York: Oxford University Press, 1965), 45.

[75]Siegbert Uhlig, "Geʿez," in *Encyclopaedia Aethiopica* (Wiesbaden: Harrassowitz, 2005), 732.

[76]A. K. Irvine, "On the Identity of Habashat in the South Arabian Inscriptions," *JSS* 10 (1965): 178.

languages that is distinct from Arabic and forms of Aramaic.[77] While there was undeniable cultural and linguistic contact that traveled both ways between the Arabian Sabeans and the ancient Ethiopians, the culture that developed in Ethiopia during the first millennium BCE was a unique and independent African culture.[78]

The question of the relationship between Ethiopia and the Sabeans is raised again when considering the long-held tradition of Ethiopian inclusion in the Solomonic lineage through the queen of Sheba mentioned in 1 Kings 10:1-13. The first detailed account of the story involving the encounter of King Solomon and the queen of Sheba appeared in a fourteenth-century Ge'ez historical account that will be given further consideration below. It is sufficient at this point to highlight the fact that, despite the fact that Sheba has been thought of by some to refer to a South Arabian context, the majority of ancient commentators on this passage take the queen to be an African.[79] The fact that *Ethiopian* was often a term used for any black person south of Egypt leaves the possibility of the queen's provenance being Ethiopia or Cush.

A similar problem arises when discussing the traditional beginning of Christianity in Ethiopia based on the story of Philip the evangelist and the eunuch in Acts 8. Despite the New Testament's identification of the eunuch as an "Ethiopian," it is more likely that this eunuch was a representative of the court of Candace, the Cushite queen of Meroë.[80] The fourth-century theologian and patriarch of Constantinople John Chrysostom mentioned in one of his homilies that there were Ethiopians present at the coming of the Holy Spirit at Pentecost.[81] However, this is not the only tradition connecting the beginning of Ethiopian Christianity to the New Testament period. Some have taken the testimony of the fourth-century Christian historian Rufinus of Aquileia to indicate that the apostle Matthew was

[77]Gene Gragg, "Ge'ez," in *The Semitic Languages*, ed. Robert Hetzrog (New York: Routledge, 1997), 242.

[78]Stuart Munro-Hay, *Aksum: An African Civilization of Late Antiquity* (Edinburgh: Edinburgh University Press, 1991), 57.

[79]Isaac, *Täwahïdo Church*, 10. The biblical account is unclear on the ethnic identity of the queen as well as the precise genealogy of Sheba as various groups by this name are listed in connection to Ham and Cush (Gen 10:7; 1 Chron 1:9; Is 43:3) as well as Shem and Abraham (Gen 10:28; 1 Chron 1:22, 32).

[80]Edwin Yamauchi, *Africa and the Bible* (Grand Rapids: Baker Academic, 2004), 161.

[81]Isaac, *Täwahïdo Church*, 17.

chosen by lot to evangelize Ethiopia. However, Rufinus's statement on the matter raises geographical complications:

> In the division of the earth which the apostles made by lot for the preaching of God's word, when the different provinces fell to one or the other of them, Parthia, it is said, went by lot to Thomas, to Matthew fell Ethiopia, and Hither India, which adjoins it, went to Bartholomew. Between this country and Parthia, but far inland, lies Further India. Inhabited by many peoples with many different languages, it so distant that the plow of the apostolic preaching had made no furrow in it, but in Constantine's time it received the first seeds of faith.[82]

While it is possible that Christianity first came to Ethiopia in the first century—especially given the high degree of contact with the Eastern Roman Empire through merchants trading across the Red Sea during that time—the earliest historically substantiated Christian period in Ethiopia was under the fourth-century king Ezana. Rufinus relates that two young Syrian brothers, Aedesius and Frumentius, came to Ethiopia from Tyre with their merchant uncle Meropius, who was killed and left the boys to be raised as slaves in the Ethiopian imperial court.[83] King Ella Amida eventually freed the Syrian boys, and the Ethiopian queen appointed them as advisors and educators for Prince Ezana. Aedesius and Frumentius used their political influence to spread the gospel, and when Ezana became king, he allowed the Syrian missionaries to return home. While Aedesius returned to his native Tyre, Frumentius—passionate for the Ethiopian church—asked the Egyptian patriarch Athanasius if he could remain in Ethiopia as bishop. Athanasius ordained Frumentius as bishop of Axum and he became the first *abuna* ("our father," i.e., patriarch), known also as *Salama, Kassate Berhan* ("Revealer of Light"), of the Ethiopian church: "Then Athanasius, for he had recently received the priesthood, after considering attentively and carefully

---

[82]Rufinus of Aquileia, *Church History: Books 10 and 11*, ed. Philip R. Amidon (New York: Oxford University Press, 1997), 18. Rufinus actually claimed that Metrodus went to "Further India" while, in the same paragraph, referred to "Ethiopia" as a distinct country that the apostle Matthew traveled to. It is likely that "Ethiopia," here means Cush while "Hither India" is Rufinus's name for the kingdom of Axum, which Athanasius names more accurately.

[83]Rufinus, *Church History*, 19. Rufinus's Roman bias is evident throughout his account as he credits Frumentius's missionary success in Ethiopia to other Roman Christian merchants who introduce Christianity to the Ethiopians "in the Roman manner."

what Frumentius had said and done, spoke as follows in the council of priests: 'What other man can we find like you, in whom is God's spirit as in you, and who could achieve such things as these?'"[84] Frumentius converted and baptized Ezana and oversaw the construction of many churches including the oldest extant church in Sub-Saharan Africa, the Church of Our Lady Mary of Zion.

Emperor Constantine's son and successor, Constantius, wrote a letter to Ezana requesting that Frumentius be examined to confirm that his theology

Figure 2.9. Imperial coin bearing the image of King Ezana and the cross

was orthodox (i.e., Arian). The letter from Constantius to Ezana survives in Athanasius's treatise against the Roman emperor, *Apologia ad Constantium*, and was the basis for Rufinus's claim that Frumentius was ordained as Ethiopia's first bishop by Athanasius:

> For of course you know and remember (unless you alone pretend to be ignorant of that which all men are well aware of) that this Frumentius was advanced to his present rank by Athanasius, a man who is guilty of ten thousand crimes; for he has not been able fairly to clear himself of any of the charges brought against him, but was at once deprived of his see, and now wanders about destitute of any fixed abode, and passes from one country to another, as if by this means he could escape his own wickedness.[85]

Constantius issued condescending warnings to the Ethiopian emperor that contained veiled threats about failing to comply with his directives: "Our fear is lest he should pass over into Auxumis and corrupt your people, by setting before them accursed and impious statements, and not only unsettle and disturb the Churches, and blaspheme the supreme God, but also thereby

---

[84]Rufinus, *Church History*, 20. Rufinus claims Frumentius's ordination occurred close to that of Athanasius (328) while Athanasius's own account in the *Apologia ad Constantinum* places the event in the mid-350s. Amidon's suggestion of an altered chronology in Rufinus to place the event during the reign of Constantine—whom the *Church History* holds in the highest regard—is likely (47n20).

[85]Athanasius of Alexandria, *Apologia ad Constantium*, ed. A. Robertson, NPNF 4 (1907), 251.

Figure 2.10. Stela attributed to King Ezana at Axum, Ethiopia

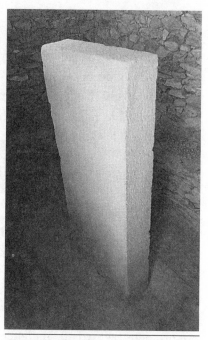

Figure 2.11. Ezana Stone outlining the king's victory and acceptance of Christianity in Ge'ez, Greek, and Sabean

Figure 2.12. Northern Stelae Park in Axum, featuring King Ezana's stela and the fallen Great Stela, which likely fell soon after its erection

cause utter overthrow and destruction to the several nations whom he visits."[86] Constantius demanded that Frumentius travel to Egypt to be examined by the Arian bishop George who had been imposed in place of the exiled Athanasius: "Now if Frumentius shall readily obey our commands, and shall submit to an enquiry into all the circumstances of his appointment, he will shew plainly to all men, that he is in no respect opposed to the laws of the Church and the established faith."[87] The Ethiopian Kingdom of Axum and its church, however, rejected the Arianism of the Roman Empire and sided with Athanasius in orthodox Christology. This is evidenced in an imperial inscription bearing dedicated to the "Father, Son, and Holy Spirit" and deploys an unprecedented reference to "Christ God," demonstrating a uniquely Ethiopian doctrine of Jesus' divinity.[88] This is significant especially when considering the common view that Christianity—and specifically the doctrine of the deity of Christ—was

Figure 2.13. Ezana Stela's curved top, possibly a continuation of pre-Christian Axumite, disk-shaped art depicting the Axumite sun god Ishtar or the moon god Almaqah

invented by the Roman Empire as a mechanism of subjugation. Quite to the contrary, at the beginning of Ethiopia's adoption of Christianity as the national religion, the Roman Empire—ruled at the time by the heretic Constantius—was attempting to introduce heretical theology subordinating the Son to the Father. Therefore, in the mid-fourth century the African churches of Egypt and Ethiopia upheld the doctrine of Jesus' divinity while the ruler of the Roman Empire was attempting, unsuccessfully, to impose the belief that Jesus was a created being.

---

[86] Athanasius, *Apologia ad Constantium*, 251.

[87] Athanasius, *Apologia ad Constantium*, 251.

[88] Stephanie L. Black, "'In the Power of God Christ': Greek Inscriptional Evidence for the Anti-Arian Theology of Ethiopia's First Christian King," *BSOAS* 71, no. 1 (2008): 102.

Material evidence indicates that Ezana, much like King Silko of Nubia, experienced a gradual conversion to Christianity. An Axumite obelisk dedicated to Ezana has images of the Ethiopian sun deity. Also located in Axum is the Ezana Stone which narrates Ezana's victory over the Meroitic Kushites in Sabean, Geʻez, and Greek. Like the Silko inscription at Kalabsha, Ezana attributes his victory to a monotheistic God and depicts himself as His divine agent:

> I set up a throne here in Shado by the might of the Lord of Heaven, who has helped me and given me sovereignty. May the Lord of Heaven make my kingdom strong! And as He has this day conquered my enemy may He conquer for me wherever I go. As He has this day conquered for me, and overthrown my enemy, I will rule the people with righteousness and justice, and will not oppress them. And may they preserve this throne, which I have set up for the Lord of Heaven, who has made me King, and the land upon which it lies. And if there shall be anyone who shall remove it, destroy it, or overthrow it, he and his kinsfolk shall be rooted out and removed from the land. I have set up this throne by the might of the Lord of Heaven.[89]

It is likely that Ezana maintained pre-Christian religious behavior while promoting and supporting the ministry of the church in a gradual Christianization of Ethiopia. It is noteworthy, however, that even centuries after the Christianization of Ethiopia, remnants of sun veneration persisted. In one of the rock-hewn churches of Lalibela, Bete Mariam (Church of Mary), an icon of the sun rests beside several typical Christian icons, which demonstrates the contextualizing of Christian iconography in Ethiopia.

Shortly after this time, Ethiopia received a group of missionaries called the Nine Saints who further advanced the growth of Christianity especially in the northern rural provinces.[90] The Nine Saints introduced monastic practices, opened monasteries that still survive today, and taught the Miaphysite doctrine of Christ existing in one person and one united nature—which was the reigning view in Egypt and Syria.[91] The Ethiopian

---

[89]Isaac, *Täwahïdo Church*, 19-20.

[90]Some content in this section previously appeared in Vince Bantu, "Early African Christianity: Ethiopia," Jude 3 Project, November 15, 2016, https://jude3project.org/blog/ethopia.

[91]The Nine Saints were originally thought to have come from Syria based on the assumption that their names were Syriac in origin. This assumption has been challenged by much of modern scholarship as the contact linguistics between Geʻez (classical Ethiopic) and various dialects of Aramaic (including Syriac) is unclear. The provenance of the Nine Saints cannot therefore be assumed with any certainty. However, it is clear that Ethiopian Christianity of the Axumite

church's name *Täwahïdo* means "being made one" or "unified" and is based on this fundamental doctrine. The Nine Saints are thought to have been the translators of the earliest biblical manuscripts into Ge'ez, a language which is still used in Ethiopian liturgy today.[92] Some of the earliest biblical manuscripts in Ge'ez were the Garima Gospels—Garima being one of the names associated with the Nine Saints. Recent radiocarbon studies have dated these Ge'ez Bible manuscripts between the fourth and thirteenth centuries.[93] However, an earlier date for these Bible translations is likely given their linguistic similarities with early Ge'ez literature.[94] While the exact author and date are not clear, what is evident is that the Bible is one of the earliest—perhaps the earliest—extant texts in the Ge'ez language. Thus Ethiopia's written history renders untenable the claim that Christianity is a white man's religion and not part of African culture. Indeed, African Christians influenced later Christian traditions in other parts of the world.

Figure 2.14. Wall painting of Mary and Jesus from Adadi Maryam Church in Lalibela, twelfth century

period had many contacts with Syriac Christianity. Aaron M. Butts, "Ethiopic Christianity, Syriac contacts with," in *Gorgias Encyclopedic Dictionary of the Syriac Heritage*, ed. Sebastian P. Brock et al. (Piscataway, NJ: Gorgias, 2011), 148.

[92]Isaac, *Täwahïdo Church*, 21.

[93]"Garima Gospels," in *The Concise Oxford Dictionary of the Christian Church*, 3rd ed., ed. E. A. Livingstone, M. W. D. Sparks, and R. W. Peacocke (New York: Oxford University Press, 2013), 224.

[94]Fr. Maximous El-Anthony, Jesper Blid, and Aaron Michael Butts, "An Early Ethiopic Manuscript Fragment (Twelfth-Thirteenth Century) from the Monastery of St Antony (Egypt)," *Aethiopica* 19 (2016): 45.

The Garima Gospels are among the earliest biblical manuscripts accompanied by decorated paintings from any country.[95]

While the Byzantine Roman Empire frequently persecuted Miaphysite ("one-nature") Christians in Syria, Egypt, and Nubia, an alliance was formed with Ethiopia to rescue persecuted Christians in the Arabian Peninsula. A South Arabian Jewish leader of the Himyarite kingdom of southwestern Arabia (modern Yemen) named Yusuf ibn Sharhabeel began forcing conversions on Christians on pain of death. This caused the Byzantine Roman emperor Justin to seek the help of the Ethiopian king Kaleb to rescue the Arabian Christians. Despite the fact that many Ethiopian and Arabian Christians maintained a Miaphysite confession—and that Roman Emperor Justin severely persecuted Miaphysite Christians in Egypt and Syria—the Romans nonetheless aided Ethiopia. Kaleb's victory over Yusuf consolidated Ethiopian control over southern Arabia, liberated the Christians from persecution, and ended the Himyarite Empire, which had been founded in the

Figure 2.15. Wall painting depicting the sun at the Adadi Maryam Church in Lalibela, twelfth century; likely a Christian contextualization of pre-Axumite sun worship

---

[95]Herbert L. Kessler, "The Word Made Flesh in Early Decorated Bibles," in *Picturing the Bible: The Earliest Christian Art*, ed. Jeffrey Spier (New Haven, CT: Yale University Press, 2009), 144.

second century BCE. Tradition holds that during the reign of Kaleb's son Gabra Masqal in the sixth century the unique Ethiopian liturgical style was developed by Saint Yared. The unique system of liturgy emerging in Ethiopia is called *Degwa* and consists of three characteristic styles of chant: *Ge'ez* (unadorned and simple), *'ezl* (deep and solemn), and *araray* (lighter, more decorative). This uniquely African Christian style of worship has been a central feature of Ethiopian Christianity for centuries.[96] Yared is said to have been transported to Paradise, where he received a vision of three celestial birds that represented the Trinity and the three Degwa chant styles that have become the cornerstone of Ethiopian liturgy.

The rise of an Islamic empire in the Arabian Peninsula severely reduced Ethiopia's influence in Red Sea and Indian Ocean trade; Ethiopia became more inwardly focused and Axum began to decline as the political center.[97] After the conquest of Axum by the Jewish queen Judith, King Gebre Mesqel recentered the Ethiopian capital at Lalibela and commissioned the construction of nearly a dozen magnificent rock-hewn churches. Ethiopian Christian literature flowered during this time with examples such as the *Kebra Negast*, *Fetha Negast* (*Law of the Kings*) and the writings of Giyorgis of Sagla.[98] Giyorgis is one of the earliest writers in Ge'ez for whom an identity can be firmly established. Giyorigs was a prolific theologian, poet, and homiletician, and some of his central texts include the *Book of the Mystery of Heaven and Earth* and the *Book of Hours*.

The writings of Giyorgis of Sagla represent the inherently poetic nature of Ethiopian literature, theology, and liturgy. This period also witnessed the development of a uniquely Ethiopian system of philosophy by seventeenth-century scholars such as Walda Heywat and Zar'a Ya'qob. Ya'qob's seminal work *Hatata* explains his construction of morality, reason, and harmony and is a landmark in African philosophy.[99] Zar'a Ya'qob reigned from 1434 to

---

[96]Solomon Addis Getahun and Wudu Tafete Kassu, *Culture and Customs of Ethiopia* (Santa Barbara, CA: Greenwood, 2014), 47.

[97]Harold G. Marcus, *A History of Ethiopia*, 2nd ed. (Berkeley: University of California Press, 2002), 12.

[98]For a modern English translation, see Miguel F. Brooks, *Kebra Nagast* (Trenton, NJ: Red Sea, 1995).

[99]For a detailed analysis of Ya'qob's work set against the political backdrop of seventeenth-century Ethiopia, see Dawit Worku Kidane, *The Ethics of Zär'a Ya'eqob: A Reply to the Historical and Religious Violence in the Seventeenth Century Ethiopia* (Rome: Editrice Pontificia Università Gregoriana, 2012).

1468 and brought peace between warring factions in Ethiopia who hotly debated the proper day of Sabbath observance—some arguing for Saturday and others for Sunday.

Zar'a Ya'qob argued in his *Maṣḥafa Berhān* (*Book of Light*) for supporters of both parties to practice the Sabbath on both days: "And if you cannot instruct them every day, teach them [at least] on Saturday and on Sunday, on which two days you have been commanded in order that you may rest in them from all your work."[100] In addition to bringing ecclesiastical unity in Ethiopia, the *Maṣḥafa Berhān* also makes clear the Ethiopian church's commitment to Christian orthodoxy: "This Book of Light tells of the abolition of magic which was being practiced in the land of Ethiopia, and it teaches the worship of God alone: without any mixing with [other] cults, astrology, or augury. Let every Christian led by this Book of Light in the light of the worship of God say [Ps 27:1], 'The Lord is my light and my salvation; whom shall I fear? The Lord is the stronghold of my life; of whom shall I be afraid?'"[101] Zar'a Ya'qob makes clear that the Ethiopian people and church were committed to the teachings of Scripture and willfully rejected traditional African religion.[102]

This fact is significant given the commonly held assumption that Christianity's beginnings in Africa were by force and that all Africans who rejected their traditional religion did so by compulsion. Zar'a Ya'qob wrote only years before Europeans began colonizing and enslaving Africans in the name of Christianity.

Figure 2.16. Bete Amanuel Church in Lalibela, Ethiopia, twelfth century

---

[100]Zar'a Ya'qob, *Maṣḥafa Berhān*, ed. Ephraim Isaac (Leiden: Brill, 1973), 83.
[101]Zar'a Ya'qob, *Maṣḥafa Berhān*, 81.
[102]Getatchew Haile, *The Homily of Zär'a Ya'eqob's Mäṣḥafa Berhān on the Rite of Baptism and Religious Instruction* (Louvain: Aedibus Peeters, 2013), xii.

Without Western influence, Zar'a Ya'qob led his people in rejecting non-biblical religious practices. Zar'a Ya'qob describes his *Maṣḥafa Berhān* as a *dersān*, which is a uniquely Ethiopian genre of literature typically consisting of exegetical, homiletical, or expository discourses. Ya'qob also describes the *Maṣḥafa Berhān* as being in the style of *Qenē*, which is a distinctly Ethiopian genre of poetry, attributed to Saint Yared, in which most Ethiopian liturgy is classified.[103] The contextualized genres of literature that originated in Ethiopia are both uniquely Ethiopian and distinctly Christian—these two aspects are interdependent.

Figure 2.17. Bete Giyorgis Church in Lalibela, Ethiopia, twelfth century

Figure 2.18. Bete Giyorgis Church from the top

---

[103]Zar'a Ya'qob, *Maṣḥafa Berhān*, 79.

During the heavy-handed reign of Zar'a Ya'qob, there was a monastic movement that originated in Ethiopia named after their founder, Stepha. These ascetic Ethiopians—Stephanites—challenged the heightened authority of the Ethiopian king in church affairs, the veneration of Mary, and the elevation of any church documents in addition to Scripture.[104] Therefore, over a century before Martin Luther nailed up the Ninety-Five Theses in Wittenberg, Ethiopia was experiencing its own Reformation that addressed many of the same theological concerns that were raised in Europe.

After the time of Ya'qob, European Christians did attempt to extend Catholicism in Ethiopia. The Ethiopian emperor Susenyos I (1606–1632) was convinced by Spanish Jesuit missionaries to enforce Catholicism in Ethiopia but was met with much resistance by local Ethiopians who preferred the indigenous Orthodox Church. Susenyos's son Fasilides (1632–1667) reestablished Ethiopian Orthodoxy as the primary faith of Ethiopia. When Emperor Fasilides heard about the Portuguese attack on Mombasa in 1632, he expelled the Jesuits from Ethiopia. However, the resistance of the ancient faith of Ethiopia was largely led by a monastic leader named Walatta Petros who defied King Susenyos and her husband's wishes by leading monastic communities against European Catholicism: "Blessed be our Lord God who did not deliver us into the treacherous net of the Europeans! Indeed, our souls fled like birds from a hunting net. Now, the net has been torn asunder, and we are safe." Honored today as one of the most revered Ethiopian saints, Walatta Petros saved her people from the "filthy faith of the Europeans" and helped restore the ancient Ethiopian faith that still stands at the core of Ethiopian identity.[105]

NORTH AFRICA

While geographically, culturally, and ecumenically distant from the various civilizations along the Nile, the Christian tradition that flourished for centuries in North Africa made significant contributions to the Christian faith. During the late ninth century BCE, a client kingdom of Phoenician Tyre became centered in the North African city of Carthage. After gaining independence

---

[104] *The Ge'ez Acts of Abba Estifanos of Gwendagwende*, ed. Getatchew Haile (Louvain: Secretariat du SCO, 2006), 69.

[105] "Gadla Walatta Petros," in *The Life and Struggles of Our Mother Walatta Petros: A Seventeenth-Century African Biography of an Ethiopian Woman*, ed. Wendy Laura Belcher and Michael Kleiner (Princeton, NY: Princeton University Press, 2015), 185.

from Tyre in the mid-seventh century BCE, the Phoenician (or Punic) speakers of Carthage led the largest empire on the Mediterranean Sea for several centuries. However, after three principal wars with the Roman Empire, North Africa fell under Roman control after the destruction of Carthage during the Third Punic War in 149–146 BCE. A new city was built on the same land and Carthage became one of the most populous and important cities in the Roman Empire.[106] In his *Geographica*, the first-century Greek historian Strabo describes the city of Carthage as a rival city to Rome and the Carthaginian Empire as stretching from Libya to Spain and "Europe."[107]

The city was expanded by Julius Caesar in the mid-first century BCE to become the fourth largest city in the empire and the capital of Roman North Africa, which included the Mediterranean coastal provinces of Mauritania (Caesariensis and Sitifensis), Numidia (Militiana and Cirtensis), Proconsular Africa, Byzacena, and Tripolitana (modern Tunisia, Libya, and Algeria). For two centuries—before a rebellion against Emperor Maximinus in 238 CE—Roman North Africa was able to prosper by establishing wealthy urban centers along the coast that the African Christians could later capitalize on in establishing a parallel ecclesiastical hierarchy.[108] Together with Egypt, the province of Proconsular Africa (modern Tunisia) was known as the breadbasket of the Roman Empire because it was the greatest contributor of grain.[109] However, unlike the Greek and Coptic-speaking Egyptians who were under the Eastern Roman Empire, the Latin and Tamazight ("Berber")-speaking people of Roman North Africa were part of the Western Empire.[110]

---

[106]Dexter Hoyos, *Mastering the West: Rome and Carthage at War* (New York: Oxford University Press, 2015), 274.

[107]Rebecca F. Kennedy, C. Syndor Roy, and Max L. Goldman, *Race and Ethnicity in the Classical World: An Anthology of Primary Sources in Translation* (Indianapolis: Hackett, 2013), 158. Strabo's account is taken to be among the most reliable for early North African geography. Elizabeth W. B. Fentress, *Numidia and the Roman Army: Social, Military, and Economic Aspects of the Frontier Zone* (Oxford: BAR International, 1979), 20.

[108]Alexander Evers, *Church, Cities, and People: A Study of the Plebs in the Church and Cities of Roman Africa in Late Antiquity* (Leuven: Peeters, 2010), 5.

[109]A. H. Merrills, *Vandals, Romans, and Berbers: New Perspectives on Late Antique North Africa* (Burlington, VT: Ashgate, 2004), 39.

[110]The modern concept of the continent of Africa did not exist in antiquity, as "Africa" did not include Egypt, Ethiopia, or Nubia as it does today. Thomas Oden, *How Africa Shaped the Christian Mind: Rediscovering the African Seedbed of Western Christianity* (Downers Grove, IL: InterVarsity Press, 2007), 83; Thomas Oden, *Early Libyan Christianity: Uncovering a North African Tradition* (Downers Grove, IL: InterVarsity Press, 2011), 151.

Only decades after the missionary activity of Jesus' disciples, one of the most prominent church fathers, Tertullian, was born and raised in Carthage. Shortly after this time the early Christian theologian Irenaeus made mention of established churches in Libya.[111] Tertullian was a highly educated Christian scholar who, through his expansive literary corpus, was the first major figure to develop Christian theology in Latin. Two centuries after his death, stories began to circulate that Tertullian was born of a centurion father, had a background as a lawyer, and served in the church as a presbyter.[112] In his own writings, Tertullian explains that he converted from paganism to Christianity in response to some significant life event. He later married and eventually became associated with a divergent strand of Christianity that he called the New Prophecy, a more theologically and socially conservative group often labeled by the dominant church as "Montanists" after one of the movements Phrygian founders, Montanus. The Montanists strongly emphasized the role of the Holy Spirit in communicating ongoing revelation and emphasized a strict social lifestyle in terms of dress, the role of women, and participation in Roman social activities. While it is unclear to what extent Tertullian broke away from mainstream Christianity and identified with Montanism, there are many Montanist elements in his writings such as *On Modesty, On Flight in Time of Persecution, Against the Valentinians,* and *On the Resurrection of the Dead.*[113] While Montanism was never officially condemned in the context of an ecumenical council, the movement received significant critique from mainstream Christians and eventually faded away in favor of the dominant church.

A younger contemporary of Tertullian named Novatian started another alternative Christian trajectory that challenged the dominant church hierarchy. When Roman emperor Decius intensified systematic persecution of Christians by demanding they all sacrifice to the Roman gods in 247, the Christian world was divided on whether to receive back into fellowship the *lapsi* (or lapsed) believers who recanted their faith to avoid persecution. At the turn of the third century, one of the earliest extrabiblical Christian texts,

---

[111]Irenaeus of Lyons, *Against Heresies*, ed. Dominic Unger (New York: Newman, 1992), 1.10.2.

[112]Eusebius of Caesarea, *Ecclesiastical History*, ed. C. F. Cruse (Grand Rapids: Hendrickson, 1998), 2.2.4; Jerome, *On Illustrious Men*, ed. Thomas P. Halton (Washington, DC: Catholic University of America Press, 1999), 74.

[113]Geoffrey D. Dunn, *Tertullian* (New York: Routledge, 2004), 7.

The Passion of St. Perpetua, St. Felicitas, and Their Companions, told the story of several North African Christians martyred during the persecution of Emperor Septimus Severus. Perpetua—a Carthaginian noble woman—and the pregnant slave Felicitas were imprisoned for their Christian faith, received a series of divine visions of their impending martyrdom, and were ultimately tortured by wild beasts and put to death by the sword. That Perpetua's husband is not directly mentioned, that she refuses the pleas of her father to apostatize, and that the central figures of this early Christian text are female challenged the male-dominant culture of early Christianity. Indeed, if the common proposition of Perpetua's authorship is correct, the *Passion* is the earliest Christian text written by a woman.[114] What is clear, however, is the significant degree to which North African Christianity was shaped by unique responses to persecution, which took further shape during the time of another of Africa's most influential Christian leaders—Cyprian of Carthage.

Cyprian, born into a wealthy family and ordained bishop just before the persecution of Decius, facilitated the various councils of Carthage—some of the earliest recorded church councils in history.[115] Cyprian wrote many letters and theological treatises, many of which, such as *On the Unity of the Catholic Church* and *On the Fallen,* dealt with the issue of the Christian response to persecution.[116] In these writings, Cyprian was addressing Novatian, the leader of an alternative church that held a more conservative view on lapsed Christians. Like Meletius of Lycopolis in Egypt, Novatian argued that the church did not have the authority to forgive the sin of idolatry. According to Cyprian, Novatian established himself as an antipope and established bishops and clerics sympathetic to his views that would rival the dominant church backed by the Roman bishop. Despite Novatian's reputation as a

---

[114]It has been suggested on the basis of philological variation in the *Passion* that Perpetua was likely one of several authors that together composed the text. Eliezer Gonzalez, *The Fate of the Dead in Early Third Century North African Christianity* (Tübingen: Mohr Siebeck, 2014), 14.

[115]Vincent Hunink, "St. Cyprian, A Christian and Roman Gentleman," in *Cyprian of Carthage: Studies in His Life, Language, and Thought,* ed. Henk Bakker, Paul van Geest, and Hans van Loon (Leuven: Peeters, 2010), 35.

[116]Cyprian's treatise *On Unity* provides an interesting window into how bishops outside of Rome understood their own authority and that of Rome at a time before the Petrine papal office developed the sense of authority that exists today. Geoffrey D. Dunn, *Cyprian and the Bishops of Rome: Questions of Papal Primacy in the Early Church* (Strathfield: St. Paul's, 2007), 6; see also a plea for being seen as equals by Carthaginian bishops addressed to Rome, in Rose Bernard Donna, ed., *Saint Cyprian: Letters* (Washington, DC: Catholic University of America Press, 1964), 21.

heretic, he actually composed one of the earliest theological defenses of the doctrine of the Trinity, *De Trinitate*, almost a century before the Council of Nicaea.[117] However, it is in his several *Epistulae* to Cyprian that he lays out the conservative view on the question of apostates. Novatian was eventually excommunicated by Cyprian's ally, the Roman bishop Cornelius. Cyprian's primary concern was not necessarily the rigid and unforgiving approach of the Novatians but the rejection of the dominant ecclesiastical hierarchy.[118] Cyprian's approach to the *lapsi* was nuanced: absolution could be granted to dying penitents while those in good health could gain forgiveness either by declaring their faith in the presence of governmental officials or waiting until the persecution ended and undergoing a formal consultation.[119] However, the unity of the church was paramount for Cyprian; apostasy could be forgiven but insubordination to the church could not.

Despite his more lenient approach in receiving the lapsed back into communion, and despite the fact that he fled during the Decian persecution, Cyprian was exiled and eventually martyred under the renewed persecution of Emperor Valerian in 258. The emperor's proconsul said to Cyprian: "'Because you in your hostility have been instructed in a wickedness like your own, you will suffer this punishment as an example. In this way, your unholy stubbornness will pay the penalty in your blood.' Cyprian said, 'Praise God!' and the believers all together said, 'Praise God!'"[120]

Another significant and uniquely North African strand of Christianity that developed less than a century after the schism between Novatian and Cyprian was the movement known among its detractors as Donatism. Named after one of its principal figures, Donatus Magnus, the Donatists expressed a similar policy toward the lapsed as the Novatians of the third century. Like the Novatian schism, the Donatist movement rose to prominence in North Africa primarily in response to Roman persecution of Christians—this time during the Great Persecution under Diocletian. In 311,

---

[117]James L. Papandrea, ed. *Novatian: On the Trinity, Letters to Cyprian of Carthage, Ethical Treatises* (Turnhout: Brepols, 2015), 9.

[118]Allen Brent, *Cyprian and Roman Carthage* (New York: Cambridge University Press, 2010), 60.

[119]J. Patout Burns Jr., *Cyprian the Bishop* (New York: Routledge, 2002), 3.

[120]Maureen A. Tilley, *Donatist Martyr Stories: The Church in Conflict in Roman North Africa* (Liverpool: Liverpool University Press, 1996), 4. Despite his rejection of Novatianism, Cyprian's authority and martyr status made him a foundational influence in the later rigorist approach of the Donatists (Evers, *Church, Cities, and People*, 297).

only a few years after the Great Persecution and just before the Edict of Milan, the newly appointed bishop of Carthage, Caecilianus, expressed the mainstream, lenient attitude toward readmitting the lapsed into communion. This led to the counterordination of a Carthaginian named Majorinus who led the rigorist party.

Shortly after his rise to prominence among the rigorists, Majorinus died and the leadership of this rigorist party fell to Donatus Magnus. Much like Novatian and his followers had rejected the *lapsi*, the Donatists conceived of those who had "surrendered" their Christian conviction—and in many cases, surrendered Bibles for burning—as *traditores* ("surrenderers"). While the Carthaginian bishop recognized by the Roman church was Caecilian, Donatus garnered a significant following, especially among the Berber communities in rural Numidia. Among the rural Numidians, there already existed a general distrust and contempt for the Roman imperial authorities who had conquered the region from the Punic ancestors of the Numidian Berbers. The fact that the Donatist position was rejected by the Roman bishop made the movement more closely associated with indigenous North African identity. Despite an appeal to Emperor Constantine for support, the Donatists were rejected at the Council of Arles in 313. The rejection of Donatism by the dominant Christian church was solidified during the time of the North African bishop Augustine of Hippo, who vehemently opposed the movement.[121] While evidence for a Donatist presence in North Africa comes as late as the sixth-century letters of Gregory the Great, the movement went into rapid decline after the Council of Carthage in 411 and the influential polemic by Saint Augustine.[122]

Augustine, who remains one of the most influential Christian theologians in history, was born in 354 in the Numidian city of Thagaste (modern Souk Ahras, Algeria). Raised in a Christian home under the strong influence of his

---

[121]Like Cyprian before him, Augustine critiqued the rigid approach toward the *lapsi* by emphasizing the authority (or ordo) of the catholic church. James P. Keleher, *Saint Augustine's Notion of Schism in the Donatist Controversy* (Mundelein, IL: Saint Mary of the Lake Seminary, 1961), 38. Adam Ployd analyzes Augustine's anti-Donatist polemic against the backdrop of his trinitarian contributions to demonstrate the continuity between Augustine's concern for ecclesiastical and theological unity. *Augustine, the Trinity, and the Church* (New York: Oxford University Press, 2015), 15.

[122]Stanisław Adamiak, "When Did Donatist Christianity End?" in *The Uniquely African Controversy: Studies on Donatist Christianity*, ed. Anthony Dupont, Matthew Alan Gaumer, and Mathijs Lamberigts, (Leuven: Peeters, 2015), 225.

mother, Monica, Augustine left the orthodox faith and joined the Manichean community popular at that time. Augustine was trained in rhetoric and Hellenistic philosophy in Carthage and taught in Rome. Due to the influence of orthodox Christian figures such as Ambrose of Milan and the stories about Anthony the Great, Augustine recanted Manichean belief and embraced orthodox Christianity. He was baptized by Ambrose and in 391 was ordained as bishop of Hippo in his native Numidia. He participated in the Council of Carthage in 397 in which one of the earliest biblical canons was decided. Although Augustine wrote in Latin as a member of the educated class, he likely spoke Numidian as well and multiple times identifies himself with pride as an African.[123] Augustine's multiethnic background as a native North African who was highly Romanized in education and culture influenced the complicated way he engaged his social setting. Augustine was the victim of Romanocentric racist attitudes because of his African identity and at various points defended the beauty of the Punic language.[124] However, Augustine felt insecure about his own ability to speak Punic and primarily spoke and wrote in Latin. Likewise, Augustine defended the faith of the dominant church centered in Rome and suppressed the indigenous Donatist faith of many native North African Christians. Rather than supporting native North African Christianity, Augustine contributed significantly to the development of Western theology, notably the development of the doctrine of original sin in his autobiographical *Confessions* and in his *City of God*, which was written in response to the destruction of Rome by the Visigoths in 410.

After the Visigoths gained control of the Western Roman Empire, including the Iberian Peninsula, the eastern Germanic Vandals who had dominated Iberia then moved further east and conquered North Africa. The Vandals established swift and complete control of North Africa and shifted the ecclesiastical landscape with a predominately Arian administration.[125] After a century of Vandal rule, North Africa was recovered by the Roman

---

[123] Augustine of Hippo, *Confessions*, ed. David Vincent Meconi (San Francisco: Ignatius, 2012), 8.6.14. This would have been countercultural for the dominant Latin-speaking, Roman-descended citizens of Carthage who tended to denigrate the indigenous Punic-speaking Numidians. Henry Chadwick, *Augustine of Hippo: A Life* (New York: Oxford University Press, 2009), 6.

[124] Justo L. González, *The Mestizo Augustine: A Theologian Between Two Cultures* (Downers Grove, IL: InterVarsity Press, 2016), 32.

[125] The Vandal ruler Geiseric expelled mainstream (or "Catholic") leadership and installed Arian bishops after his conquest of Africa (Merrills, *Vandals, Romans, and Berbers*, 44).

emperor Justinian in 533. Originally incorporated into the Byzantine Roman Empire as a prefecture, Emperor Maurice extended the autonomy of Africa as an exarchate in 585. The military and political power of Byzantine Africa proved vital to the ascension of Emperor Heraclius, who used the military power of the Numidians to usurp the throne from Emperor Phocas in 608. The rise of Islam and the Arab Muslim conquest of the mid-seventh century ushered in a new and final era for North Africa and its Christian presence.

After swiftly conquering Egypt in 640, the Muslim forces led by 'Amr ibn al-'As also conquered eastern portions of North Africa (modern Libya). Despite the dwindling strength of Roman North Africa during Islamic incursions, an African victory was won against the Arabs during the Battle of Vescera in 682. Muslim forces led by 'Amr ibn al-'As's nephew Uqba ibn Nafi were defeated by the Romans, who were supported by the Amazigh ("Berber") independent Christian nation of Altava led by king Akzel (Latin "Caecilius"). This victory was short, as the Muslim commander of the Umayyad army, Hasan ibn al-Nu'man, defeated the Romans and destroyed Carthage in 698. While the Roman forces fled to Italy after this devastating loss, a final resistance was mounted by the indigenous Numidians led by

Figure 2.19. Christian baptistery from Bekalta, Tunisia, sixth century

Queen Dihya (or Kahina), who pushed the Muslims back to Libya. Shortly thereafter, Umayyad caliph Abd al-Malik defeated Queen Dihya at the Battle of Tabarka in 702. Abd al-Malik then established the city of Tunis as the new administrative center of the region near the destroyed Carthage.

W. H. C. Frend argues that North African Christianity did not survive the Islamic conquest because of the marginalization of the Donatists, whom he contends represented the faith of the indigenous Numidians.[126] The Donatist movement should not be reduced merely to a nationalist movement. As Alden Bass points out, much of the Donatist rhetoric that has been understood as anti-nomian (or "against the law") should be read in light of their understanding of the apostle Paul's theological construction of the law rather than a nationalist movement.[127] However, archeological evidence in North Africa demonstrates ethnic and socioeconomic differentiation between the dominant church and the Donatists by revealing separate, competing, neighboring church structures.[128] Available textual evidence demonstrates that many of the Catholic figures opposing the Donatists, such as Augustine, also supported the aristocratic landowners, who often used their social position to enforce Catholic belief over the Donatists.[129] Conversely, Donatists often aligned themselves with

Figure 2.20. The Great Mosque of Kairouan, Tunisia, seventh century

---

[126]W. H. C. Frend, *The Donatist Church: A Movement of Protest in Roman North Africa*, 2nd ed. (New York: Oxford University Press, 2003), 336.

[127]Alden Lee Bass, "Justus sib ilex est: The Donatist Interpretation of the Law in Romans 2:14," in *Sacred Scripture and Secular Struggles*, ed. David Vincent Meconi (Leiden: Brill, 2015), 163.

[128]J. Patout Burns Jr. and Robin M. Jensen, *Christianity in Roman Africa: The Development of its Practices and Beliefs* (Grand Rapids: Eerdmans, 2014), xlix.

[129]Cam Grey, "Rural Society in North Africa," in *The Donatist Schism: Controversy and Contexts*, ed. Richard Miles (Liverpool: Liverpool University Press, 2016), 135. Grey points out that this type of theological strong-arming on the part of landowners also occurred among Donatists aristocrats.

resistance movements against Roman hegemony—as was the case with Donatist bishop Optatus of Thamugadi, the largest Donatist stronghold in North Africa— who led a failed coup with the Numidian general Gildo in 398.[130] Perhaps more significant is the fact that Christian literature did not survive in Punic or Tamazight ("Berber") languages; all the

Figure 2.21. Roman-era pillar with cross icon, re-purposed in the construction of the Great Mosque of Kairouan, seventh century

available evidence is in Latin. These factors indicate the degree to which Christianity in North Africa was in large part centered on the wealthy, educated, Latin-speaking, urban population and was not supported among the rural Amazigh who maintained an alternative theology. It is important to note, however, that Muslim sources in Arabic indicate continuing Christian

Figure 2.22. Remains of the Donatist Cathedral of Timgad, Algeria, fourth century

[130]Burns and Jensen, *Christianity in Roman Africa*, 592.

presence in North Africa for centuries after the conquest. Interestingly, one of the most common terms for Christians in Arabic sources is *afariqa*—indicating a significant degree to which "Christian" and "African" were synonymous concepts.[131] It is more likely that the disappearance of the Christian presence in Numidia was due to increasing persecution and social marginalization. Before this period, however, North Africa had been a Christian region from the New Testament period that profoundly shaped much of Christian life and thought.

---

[131]Merrills, *Vandals, Romans, and Berbers*, 303.

3

The Early Church in the Middle East

SYRIA

Over the centuries there have been many Christian communities from various ecclesiastical, national, and ethnic affiliations that shared a common heritage rooted in the Syriac-speaking world. Syriac is a Northwest Semitic dialect of Aramaic that originated in an ancient city named Urhoy (modern Urfa, Turkey) and spread via Christian missions through the continent of Asia. Modern churches that still use Syriac in liturgy include the Syrian Orthodox Church (also called Jacobite, after Jacob Baradaeus, a sixth-century bishop of Urhoy), the Assyrian Church of the East (often erroneously labeled "Nestorian"; including a substantial constituency in China during the medieval period), the Maronite Church, the Chaldean Catholic Church, and the various Saint Thomas Christian communities of Kerala, India. Over two millennia across the continent of Asia, various Christian communities have expressed diverse forms of worship grounded in different (and often opposing) theological positions united primarily by their shared heritage of this dialect.

Christianity had one of its strongest and earliest constituencies in the nearby Roman province of Syria, where the term *Christian* was first used in the capital city of Antioch (Acts 11:26). Because of Peter's activities in Antioch (Gal 2:11), several modern ecclesiastical communities centered in Antioch claim Petrine apostolic succession. Ignatius of Antioch, a younger contemporary of Peter and disciple of the apostle John, served as one of the earliest bishops of Antioch and was one of the earliest nonbiblical Christian writers. Tatian the Syrian, a pupil of the Palestinian theologian Justin Martyr, was another second-century theologian. Like Justin, Tatian wrote treatises critiquing Hellenistic philosophy and focused heavily on Christ as the divine Logos. Tatian also composed a four-part Gospel harmony called the *Diatessaron*, which only survives in a commentary on the text by Ephrem the Syrian. During the late second century, a theological academy developed in Antioch that would later produce figures such as Theophilus of Antioch, Diodore of Tarsus, John Chrysostom, and Theodore of Mopsuestia. Antiochene Christianity was deeply influenced by rabbinic Judaism and tended to emphasize a more literal approach to biblical interpretation. As one of the most significant cities of the Roman Empire, the patriarchate of Antioch extended through the majority of what is now known as the Middle East. While the Greek-speaking theologians of Antioch would continue to profoundly shape Middle Eastern Christianity, Syriac would become the dominant language of Asian Christianity. Both the Syriac language and Christian tradition were originally centered in Urhoy (or Edessa), which was incorporated into the Roman Empire through the early second to mid-third centuries.

The culture of Urhoy has always been cosmopolitan as there have been several ruling powers over the centuries.[1] Although Urhoy does not enter the written record until the Hellenistic period, it is of little doubt that this well-watered site was frequently visited and possibly settled during the Persian Achaemenid Empire (550–330 BCE).[2] Following the conquest of the region by Alexander the Great in 334 BCE, Urhoy was officially settled in the Hellenistic Seleucid kingdom and named Edessa after a city of the same name in the Macedonian homeland.

At the end of the second century BCE the Persian Parthian Empire took advantage of the increasing internal rivalries between the Seleucid, Ptolemaic, and ascendant Roman kingdoms and assumed control of the region. During Parthian rule Urhoy, including its surrounding region Osrhoene, established a local kingship system called the Abgarid dynasty.[3] During Parthian hegemony, Urhoy developed a friendly relationship with Rome, though there was no attempt at incorporating Urhoy into the Roman Empire

---

[1] The Antiochene orator Malalas reports that Seleucus I referred to Urhoy as a "half-barbarian Antioch." Steven K. Ross, *Roman Edessa: Politics and Culture on the Eastern Fringes of the Roman Empire, 114-242 CE* (New York: Routledge, 2001), 8.

[2] Ross, *Roman Edessa*, 5; J. B. Segal, *Edessa: The Blessed City* (New York: Oxford University Press, 1970), 3.

[3] After the royal name Abgar that appears most often during this dynasty.

until the second century CE. Urhoy/Osrhoene's incorporation into Roman territory was a century-long process that began with Trajan's campaign against Parthia in 114 CE and culminated with the last native king of Urhoy, Abgar X, becoming a Roman consul in 242.

The *Teaching of Addai* is an early fifth-century Syriac text that narrates the legend of how Christianity came to Urhoy through a personal correspondence between King Abgar Ukkama ("Black") and Jesus, which resulted in the apostle Thaddeus evangelizing Urhoy and establishing the first Syriac-speaking church.[4] Although the historicity of the Abgar legend is largely dismissed by contemporary scholarship,[5] an earlier account of the same story appears in Eusebius's *Ecclesiastical History*.[6] The establishment of Christianity in Syria is also the account accepted by the early third-century heresiarch Bardaisan in his *Book of the Laws of the Countries*.[7] It is generally accepted that Christianity came to Urhoy no later than the late second century and to the neighboring city of Nisibis soon after.[8]

Likewise, the Syriac version of the Bible may have been translated in the first century but no later than the second.[9] The Syriac Old Testament is unique among early biblical translations as it came directly into Syriac from Hebrew and not the Greek Septuagint.[10] Like the majority of the Roman Empire, earliest Christianity in Urhoy was theologically varied. Christians

---

[4]The apostle referenced is Saint Addai or Thaddeus of Edessa, alleged to be one of the seventy apostles, not to be confused with Thaddeus of the twelve apostles. *The Teaching of Addai*, ed. George Howard (Atlanta, GA: Society of Biblical Literature, 1981).

[5]Ross, *Roman Edessa*, 136; Walter Bauer, *Orthodoxy and Heresy in Earliest Christianity* (Philadelphia: Fortress, 1971), 11.

[6]Eusebius of Caesarea, *Ecclesiastical History*, ed. C. F. Cruse (Grand Rapids: Hendrickson, 1998), 1.12.

[7]Bardaisan, *Book of the Laws of the Countries*, ed. William Cureton (London: Francis and John Rivington, 1855), 31-32.

[8]Ross, *Roman Edessa*, 117; Bauer, *Orthodoxy and Heresy*, 13; Wilhelm Baum and Dietmar Winkler, *The Church of the East: A Concise History* (New York: Routledge, 2003), 8. An inscription attributed to Bishop Aberkios attests the existence of Christianity in Nisibis no later than the late second century. Ephrem the Syrian, *Hymns*, trans. Kathleen E. McVey (New York: Paulist, 1989), 6.

[9]M. P. Weitzman, *The Syriac Version of the Old Testament: An Introduction* (New York: Cambridge University Press, 1999), 2. The Old Testament was translated no later than the second century, and the Old Syriac New Testament was also composed as early as the second century. The standard Syriac Bible today is known as the Peshitta ("simple," "straightforward"), a version that emerged no later than the ninth century, combining the standard OT and NT in order to distinguish them from contemporary translations. Sebastian Brock, *The Bible in the Syriac Tradition* (Piscataway, NJ: Gorgias, 2006), 23.

[10]Brock, *Bible in the Syriac Tradition*, 17.

of Urhoy were strongly influenced by the writings of Marcion, Bardaisan, and Mani, all of whom were later declared heretics by the greatest Syriac champion of Nicene orthodoxy, Ephrem the Syrian (306–373). Not until the fourth century did orthodox theology, as represented by figures such as Ephrem and his older Persian contemporary Aphrahat, become the mainstream doctrine.[11]

Ephrem was born in Nisibis to Christian parents, served as a deacon and *malphono* ("teacher"), and fled to Urhoy after the Persian conquest of Nisibis.[12] Ephrem is often associated with an indigenous Syrian form of protomonasticism and he lived in ascetic solitude while also providing aid for the poor and sick in Urhoy.[13] During his time as the malphono of the School of the Persians in Urhoy, Ephrem wrote the majority of his Syriac literary corpus, which focused primarily on combating the theological views

---

[11]This fact has led Robert Murray to argue that in the Syriac-speaking world what later became declared orthodox Christianity developed first in Nisibis and not Urhoy. This argument is based largely on the fact that Nisibis produced orthodox Syriac Christianity's earliest figures, Aphrahat and Ephrem, whereas the earliest Christian figures of Urhoy were heretics such as Bardaisan, Marcion, and Mani. *Symbols of Church and Kingdom: A Study in Early Syriac Tradition* (New York: Cambridge University Press, 1975), 6-9; see also Segal, *Edessa*, 62. This view is rooted in Bauer's thesis that orthodox Christianity developed in the fourth century while the Christianities of the second and third centuries were theologically diverse as there was not yet a dominant "orthodox" view. Bauer also claims that what later became known as orthodoxy developed primarily in Rome while heretical movements came from exterior territories of the empire (Bauer, *Orthodoxy and Heresy*, 229). This Eurocentric view fails to account for the presence of heretics in Rome such as Valentinus as well as early pillars of orthodoxy in Syria and Egypt such as Tatian and Clement of Alexandria. It is most probable that Nisibene Christianity was as theologically varied in the second century as Urhoy.

[12]St. Ephrem the Syrian, *Hymns on Paradise*, trans. Sebastian P. Brock (Crestwood, NY: St. Vladimir's Seminary Press, 1990), 9; Sebastian P. Brock, *The Luminous Eye: The Spiritual World Vision of Saint Ephrem the Syrian* (Kalamazoo, MI: Cistercian Publications, 1985), 16. Although Ephrem initially found the conditions of Persian Nisibis agreeable and encountered no opposition, he eventually made his way to Urhoy. Arthur Vööbus, *Literary Critical and Historical Studies in Ephrem the Syrian* (Wetteren: Imprimerie Cultura, 1958), 51.

[13]Syriac ascetics existed in several categories: *ihidaye* ("single," "celibate," "single-minded"), *bthule* ("virgins"), and *qaddishe* ("sanctified," i.e., married persons who had renounced marital intercourse). Syrian monasticism developed independently from that practiced in Egypt and retained its own distinctives in architecture and practice. R. M. Price, *A History of the Monks of Syria by Theodoret of Cyrrhus* (Kalamazoo, MI: Cistercian Publications, 1985), xx. Ephrem was known as the "prince of the monks," Vööbus, *Literary Critical and Historical Studies*, 112. Brock has cautioned against using the term *monk* in order to avoid confusion with the later form of monasticism that would develop in Egypt (Ephrem, *Hymns on Paradise*, 26). It is not necessary to avoid using the term in reference to Ephrem, but it is important not to associate Syrian asceticism with Pachomian coenobitic monasticism. The early fifth-century historian Palladius reports on the leadership provided by Ephrem during a severe famine in Urhoy. Palladius, *Lausiac History*, ed. Robert T. Meyer (Mahwah, NJ: Paulist, 1964), 116-17.

Figure 3.1. Church of Saint Jacob in Nisibis, fourth century

of the followers of Bardaisan, Marcion, and Mani—three of his heavily influential predecessors.[14]

Like the culture of Urhoy, Ephrem's thought and writing style were rooted in three primary influences: indigenous Mesopotamian tradition, Judaism, and Hellenism.[15] Whereas the Hellenistic theological method of Ephrem's day sought out definitions or boundaries (Greek *horoi*) with which to speak of God, this approach appeared dangerous, if not blasphemous, to Ephrem. Rather, Ephrem used his poetic *madrāshe* to speak of God by means of flexible symbols and dynamic paradox.[16] Written in syllable patterns,

---

[14]Adam H. Becker, *Fear of God and the Beginning of Wisdom: The School of Nisibis and the Development of Scholastic Culture in Late Antique Mesopotamia* (Philadelphia: University of Pennsylvania Press, 2006), 41. The sixth-century *Life of Ephrem* claims that Ephrem was instantaneously endowed with the ability to speak Greek upon hearing the preaching of Basil of Caesarea (Ephrem, *Hymns on Paradise*, 21); however, most of his writings survive in Syriac. Brock also points out that many works attributed to Ephrem in Greek, as well as Latin, Arabic, and Slavonic, were not originally composed in Syriac at all (36).

[15]It is true that Ephrem "expresses contempt for Greek thought" (Murray, *Symbols*, 30). However, Ephrem finds use of Hellenistic culture and philosophy where it is compatible with and subject to Scripture in a manner common to early Christians such as Tatian and Basil of Caesarea. Jeffrey Wickes, *Bible and Poetry in Late Antique Mesopotamia: Ephrem's Hymns on Faith* (Oakland, CA: University of California Press, 2019), 13.

[16]Ephrem and Syriac literature as a whole have been met, unfortunately, with not a small amount of Eurocentric condescension labelling Semitic modes of theology as demonstrating "little profundity

madrāshe (often called "hymns") and *memre* (often called "homilies") were genres of literature unique to the Syriac language. Most associated with Ephrem, *madrāshe* were set to music and performed in a call-and-response communal setting. Some prominent features of Ephremian theology are a high value on the corporeal world (in contrast to Platonic dualism), the juxtaposition of opposing elements, and the primacy of faith over reason: "Through faith God reveals Himself to you."[17] Like all cultures, Syriac culture had many influences as it existed at the intersection of the Roman and Persian Empires.[18] The Syriac-speaking Christian tradition developed significantly by Ephrem was quite culturally distinct from that of the Greco-Roman Christian world.

Despite some of the racist dismissal of Syriac theological poetry as less sophisticated than Greco-Roman, Hellenized theology, thankfully much contemporary Syriac scholarship has come to value the theological and cultural approach of Ephrem on its own Semitic, Mesopotamian terms. Similarly, styles of worship and theology that emerge from non-Western cultures in the modern world are often dismissed as less refined or even less theologically informed—judgments often cloaked in problematic language such as "high" and "low" liturgy. Non-Western Christians of the modern world can find a model in the Syriac approach to theology as established by Ephrem the Syrian that was already an alternative to the dominant Roman church in the patristic period.

The core feature of Ephrem's theological method is his understanding of God's self-revelation through "hidden meaning" (*hayla kasya*) discerned through the eye of faith by means of symbols (*raze*).[19] The *raze* typologically connect two different modes of reality on a much deeper level than is implied by the modern word *symbol*. The process of instruction by means

---

or originality of thought . . . turgid, humourless, and repetitive" (Segal, *Edessa*, 89). Fortunately, this approach has largely faded from Syriac studies: Ephrem is indeed an accomplished poet, yet his specific form of orthodoxy employs the art of language in such a way as to surpass the clarity of well-defined terminology and logical demonstration with the clarity of a more comprehensive and superior form of intelligence. Kees den Biesen, *Simple and Bold: Ephrem's Art of Symbolic Thought* (Piscataway, NJ: Gorgias, 2006), xix.

[17]Brock, *Luminous Eye*, 29; den Biesen, *Simple and Bold*, 324.

[18]David Allen Michelson, *The Practical Christology of Philoxenus of Mabbug* (New York: Oxford University Press, 2014), 121; Justo L. González, *The Mestizo Augustine: A Theologian Between Two Cultures* (Downers Grove, IL: InterVarsity Press, 2016), 171.

[19]*Raze* is the Semitic concept behind Paul's use of the Greek *mystērion* (Ephrem, *Hymns on Paradise*, 42).

of symbols and meaning is for Ephrem the sum of theology.[20] In his
Madrāshe on Paradise, Ephrem imagines the glory of heaven by means of
God's self-revelation:

> For him who would tell of it
> there is no other means
>> but to use the names
> of things that are visible,
> thus depicting for his hearers
> a likeness of things that are hidden.
> For if the Creator
> of the Garden
> has clothed His majesty
> in terms that we can understand,
>> how much more can His Garden
> be described with our similes?[21]

Throughout the *Madrāshe on Paradise* and his entire corpus, the two principle witnesses through which divine symbols are perceived for Ephrem are
creation and Scripture. A prominent example is Ephrem's *Madrāshe on the
Pearl*: "One day, my brothers, I held a pearl; I saw in it symbols [*raze*], witnesses to the Kingdom, images and signs of His majesty. It became a fountain
from which I drank the mysteries of the Son."[22] Ephrem continues to describe how the luminosity of the pearl represents the glory of God. Similarly,
the spherical shape of the pearl represents the eternality and incomprehen-
sibility of God. Ephrem often warns his readers against any attempt to investigate the mysteries of God. Indeed, Ephrem stands as an "ambassador to
Asian Christianity," providing an indigenously Syrian approach to theology
that is free from Western cultural trappings and a more relevant inroad for
Christians of Eastern cultural descent.[23]

---

[20]Sidney H. Griffith, *'Faith Adoring the Mystery': Reading the Bible with St. Ephraem the Syrian*
(Milwaukee: Marquette University Press, 1997), 29. One such example is the symbol of the "eye,"
or soul, through which the individual perceives the *raze* of God, which Ephrem develops in his
Madrāshe on the Church 37.6-7 (*Hymns on Paradise*, 72-73).

[21]Ephrem, *Hymns on Paradise*, 155.

[22]The passage is translated from Ephrem, *Madrāshe on Faith*, ed. Edmund Beck, *Des heiligen
Ephraem des Syrers: Hymnen de Fide*, Corpus Scriptorum Christianorum Orientalium 154 (Louvain: Imprimerie Orientaliste, 1955), 248-49.

[23]Ephrem, *Hymns on Paradise*, 15.

While Ephrem wrote much prose and artistic literature common in early Christianity, his thought comes forth most powerfully in his *memre* and especially in his *madrāshe*.[24] It is the symbolic complexity and theological depth found in the *madrāshe* that have earned Ephrem, also called the "Harp of the Spirit" by his contemporaries, the reputation as the most significant figure in the history of Syriac Christianity and the greatest poet-theologian equaled only by Dante. Ephrem ingeniously appropriated this deeply influential art form to polemicize against one of its forerunners (Bardaisan) while promoting Nicene orthodoxy.[25] While Bardaisan preceded Ephrem in his use of *madrāshe*, Ephrem is generally considered the master of this literary art form.[26] By appropriating such a significant aspect of Urhoy culture for the promotion of orthodox Christianity, Ephrem became a missiological exemplar for theological contextualization and set the trajectory for theology and literature for the entire Syriac Christian tradition that would follow him.

The second most influential Syriac Christian writer—known as the "Flute of the Spirit"—was the late fifth/early sixth-century poet-theologian and bishop, Jacob of Serugh. Jacob continued the Syriac Christian tradition of Ephrem after being educated at the School of Edessa (Urhoy) and composing over seven hundred *memre*, most of which have still not been translated.[27] Jacob was born the same year as the controversial Council of Chalcedon and maintained the Miaphysite position—the dominant view in the Syrian region. At the time of the council in 451, both Maximus II, bishop of Antioch, and Ibas, bishop of Urhoy, accepted the two-nature position of Chalcedon. However, Severus, the bishop of Antioch (508–518), vehemently opposed Chalcedonian theology and was replaced by the Chalcedonian emperor Justin I. Severus lived the last twenty years of his life in exile in Egypt where he continued to write letters in support of the Miaphysite church. In these letters Severus presents Miaphysite theology as the faith of

---

[24]While "hymn" is the most frequent English rendering, scholars remain divided on how to translate *madrāshe*. Kees den Biesen calls them "teaching songs" (*Simple and Bold*, vii). A more apt equivalent in the contemporary world is the African-American spiritual, which also involves the musical, call-and-response expression of a culturally specific religious community.

[25]Whose name literally means "son of the Daisan," the river of Urhoy (Segal, *Edessa*, 35).

[26]Murray, *Symbols*, 30.

[27]Philip Michael Forness, *Preaching Christology in the Roman Near East: A Study of Jacob of Serugh* (Oxford: Oxford University Press, 2018), 9.

Syrians and Egyptians and associates Chalcedonian theology with the oppressive Roman Empire:

> However, because making accusations is not pleasing to me, I will make clear
> and expound to those who are mine and who love me what it (my opinion)
> is to them, and proclaim it also to those who are against me; the communion
> that now prevails in the persecuted church [*'idtah radiyptah*] of the East and
> in all the Egyptian church, and is pure in the proclamation of the faith, and
> in the rejection of the evil Chalcedonian ungodliness [*biyshut rush'ah*], and
> in purification and no commingling with heretics—I thus hold and I thus
> draw near to this (communion), in like manner I drew near it with the highest
> conviction and coherent thought.[28]

Because Severus's successors were Chalcedonians and loyal to the doctrine and politics of the Roman emperor Justin and his nephew Justinian, the name for Christians in the Syrian region who maintained a two-nature Christology was "Melkites" (lit., "of the king"). However, the majority of the Syrian populace saw Severus as their rightful leader and remained loyal to Miaphysite doctrine.

Much like Egypt, the oppressive tactics of Roman Chalcedonians instigated by Justinian exacerbated the process by which Syrian Christians associated Miaphysite doctrine with Syrian identity and was the principal impetus in creating an independent Syrian Orthodox Church.[29] While many Syrian Miaphysites feared the establishment of a separate church due to the resultant persecution, a bishop named John in the Syrian city of Tella requested permission from Severus of Antioch in the early 520s to begin mass ordinations for an indigenously Syrian Miaphysite hierarchy.[30] The deeds of John of Tella as recorded in John of Ephesus's *Lives of the Eastern Saints* served as an inspiration to Syrian Christians in the establishment of their own ecclesiastical hierarchy in contrast to that of the Roman Empire.

Another prominent figure in John of Ephesus's chronicle was Jacob Baradaeus, who like John of Tella ordained thousands of Syrian priests and fortified

---

[28]Severus of Antioch, *The Sixth Book of the Select Letters of Severus, Patriarch of Antioch: In the Syriac Version of Athanasius of Nisibus*, ed. E. W. Brooks (London: Williams & Norgate, 1904), 370.

[29]Volker L. Menze, *Justinian and the Making of the Syrian Orthodox Church* (New York: Oxford University Press, 2008), 249.

[30]John of Ephesus, *Lives of the Eastern Saints*, ed. Ernest W. Brooks, PO 18 (1924), 59.

the Syrian Orthodox Church to the point of its adherents bearing his name as "Jacobites." In 553 Emperor Justinian convened the Second Council of Constantinople in an attempt to win back the Syrian Miaphysites and reunite the Christians of his empire. Justinian's attempt at reconciliation by condemning Theodore of Mopsuestia—a formative theologian for the Syrian church's rival, the Persian Church of the East—ultimately failed due to decades of Roman oppression in Syria.

After a short occupation by the Persian Empire, Syria was recaptured by the Byzantine Roman Empire in 628 only to be conquered by the Arabs in 640. While Christians who accepted the Council of Chalcedon (Melkites) expressed hope for a Byzantine recovery of Syria, the Miaphysites expressed no loyalty to either Byzantine or Muslim rule.[31] In 661, the founder of the Umayyad caliphate Mu'awiya centered the dynasty in Damascus where he ruled a predominately Christian population and allowed for a significant degree of religious freedom.[32] One of the most prominent eighth-century Christians, John of Damascus, was born into a family of Christian leaders in the Umayyad government and served in government himself before entering the Mar Saba Monastery.[33]

Another prominent Syrian Christian from the Mar Saba Monastery was Theodore Abū Qurrah, a Melkite (Chalcedonian) theologian born in 750, right at the time that John of Damascus died and the Abbasid caliphate supplanted the Umayyads. During the iconoclastic controversy of the eighth century, both John and Theodore argued as *iconodules* (lit., "guardians of icons"), who supported the veneration of holy icons. John and Theodore supported icon veneration despite the fact that both of them lived in the Muslim world in which iconographic depiction of holy figures would have been highly disfavored. Born in Urhoy, Theodore served as bishop of Harran, engaged in public debate with Miaphysite and East Syriac theologians, and was a leading figure in a massive translation movement at the

---

[31]Indeed, Christians living under Arab Muslim rule did not understand the conquest as religious in nature; G. J. Reinink, *Syriac Christianity Under Late Sasanian and Early Islamic Rule* (Aldershot, NH: Ashgate, 2005), 157.

[32]Robert G. Hoyland, *In God's Path: The Arab Conquests and the Creation of an Islamic Empire* (New York: Oxford University Press, 2015), 130.

[33]Robert Hoyland, *Seeing Islam as Others Saw It: A Survey and Evaluation of Christian, Jewish, and Zoroastrian Writings on Early Islam* (Princeton, NJ: Darwin Press, 1998), 481.

beginning of Islam where Syriac-speaking Christians translated Greek literature into Arabic, often through Syriac.[34] As the first known Christian author to write in Arabic, Theodore's theological approach was largely influenced by Islam and was foundational for the bourgeoning production of Christian theology in Arabic.

As discussed above, the earliest extant Christian text written in Arabic—*On the Triune Nature of God*—articulates trinitarian theology using Islamic concepts of God, his Word, and his Spirit: "We worship no other god with God in His Word and His Spirit."[35] The author of this text masterfully explains the doctrine of the Trinity while avoiding sonship language that is problematic for Muslims and relying on relevant concepts such as the Law, the Prophets, and the Gospels. As Islamic theology received significant challenges from Christianity and Judaism, the systematic and philosophical defense of the tenets of Islam developed into a unique form of theological argumentation called *kalam* (discourse). In order to provide answers to the objections against Islam, the school of *kalam* practitioners—the *mutakallimūn*—grappled with issues such as predestination, hell, salvation, and the Word of God. One early prominent school of *kalam* were the Mu'tazilites who were rejected by many Islamic scholars for their denial that the Qur'an was eternally preexistent with God. The Mu'tazilites were at the height of their influence during the ninth- and tenth-century Abbasid caliphate and Theodore publicly disputed the Mu'tazila *mutakallimūn*.[36] In debating Miaphysite and East Syriac Christians as well as Muslims, Theodore appropriated the methodology of public discourse as developed by the *mutakallimūn* in his own defense of Melkite Christian theology.

Despite their divergent theological positions, Miaphysite and East Syriac theologians who began to write in Arabic would follow Theodore in engaging

---

[34]David Thomas and Barbara Roggema, *Christian-Muslim Relations: A Bibliographical History (600–900)* (Leiden: Brill, 2009), 568-69. Theodore translated the pseudo-Aristotelian text *De virtutibus animae* into Arabic in the early ninth century at the request of an Abbasid general. Sidney H. Griffith, *The Church in the Shadow of the Mosque: Christians and Muslims in the World of Islam* (Princeton, NJ: Princeton University Press, 2008), 107.

[35]*On the Triune Nature of God*, in *An Arabic Version of the Acts of the Apostles and the Seven Catholic Epistles*, ed. Margaret Dunlop Gibson (London: C. J. Clay and Sons, 1899), 3.

[36]Sidney H. Griffith, *A Treatise on the Veneration of the Holy Icons Written in Arabic by Theodore Abū Qurrah, Bishop of Harrān (c. 755–c. 830 AD)* (Leuven: Peeters, 1997), 17.

in "Christian *kalam*."[37] One such example was a Syrian Miaphysite apologist from Takrit named Abu Raita. Through translating Greek philosophy, engaging in theological discourse in the early Islamic world, and contextualizing Christian theology through Arabic cultural methods, Syrian Christians such as Theodore and Abu Raita helped chart a new course in the development of Syrian Christianity. Even as spoken Syriac began to give way to Arabic for many Christians in Syria, there were still many Syriac-speaking Christians well into the medieval period—most notably the thirteenth-century theologian, philosopher, and scientist Gregory II Abu'lfaraj bar Ahron, also known as Bar Hebraeus. Originally trained in medicine, Bar Hebraeus wrote numerous works of philosophy, theology, biblical exegesis, and history. He served as *maphrian* (deputy patriarch) of the Syrian Orthodox Church and strengthened the West Syriac (or Jacobite) community. In the writings of Bar Hebraeus, the association of the Miaphysite (Jacobite) Christian identity with the Syrian people became more evident. In his *Ecclesiastical Chronicle*, Bar Hebraeus draws from the work of the twelfth-century patriarch Michael the Syrian and describes difficulties with the Greek ecclesiastical authorities. In protest, the reigning Syrian bishop refused to bless the Greek patriarch and proclaimed: "You are Greek! We are Syrians!"[38] Even at the end of Syriac literary production, the ethnoreligious character of Syrian Christians was being reified in prominent ways as this ancient Christian community is principally defined by Syrian identity.

LEBANON

The land and people of Lebanon are mentioned across the Scriptures. The Old Testament speaks of the renown of the "cedars of Lebanon" and Jesus himself visited the Lebanese town of Tyre, where he healed a demon-possessed girl (Ps 92:12; Is 2:13; Mk 7:24-30; called a "Canaanite" in Mt 15:21-28). Modern and ancient Christians—such as Eusebius of Caesarea—have identified the Lebanese town of Qana as the site where Jesus turned water into wine.[39] Early Christians such as the apostle Paul evangelized the environs

---

[37]Griffith, *Church in the Shadow*, 90.

[38]Bar Hebraeus, *The Ecclesiastical Chronicle*, ed. David Wilmshurst (Piscataway, NJ: Gorgias, 2016), 160.

[39]C. Thomas McCollough, "Khirbet Qana," in *Galilee in the Late Second Temple and Mishnaic Periods*, vol. 2: *The Archaeological Record from Cities, Towns, and Villages*, ed. David A. Fiensy and James Riley Strange (Minneapolis: Fortress, 2015), 129.

of Phoenicia throughout the book of Acts (Acts 11:19; 15:3; 21:2-3). While it is highly likely that Christianity continued to grow in Lebanon from New Testament times, literary evidence of Lebanese Christianity comes later in the mention of Christian figures such as the martyr Pamphilus and the Arian bishop Eusebius of Nicomedia. Beirut was also a major seat of education and many Christians, such as the Miaphysite patriarch Severus of Antioch during the fifth century and the historian Zacharias of Mytilene, studied there.[40] Eventually Lebanese Christianity would be associated with an ancient, Syriac-speaking community called the Maronites.[41] The Maronite Church came into form during Late Antiquity and has traditionally been associated with two Syrian missionaries to Lebanon with similar names: Maroun and John Maron.

Maroun was born in the mid-fourth century in Syria and later became a Christian hermit, living in the mountains near Antioch. He was a close associate of John Chrysostom and gained great renown as an ascetic recluse like Anthony of Egypt.[42] Maroun engaged in fervent spiritual disciplines and converted a local temple to a church: "Embracing the open-air life, he repaired to a hill-top formerly honored by the impious. Consecrating to God the precinct of demons on it, he lived there, pitching a small tent which he seldom used."[43] Due to the fame and many miracles of Maroun, many local Christians entered the monastic life and became his disciples: "He [Maroun] produced many plants of philosophy, and it was he who planted for God the garden that now flourishes in the region of Cyrrhus."[44]

While Maroun's life and ministerial career was centered in Syria, some of his early followers were Lebanese and among the first to introduce Christianity in Lebanon.[45] One of Maroun's disciples, Abraham of Cyrrhus, is

---

[40]Pauline Allen and Robert Hayward, *Severus of Antioch* (New York: Routledge, 2004), 6.

[41]The spread of Maronite Christianity in Lebanon is thought to have happened between the seventh and tenth centuries; C. Korolevskij, "Beyrouth," in *Dictionnaire d'histoire et de géographie ecclésiastiques* (Paris: Letouzey et Ané, 1935), 8:1312.

[42]Maroun is said to have received a letter from Chrysostom; Theodoret of Cyrrhus, *Religious History*, ed. R. M. Price (Kalamazoo, MI: Cistercian Publications, 1985), 119n1.

[43]Theodoret, *Religious History*, 117. The text later explains that Maroun's followers constructed a shrine at the same site.

[44]Theodoret, *Religious History*, 118.

[45]The traditional view of many Lebanese Christians that the Maronites grew in Lebanon has been challenged with some scholars claiming that the Maronites did not come to Syria and Lebanon until the sixth century in a migration fleeing the persecutions of Najran in Arabia. Kamal Salibi,

known as the "apostle of Lebanon" as he introduced the monastic practices
of Maroun in Lebanon soon after Maroun's death in 410.[46] After significant
growth in ascetic piety and training, Abraham traveled to Lebanon as a
missionary: "He [Abraham] resolved to run the risks of piety as the price of
divine favor, and repaired to Lebanon, where, he had heard, a large village
was engulfed in the darkness of impiety."[47] Although initially met with
severe persecution in the Syrian town of Emesa, Abraham's commitment to
the gospel eventually won over many locals who then received Abraham as
chief financial officer, bishop, and monastic leader. The tenth-century Arab
historian al-Mas'udi describes the monastery of Maroun's followers: "There
was dedicated to him [Maron] a great monastery located to the east of Hama
and Shayzar. It was a splendid building. Around it were three hundred cells
inhabited by monks. . . . The monastery and the cells around it were eventually destroyed by the many raids of the Arabs and by the injustice of the
sultan."[48] It is likely that the Monastery of Maroun was founded in Syria and
that the center of Maronite Christianity shifted to Lebanon after the destruction of the monastery in the tenth century.[49] The followers of Maroun
had established over fifty monasteries across Syria that became centers for
support of Chalcedonian theology in the mid-fifth century.

Immediately following the Council of Chalcedon in 451, Byzantine emperor Marcian enlarged the monastic complex of Maroun, whose inhabitants strongly supported the two-nature theology of Chalcedon. Because
the majority of the Syriac-speaking world in Mesopotamia were Miaphysite, Maronites endured persecution. Modern Maronite chronicles tell of
Miaphysites burning Maronite churches and monasteries and killing approximately 350 Maronite ascetics.[50] Early modern Maronite chronicles
claim that the Maroun monastery appealed to the Roman pope Hormisdas

---

"The Maronite Experiment," in *Conversion and Continuity: Indigenous Christian Communities
in Islamic Lands Eighth to Eighteenth Centuries*, ed. Michael Gervers and Ramzi Jibran Bikhazi
(Toronto: Pontifical Institute of Mediaeval Studies, 1990), 425.

[46]Theodoret, *Religious History*, 120.

[47]Theodoret, *Religious History*, 120.

[48]Gervers and Bikhazi, *Conversion and Continuity*, 411.

[49]Lucas Van Rompay, "Excursus: The Maronites," in *The Oxford History of Christian Worship*, ed.
Geoffrey Wainwright and Karen B. Westerfield Tucker (New York: Oxford University Press,
2006), 170.

[50]Gervers and Bikhazi, *Conversion and Continuity*, 411.

for support, which initiated the subservience of the Maronites to the See of St. Peter in Rome. However, this account likely reflects a desire for late medieval and early modern Maronites to demonstrate an unbroken connection to Rome.

In the early seventh century, John Maron (taking the name of the fourth-century Maroun) is believed to have been born in Syria and was educated in the monastery of Maroun. According to Maronite tradition, John Maron rose to prominence in the Maroun monastery and combatted both Miaphysitism and Monothelitism, the latter of which was prevalent among seventh-century Maronites. Because the Maronites now lived under Islamic hegemony and were theologically at variance both with Chalcedonian Byzantines and Miaphysite Syrians, they were severely persecuted. After various attacks on the Maroun monastery by both Greeks and Arabs, John Maron is believed to have led the Maronites into hiding in the Qadisha Valley where the community continued to develop relatively free of Western Christian influence. Lebanese tradition holds that John Maron established Chalcedonian theology at the heart of Maronite identity, and this national Lebanese church takes its name from the seventh-century figure.

Like other Melkite Christians in the Middle East, the seventh-century Maronites expressed loyalty to the Roman Empire and did not fare as well under Islamic rule as the Miaphysites. Because the Maronites shared the Chalcedonian Christology of Byzantium, they openly represented allegiance to the Romans and hoped for an overthrow of Arab hegemony. The *Maronite Chronicle* of 664, for example, describes in detail the slightest Roman victory over Arab Muslims and gives cursory attention to much more decisive Arab victories over the Romans.[51] This stands in stark contrast to the Miaphysite chronicles of Syria, which display no restraint in exposing Roman defeat at the hands of Arab Muslims.[52] While Miaphysites were critical of Islamic rule, their strained relationship with the Byzantine Chalcedonians allowed them to function with more ease under Muslim rulers than the Maronites and other Melkite Christians:

---

[51]The *Chronicle* outlines in detail the Arab retreat at Thrace but only mentions in one sentence that the Arab commander Ibn Khālid captured the fortresses of Pessinus, Cius, and Pergamum, and the entire city of Smyrna. *Maronite Chronicle*, in *The Seventh Century in the West-Syrian Chronicles*, ed. Andrew Palmer (Liverpool: Liverpool University Press, 1993), 33-35.

[52]For example, *Chronicle of James of Edessa*, in Palmer, *West-Syrian Chronicles*, 39.

In the same month the bishops of the Jacobites, Theodore and Sabūkht, came
to Damascus and held an inquiry into the Faith with the Maronites in the
presence of Muʿāwiya. When the Jacobites were defeated, Muʿāwiya ordered
them to pay 20,000 denarii and commanded them to be silent. Thus there
arose the custom that the Jacobite bishops should pay that sum of gold every
year to Muʿāwiya, so that he would not withdraw his protection and let them
be persecuted by the members of the (Orthodox) Church. The person called
ʿpatriarchʾ by the Jacobites fixed the financial burden that all the convents of
monks and nuns should contribute each year towards the payment in gold
and he did the same with all the adherents of his faith. He bequeathed his
estate to Muʿāwiya, so that out of fear of that man all the Jacobites would be
obedient to him.[53]

The *Maronite Chronicle* depicts the Miaphysites as subservient to Islamic
rulers, who must be paid for the protection of the anti-Chalcedonian Christians. It is interesting that while Miaphysite sources depict Maronite and
other Chalcedonian Christians of the Middle East as Roman sycophants, in
a similar fashion Maronite sources portray Miaphysites as submissive to
Muslim rulers.[54]

Shortly after the Islamic conquest, the Maronites distinguished themselves from both their dominant Syrian Miaphysite neighbors and other
Chalcedonian Melkite Christians. From the time of Emperor Heraclius just
before the Islamic conquest, the doctrine of monothelitism (lit., "one will")
was promulgated in an attempt to reconcile the Chalcedonians and Miaphysites by asserting that, while Christ existed in two natures, he had one will.
This doctrine was unsuccessful in reconciling the various parties and was
ultimately condemned at the Third Council of Constantinople in 680–681.
However, while modern Maronite sources deny ever having been at variance
with the Catholic Church, seventh-century sources indicate that the Maronites rejected the dythelitism ("two wills") of the Third Council of Constantinople and embraced monothelitism.[55] Indeed, it has been suggested

---

[53]*Maronite Chronicle*, 30-31. Muʿāwiya was the founder and first caliph of the Umayyad dynasty
centered in Damascus.

[54]Though there is evidence that Muslim rulers in the eighth century enforced dytheletism on the
Maronites. Jack Tannous, "In Search of Monotheletism," *DOP* 68 (2014): 32.

[55]Palmer, *West-Syrian Chronicles*, 25. Aziz Atiya claims that Byzantine Emperor Heraclius promoted monothelitism in Lebanon before its condemnation several decades later. *History of
Eastern Christianity* (Notre Dame, IN: University of Notre Dame Press, 1968), 395.

that the Maronites were the most influential Chalcedonian Christian community of the Umayyad period.[56]

Similarly, the Maronites embraced the longer form of the Trisagion prayer, which was a continued point of contention between the Syrian and Roman churches. The prayer used in the Roman church ("Holy God, Holy Strong, Holy Immortal, have mercy on us") had a longer form that was popular in the Middle East and included an additional phrase: "Holy God, Holy and Strong, Holy and Immortal, Christ, King, who was crucified for us, have mercy on us." The Trisagion (lit., "three holies") in its different versions became a marker for the rival christological positions. This could be because its earliest attestation was at the Council of Chalcedon in 451.[57] During this period, the Muslim rulers favored both the Maronites and the Miaphysites, whose liturgical practice was at variance with Byzantium.[58] This would indicate that Middle Eastern Christians experienced a higher degree of favor by Muslim rulers to the degree to which they were distinct from or at odds with dominant Roman (Byzantine) Christianity. While many modern Maronites deny this divergence from the dominant Roman church,[59] the twelfth-century patriarch Michael the Syrian claimed that Roman Chalcedonians persecuted the Maronites during the eighth century: "They (Maronites) confess one will in Christ and say 'who was crucified for us,' but they accept the Council of Chalcedon. Bar Qanbara came to Mabbug and began battling with the Chalcedonians who were there, but they would not accept to speak of two wills and did not cease from the expression 'who was crucified.'"[60] Theodore Abū Qurrah serves as an earlier source who also claimed that the Maronites rejected the "two-will" theology of the Roman (Byzantine) church.[61]

The relationship between medieval Maronite, Miaphysite, Islamic, and dominant Roman Christianity is similar to intercultural dynamics in Christianity

---

[56]Tannous, "Monotheletism," 52.

[57]Sebastian Brock, "The Thrice-Holy Hymn in the Liturgy," *Sobornost* 7 (1985): 28.

[58]Palmer, *West-Syrian Chronicles*, 26.

[59]It has been suggested that Maronite history written before the union with Rome was destroyed in order to conceal the previous discord between the Roman and Maronite Churches. Kamal Salibi, "The Traditional Historiography of the Maronites," in Bernard Lewis, *Historians of the Middle East* (New York: Oxford University Press, 1962), 213.

[60]Michael the Syrian, *Chronicle*, ed. Gregorios Yohanna Ibrahim (Piscataway, NJ: Gorgias, 2009), 470.

[61]Tannous, "Monotheletism," 62.

today. Because of Western, white cultural captivity, often non-Western Christians who espouse theological rhetoric of Western Christianity or are connected to a Western denomination are supported to a greater extent. On the other hand, non-Western Christians who belong to Western denominations are often seen as more foreign both by other non-Western Christians who belong to indigenous churches (like the early Syrian Miaphysites) and by non-Western non-Christians. The late antique and early medieval Maronites found themselves in a similar situation where they lived on the margins of the Roman Empire and later as minorities under Islamic rule and embraced the Syriac-speaking Christian tradition of the land now called the Middle East. Yet, because they were aligned with the dominant Roman (Byzantine) theology of Chalcedon, they experienced marginalization by their neighboring Miaphysite Christians as well as Muslim leaders. However, they did not agree with Roman Christians on everything as they rejected the doctrine of dytheletism. Therefore, the early Maronites represented a nuanced, Middle Eastern Christian community that asserted their autonomy by choosing those elements of mainstream Syriac Christianity and the dominant Roman church with which they wanted to identify.

The relationship of the Maronites and Roman (Byzantine) church shifted drastically during the Crusades when the Maronites aided the Western invaders, which resulted in a higher degree of Romanization of Maronite liturgy and intermarriage between Europeans and the Lebanese. Some believe that it was during the early middle ages that the Maronite tradition became primarily associated with Lebanon. Ties between Lebanese Maronites and Western Christianity increased after the conquest of the Levant by the Mamluk Sultanate in the twelfth century. The racist, condescending attitude of the Roman church toward Middle Eastern Christians was made plain in the papal bull of Pope Leo X when the Maronites officially came under the authority of Rome:

> We thank Divine Providence . . . since, among the Eastern churches, placed among infidels as in a field of error, the Almighty had deigned to keep His faithful servants as a rose among the thorns . . . and had made you piously and bravely keep to the faith and discipline of the Holy Roman Catholic Church in spite of the persecutions and difficulties you had to stand from the infidels.[62]

---

[62]Kamal Salibi, "The Maronite Church in the Middle Ages and its Union with Rome," *OC* (1958): 104.

While theological polemic was common to medieval Christianity, the normal epithets deployed would be *heretic* or *impious* rather than racialized terms such as *infidel*. Statements such as these represent the degree to which Western Christianity has placed itself as a standard against which all other Christian communities must be measured.

Questions surrounding cultural autonomy and Eurocentricity have continued to frame much of Maronite Christian history and identity. As Maronite presence was at this point largely consolidated in Lebanese territory, this national church has continued to shape the fundamental character of Lebanese identity as modern Lebanon has the largest Christian percentage in the Middle East. While Christianity in Lebanon has always included various theological camps, the Maronite Church has been the dominant form of Christianity for centuries. Maronite identity has been described as paradoxical in the sense that, even in modern times, this ancient church sees itself both as an uninterrupted part of the Roman Catholic Church and as a national, independent church rooted in the Syriac liturgical tradition that is synonymous with Lebanese identity.[63] As with many marginalized groups, the Maronites have had to navigate between self-definition and the temptation to define themselves according to the standards of the dominant culture.[64]

ARABIA

The New Testament identifies Arabia as one of the earliest regions where Christians were present. In his letter to the Galatian church, the apostle Paul recounts the events surrounding his conversion and reports that, instead of going to Jerusalem for instruction in the faith, he "went into Arabia" (Gal 1:17). The mention of "Arabia" in the New Testament likely refers to Arabia Petraea, or the Nabataean kingdom, in what is now northwest Arabia and Jordan. There are early fourth-century attestations of Christians further east and south in the Arabian Peninsula. The sixth-century Persian Christian historian Msiha Zkha reports the existence of Christian bishops in the year 310 in Beth Qatraye, the name given by Syriac-speaking Persian Christians

---

[63]Atiya, *Eastern Christianity*, 403.
[64]W. E. B. DuBois, *The Souls of Black Folk* (New Haven, CT: Yale University Press, 2015), 8.

to the eastern Arabian Peninsula in present-day Qatar; it had a strong Christian presence until the ninth century.[65]

It is likely that Arabian Christians predated the earliest recorded evidence indicating established bishoprics. In the early fifth century, the Arian historian Philostorgius reported that the Southern Arabian ruler accepted Christianity due to the missionary Theophilus the Indian, sent by the Roman emperor Constantius. Philostorgius depicts the "Sabeans" as descendants of Abraham who had lost their way in paganism. Constantius sent Theodore the Indian with many gifts in order to impress the Arabian ruler:

> Accordingly, Theophilus, on his arrival among the Sabeans, endeavored to persuade the ruler of the tribe to become a Christian, and to give over the deceits of heathenism. Hereupon the customary fraud and malice of the Jews was compelled to shrink into deep silence, as soon as ever Theophilus had once or twice proved by his wonderful miracles the truth of the Christian faith. The embassy turned out successfully; for the prince of the nation, by sincere conviction, came over to the true religion, and built three churches in the district, not, however, with the money which the emperor's ambassadors had brought with them, but out of sums which he voluntarily supplied out of his private resources, with a laudable strife to show that his own zeal was a match for the wonders performed by Theophilus.[66]

The account provided by Philostorgius is echoed by that of the early fifth-century Palestinian church historian Sozomen and his account of early evangelization in Northern Arabia. In his *Ecclesiastical History*, Sozomen also describes the "Saracens" as being of Abrahamic descent and having fallen into paganism:

> Some of the Saracens were converted to Christianity not long before the accession of Valens. Their conversion appears to have been the result of their intercourse with the priests who dwelt among them, and with the monks who dwelt in the neighboring deserts, and who were distinguished by their purity

---

[65]Msiha-Zhka, *Church History*, ed. Alphonse Mingana in *Sources Syriaques* (Leipzig: Otto Harrassowitz, 1908), 106. A Syrian ascetic named Pamphilos, who attended the Council of Nicaea, was known as "the first bishop of nomad Arabs"; Samuel Hugh Moffett, *A History of Christianity in Asia*, vol. 1: *Beginnings to 1500* (Maryknoll, NY: Orbis, 1998), 273.

[66]Philostorgius, *Ecclesiastical History*, ed. Edward Walford (London: Henry G. Bohn, 1855), 444-45.

of life, and by their miraculous gifts. It is said that a whole tribe, and Zocomus, their chief, were converted to Christianity and baptized about this period.[67]

Sozomen goes on to explain that the Arab ruler Zocomus and his wife were blessed through the monk to be able to have a son, which led to the conversion and baptism of Zocomus and his tribe. Later, the Arab queen Mania (or Mavia) was at war with the Romans and was successfully pushing them back across Palestine, which led to a Roman appeal for peace. Mania granted a peace treaty with the Romans on the condition that an orthodox (i.e., Nicene)[68] bishop named Moses be consecrated to oversee the Arabian churches: "Having again protested, upon oath, that he (Moses) would not receive ordination at the hands of Lucius, the Roman rulers conducted him to the bishops who were then in exile. After receiving ordination from them, he went to exercise the functions of his office among the Saracens. He concluded a peace with the Romans and converted many of the Saracens to the faith."[69] Sozomen's account indicates that Moses was an Arabian Christian ascetic whose miraculous power and ministerial exploits made such an impression on the Arabians that he even led queen Mania to the Christian faith.[70] So at a time when the Roman Empire was under the leadership of heretical Arians, the Arabians maintained orthodox doctrine and made the orthodox leadership of an indigenous Arabian bishop the central stipulation of their truce with the Romans. For the Arabian queen Mania, the "right sort of bishop" to minister to her people was an orthodox, Nicene bishop.[71]

This is significant given the common belief that the divinity of Christ was a doctrine that was invented by Constantine as part of an overall plan to use Christianity as a mechanism of subjugation. The primary sources narrating the earliest years of Christianity in Arabia paint a starkly different picture than such unsubstantiated theories. Christians of Arabia maintained their belief in the deity of Christ despite the heretical influence of the Roman

---

[67]Sozomen, *Ecclesiastical History*, ed. Edward Walford (London: Henry G. Bohn, 1855), 310.

[68]Menze, *Justinian*, 222n104. While Sozomen does not specify the theological controversy that divides Moses and Lucius, Menze claims that this was the Arian controversy of the fourth century. This interpretation is supported also in Greg Fisher, *Arabs and Empires Before Islam* (New York: Oxford University Press, 2015), 81.

[69]Sozomen, *Ecclesiastical History*, 309.

[70]G. W. Bowersock, Peter Brown, and Oleg Grabar, *Late Antiquity: A Guide to the Postclassical World* (Cambridge, MA: Harvard University Press, 1999), 569.

[71]Fisher, *Arabs and Empires*, 82.

emperor who denied this foundational belief. Today many liberal, mainline Christian communities have strayed from biblical orthodoxy and have influenced many scholars of color to do the same.[72] Contemporary discourse often identifies theological reflection from marginal communities with liberal biblical scholarship and theological claims that ironically emerged in nineteenth-century Europe. Despite the prevalence of problematic views of Scripture and Christology among many scholars of color today, most church communities among people of color hold deeply to the historic Christian faith. Just like fourth-century Christians of Arabia, the heretical theology of the dominant culture is not embraced by marginal Christian communities in the modern world. Contemporary theologians of color must emulate the faith and courage of Queen Mania, who did not submit to the heretical faith of colonial powers. This may have been easier given that—unlike most Christians of color today—Christianity entered ancient Arabia free of Western colonialism.

It is noteworthy that Roman sources such as Sozomen are not the earliest witnesses to Christianity in Arabia. Rather, the activity of Persian Christians on the Eastern Arabian coast provides the earliest documentation for Christian presence on the peninsula. As the Sasanian Persian Empire controlled Eastern Arabia, East Syriac Christians from Persia capitalized on the opportunity to bring Christianity to the Arabs of Qatar and Oman:

> From the biography of a monk named Jonah we learn that in the region of Qatar there existed a monastery in the 340s AD. Around 390 a certain 'Abdisho' left southern Iraq for 'an island of Yamama and Bahrain,' where 'he lived an ascetic life, baptized its inhabitants and built a monastery' (*Chron. Siirt* 5.310). In the year 410 Batai, bishop of Mashmahig (modern Muharraq island next to Bahrain), was excommunicated and replaced by a certain Elias (*Synod Or.* 34, 36). And the acts of a synod of 424 record a John, bishop of Mazun (Oman), in attendance (*Synod Or.* 43). Though as yet scanty, there is also archaeological evidence for Christianity in this region. This consists of two monasteries on islands off the coast of Abu Dhabi, the remains of churches on the island of Failaka and at Jubayl and Thaj in northeast Arabia,

---

[72]E.g., James Cone's assertion, in conjunction with Gustavo Gutiérrez, that Christian concern with unbelief is rooted in the European Enlightenment—a claim that this present study demonstrates to be inaccurate. *For My People: Black Theology and the Black Church* (Maryknoll, NY: Orbis, 1984), 70.

sundry crosses and possibly a cemetery at Hinna near Thaj (six stones found bearing crosses).[73]

At the turn of the sixth century, the situation became stormy for the Christians of Arabia especially in the southern region of the Himyarites. During this time Christianity had spread from the northern Transjordan region of Arabia into the southern portions of the peninsula. Under the leadership of Dhu Nuwas, the Jewish kingdom of the Himyarites (modern Yemen) began to persecute Himyarite Christians. Dhu Nuwas desired to create a Judaic kingdom in the Arabian Peninsula that would be independent of Roman, Persian, and Ethiopian authority. For this reason, he attacked Ethiopian Christians in the Himyarite settlement at Zafar and the Christian community in Najran.[74] The persecution was also instigated by the burning of a synagogue by local Christians. Despite the newness of Himyarite Christianity just before the persecution, the sixth-century *Book of the Himyarites* presents the inhabitants of Najran as heavily Christian; the "believing Najranites" are often referred to as representing the collective attitude of the entire city.[75] Despite the Christians' attempts to appease the Himyarite king by paying alms, Dhu Nuwas continued his persecution and ordered approximately five thousand Christians to be thrown into burning pits and more than one thousand Christian children enslaved.[76] Among the martyred was even the bishop of Najran al-Harith (or Arethas) who has since been venerated in the Roman Catholic Church despite the likelihood of his confession being that of the Church of the East. The *Book of the Himyarites* vividly displays the severity of the persecution and the resolute posture of the Himyarite Christians:

> And they said to him: "Art thou a Christian?" He answered them: "If I am worthy I am Christian." These unclean ones said to him: "If you art a Christian stretch thy hand up." And he immediately stretched up his right hand, and a man swiftly drew his sword, smote him, and cut it off. Again he said to him: "If thou art a Christian stretch up the other." And immediately with joy he

---

[73]Robert G. Hoyland, *Arabia and the Arabs: From the Bronze Age to the Coming of Islam* (New York: Routledge, 2001), 30.

[74]*Book of the Himyarites*, ed. Axel Moberg, *The Book of the Himyarites: Fragments of a Hitherto Unknown Syriac Work* (New York: Oxford University Press, 1924), cv.

[75]*Book of the Himyarites*, cviii.

[76]Maxime Rodinson, *Muhammad* (New York: Taurus, 1971), 31.

stretched up the left one also, and then that crucifier smote and cut off that as well. Again they asked him and said to him: "Art thou still a Christian?" And he said to them: "In life and in death I am a Christian, and praise be to God, our Lord Jesus Christ, who has deemed me worthy of this." When they heard this, those foes of righteousness became angry and smote his feet also from behind and cut them both off.[77]

The severity of the persecutions in Najran and of the Ethiopians who were attacked at Zafar prompted the Ethiopian king Caleb to intervene. Caleb sent massive forces across the Red Sea into Southern Arabia and leveled a defeat against the Himyarites so devastating that it brought an end to the entire kingdom.[78]

The martyrdom of the Najran Christians is even mentioned in the Qur'an, where the Christian martyrs are praised and the forces of Dhu Nuwas are condemned:

> Woe to the makers of the pit (of fire), fire supplied (abundantly) with fuel: Behold! They sat over against the (fire), and they witnessed (all) that they were doing against the Believers. And they ill-treated them for no other reason than that they believed in Allah, Exalted in Power, Worthy of all Praise! Him to Whom belongs the dominion of the heavens and the earth! And Allah is Witness to all things. Those who persecute (or draw into temptation) the Believers, men and women, and do not turn in repentance, will have the Penalty of Hell: They will have the Penalty of the Burning Fire. For those who believe and do righteous deeds, will be Gardens; beneath which rivers flow: That is the great Salvation, (the fulfillment of all desires).[79]

The late fifth and early sixth century witnessed significant growth of Christianity in Arabia. One of the earliest extant archaeological sites for Christian activity in Arabia is the remains of a fifth/sixth-century church near Jubail, Saudi Arabia. The Jubail church was discovered by accident in 1986 when a Saudi oil company was digging one of its trucks out of the sand. The Saudi government has sealed off the site and no official excavation and

---

[77] *Book of the Himyarites*, cvi-cvii.

[78] An interesting and perhaps surprising example of late antique geoethnic constructions of the Other is in the *Book of the Himyarites* when the Ethiopian bishop Euprepios refers to the Himyarites as "barbarians," a term often used by Hellenists in reference to Ethiopians and Cushites (cxli).

[79] *Surah Al-Buruj* 4-9. From the translation of the Qur'an by Abdullah Yusuf Ali.

publication of the church has been possible. Thankfully, several of the ARAMCO employees provided photos of the site that serve as a limited window into this ancient Arabian church.[80] While the funerary inscriptions clearly identify the structure as a Christian church, the architecture of the columns and archways display a unique style similar to that of the later Umayyad period.[81]

The Ghassanid territory further west from Jubail also witnessed increased church construction during the sixth century, with at least seven churches attested in the Ghassinid town of Gerasa and approximately seventeen churches in Umm al-Jimāl.[82] In addition to mentioning numerous Arabian churches, a letter from an Arabian archimandrite reported the existence of 137 monasteries in Arabia. The tenth-century Persian historian Isfahānī reported that various Arab tribes competed over the construction of the

Figure 3.2. Remains of a Church of the East church in Jubail, Saudi Arabia, possibly dating as early as the fourth century

[80]Barbara Finster, "Arabia in Late Antiquity: An Outline of the Cultural Situation in the Peninsula at the Time of Muhammad," in *The Qur'ān in Context: Historical and Literary Investigations into the Qur'ānic Milieu*, ed. Angelika Neuwirth, Nicolai Sinai, and Michael Marx (Leuven: Brill, 2010), 87.

[81]Robert A. Carter, "Christianity in the Gulf after the Coming of Islam: Redating the Churches and Monasteries of Bet Qatraye," in *Les preludes de l'Islam: Ruptures et continuités dans les civilisations du Proche-Orient, de l'Afrique orientale, de l'Arabie et de l'Inde à la Vielle de l'Islam*, ed. Christian Julien Robin and Jérémie Schiettecatte (Paris: De Boccard, 2013), 323.

[82]Irfan Shahîd, *Byzantium and the Arabs in the Sixth Century*, vol. 2, part 1: *Toponymy, Monuments, Historical Geography, and Frontier Studies* (Washington, DC: Dumbarton Oaks, 2002), 146.

Figure 3.3. Late antique Christian church in Arabian Peninsula

monasteries with which they took great care. Isfahānī describes a Lakhmid Arab monastery that would be visited by the Lakhmid king al-Nuʿmān:

> And it was related that al-Nuʿmān used to pray in it and receive communion; that he hung in its haykal [chapel] five hundred lamps [qindīls] made of gold and silver. Their oil during feast days were oils of lily [iris; zanbaq] and of willow [bān] and others that were similar to these. And the wood he used to burn (for censing in it) consisted of Indian aloes and of ambergris, in quantities that defy description.[83]

One of the most prominent churches in sixth-century Arabia was located in the city of Jābiya, named for Sergius, the patron saint of the Ghassanid Arab tribe. The fact that Sergius—an Arab soldier who fought the Persians—received the highest amount of Christian devotion in late antique Christian Arabia attests to the uniquely militaristic nature of this society.[84]

The sixth century was also a period of heightened missionary activity among the Arabs, notably that of the Syrian Miaphysites. As in Nubia, both the oppressive Chalcedonian policies of Justinian and the resultant Miaphysite

---

[83]Shahîd, *Byzantium and the Arabs*, 163.
[84]Irfan Shahîd, "Arab Christian Pilgrimages in the Proto-Byzantine Period," in *Pilgrimage and Holy Space in Late Antique Egypt*, ed. David Frankfurter (Leiden: Brill, 1998), 379.

missions supported by Empress Theodora played a decisive role in the development of Christianity in Arabia. The ruler of Roman Arabia, Al-Harith ibn Jabalah, made a request to the Miaphysite-sympathizing empress Theodora for a Miaphysite bishop to be sent to Arabia:

> When a lack of priests had consequently arisen in the countries of the east and of the west, and especially of bishops, then the glorious Hereth Bar Gabala, the great king of the Saracens, with many others asked the Christ-loving queen Theodora to give orders that two or three bishops might immediately be instituted by the orthodox in Syria. And, since the believing queen was desirous of furthering everything that would assist the opponents of the synod of Chalcedon, she gave orders and two blessed men, well tried and divine persons, whose names were James and Theodore, were chosen and instituted, one for Hirtha of the Saracens, that is Theodore, and James for the city of Edessa . . . the blessed Theodore exercised authority in the southern and western countries and the whole of the desert and Arabia and Palestine, as far as Jerusalem.[85]

Like James (Jacob Baradaeus) in Syria, Theodore had a long career of over thirty years as he fortified the Arabian Christian community. It is likely not a coincidence that during Theodore's tenure in the later sixth century a spring of churches and monasteries across Arabia were constructed and that Theodore had a direct role in these projects. As John of Ephesus explains, the Arab ruler Harith ibn Jabalah supported the Miaphysite cause as both Arabian Christians and political rulers remained predominately anti-Chalcedonian. During the time of Byzantine emperor Maurice, an unsuccessful attempt was made to convert the Jafnid tribe of Northern Arabia.[86] However, under the indigenous leadership of Harith, the Jafnids supported Miaphysite Christianity throughout the lifetime of Harith. At the same time, many churches and monasteries were constructed in the eastern regions of the

---

[85]John of Ephesus, *Lives of the Eastern Saints*, 153-54. *Hirtha*, a Syriac loanword from pre-Islamic Arabic/Sabaic, is not a proper name but refers to an enclosure for a military camp (Shahîd, *Byzantium and the Arabs*, 14). The Syriac word used here by John of Ephesus translated "Saracens" is actually *tayāyē*, referring to the Southern Arabian Tayy tribe and Arabs in general. Although it does not survive, John also included an entire chapter in his *Ecclesiastical History* focused solely on the growth of the church among the Ghassanid Arabs (Shahîd, *Byzantium and the Arabs*, 156).

[86]Geoffrey Greatrex and Samuel N. C. Lieu, *The Roman Eastern Frontier and the Persian Wars, Part 2: AD 363-630: A Narrative Sourcebook* (New York: Routledge, 2002), 112.

peninsula that would have predominately belonged to the Church of the
East centered in Persia.[87]

The Islamic conquest during the seventh century did not hinder the
production of Christian theological and literary material. Syriac literature
immediately following the Islamic conquest portrayed Islam and Muhammad in nonpolemical terms and only in the early eighth century was
literature critical of Islam written.[88] However, the conquest did not come
without its complications for Arabian Christians. The catholicos of the
Church of the East based in Persia wrote a series of letters to his Qatari
constituents, who had apparently begun to distance themselves from his
authority based in Celeucia-Tsesiphon:

> For the devil, their departure from the faith alone was perhaps enough, as to
> that of the Mazunaye. But the bishops of Fars and of Beth Qatraye, eager also
> about how they could deny Christianity with books of folly and with seals of
> impiety beyond what the devil wished, wrote, sealed and sent a denial of com-
> munion with the Church of God, that is, with Christianity, and presented it
> sealed, so that the denial of the faith would not only be limited to them, as it
> was in the Mazunaye, but also their descendants, if truly they shall have sons
> who are wicked like them.[89]

Catholicos Isho'yahb III displays concern about the increasing reality of
Arabian Christians converting to Islam, as had apparently occurred among
Christians in Oman. Yet, despite the increasing pressure for Christians in
the seventh-century Arabian Peninsula, theological production did not
cease after the conquest. One of the most significant Christian theologians
who lived in Arabia before, during, and after the conquest was Isaac of Ni-
nevah, or Isaac the Syrian. Isaac was born in Beth Qatraye in 613 and entered
the monastic life at an early age. He rose to prominence in Beth Qatraye
both as an ascetic and a theologian. Isaac was ordained bishop of Nineveh
but quickly left office and lived the rest of his life in the Mesopotamian
desert as an ascetic. While a part of the Church of the East, Isaac's writings

---

[87]Robert A. Carter, "Christianity in the Gulf During the First Centuries of Islam," *AAE* 19 (2008): 71.
[88]Reinink, *Syriac Christianity*, 182.
[89]Isho'yahb III, *Letter to the People of Qatar*, ed. Mario Kozah, *An Anthology of Syriac Writers from Qatar in the Seventh Century* (Piscataway, NJ: Gorgias, 2015), 50. *Mazunaye* is Syriac for "citi-zens of Oman."

did not directly engage theological disputes but focused primarily on the ascetic life and spirituality. Isaac's emphasis on God's revelation through nature and the spiritual pursuit of theological mystery displays the degree to which he stands in the Syriac theological tradition of Ephrem: "The natures endowed with intellect infinitely surpassed in knowledge what they comprehended in our Lord Christ—what they had not known before—who came for the sake of their and our liberation and perfection."[90] Here Isaac expounds on the nature and limits of human knowledge which for him, like Ephrem, are activated only by God's self-revelation in Christ. Because of the general Christian applicability of Isaac's writings, they have been translated into various languages and his renown has gone beyond the Church of the East.[91] Isaac was one of the most influential Christian theologians who lived during the early years of Islamic rule in the Arabian Peninsula. Christianity still persisted in Arabia, especially in Beth Qatraye, after the Islamic conquest, as is evidenced by extant church remains from the eighth and ninth centuries.[92] Although textual references to the Christians of Arabia began to wane after the Islamic conquest, this was the beginning of the flourishing of Arabian Christian architecture. The seventh to ninth centuries may have been the high point of Christian church construction precisely because of the newly Islamicized Arabian Peninsula, resulting in the Christians' desire to refortify their community.[93] During this time, Christians began writing theology in Arabic in various parts of the Islamic world. However, some of the earliest Arabic inscriptions date back as early as 340—two centuries before the birth of Muhammad—and were Christian in nature.[94] Some of these recently discovered Christian inscriptions were also accompanied with crosses. This means that the gospel of Jesus Christ was proclaimed in some of the earliest words written in the Arabic language.

---

[90]Isaac of Nineveh, *Chapters on Knowledge*, ed. Grigory Kessel, *An Anthology of Syriac Writers from Qatar in the Seventh Century* (Piscataway, NJ: Gorgias, 2015), 273.

[91]Sebastian Brock, *The Wisdom of Saint Isaac the Syrian* (Oxford: Fairacres, 1997), 1.

[92]Carter, "Christianity in the Gulf," 98.

[93]Carter, "Redating the Churches and Monasteries of Bet Qatraye," 327.

[94]For copious examples of pre-Islamic Christian inscriptions in Arabic adorned with crosses, see C. Robin, A. I. Al-Ghabban, and S. F. Al-Sa'īd, "Inscriptions antiques de la région de najrān (arabie séoudite méridionale): nouveaux jalons pour l'histoire de l'écriture, de la langue et du calendrier arabes," *Comptes rendus des séances de l'académie des inscriptions et belles-lettres* 3 (2014), 1093-1109. While these examples largely come from the sixth-century, Christian inscriptions in Arabic go back to the fourth century (Fisher, *Arabs and Empires*, 350).

ARMENIA

The highlands surrounding the biblical Mount Ararat, known as Armenia since Achaemenid times, have been occupied since the Bronze Age. Armenia was at the height of its power when the Artaxiad dynasty ruled from the early second century BCE until its fall to the Roman Empire at the beginning of the first century CE. From that time until the dissolution of the Soviet Union in 1991, Armenia was under constantly shifting foreign domination including Romans, Persians, Arabs, Turks, and Russians.[95] Lodged between the Black and Caspian seas and straddling the Roman and Persian Empires of Late Antiquity, Armenia found itself the victim of constantly shifting political borders. Yet what has profoundly shaped Armenian identity and united its people throughout centuries of oppression is its unique Christian tradition.

Like other orthodox Christian communities, the Armenian Apostolic Church celebrates its tradition of apostolic founding, which is highlighted even in its name. Armenian church tradition holds that the apostle Thaddeus came to Armenia before converting Abgar of Urhoy and was martyred in Armenia after converting some of the imperial court.[96] Thaddeus was followed by the apostle Bartholomew, who was also martyred in Armenia.[97] It is likely that Christianity took early root before the significant developments of the fourth century. Eusebius of Caesarea indicates the presence of Christians in the mid-third century: "He [Dionysius of Alexandria] wrote in like manner to the Armenians, *On Repentance*, where Meruzanes was bishop."[98] Eusebius here provides a list of the encyclicals written by Dionysius, pope of Alexandria (248–264), which included a letter written to the bishop of Armenia.[99] Before the fourth century the Christians would have been the minority, as the dominant religion in Armenia was the Zoroastrian practice of

---

[95]The history of persecution has resulted in a heightened focus on martyrdom in Armenian Christianity; Abraham Terian, *Patriotism and Piety in Armenian Christianity: The Early Panegyrics on Saint Gregory* (Crestwood, NY: St. Vladimir's Seminary Press, 2005), 18.

[96]*Acts and Martyrdom of the Holy Apostle Thaddeus*, ed. S. C. Malan (Oxford: Rivingtons, 1868), 68. This account became normative in Armenian historiography especially after the monumental fifth-century account of Moses Khorenats'i, *History of the Armenians*, ed. Robert W. Thomson (Cambridge, MA: Harvard University Press, 1978), 174.

[97]Malachia Ormanian, *The Church of Armenia: Her History, Doctrine, Rule, Discipline, Liturgy, Literature, and Existing Condition*, trans. G. Marcar Gregory (Burbank, CA: Armenian Church of North America Western Diocese, 1955), 3.

[98]Eusebius, *Ecclesiastical History*, 255.

[99]Atiya, *Eastern Christianity*, 316.

the Persians who ruled over them. The Armenian *Acts of Thaddeus* depicts first century Armenia as a predominately pagan context: "Many others at that hour believed in Christ. But the priests of the idols went and told it all to their lawless and wicked king Sanadrug. Then that abandoned king gave orders that all the believers should be put to death. But a sign from heaven appeared over them, and many believed in Christ, and fear came upon the heathens, many of whom were terrified by the brilliant light."[100] Likewise, the *Life and Times of Saint Gregory the Illuminator* describes Armenia as "a nation in which no trace of the worship of God existed anywhere."[101]

At the beginning of the fourth century, an Armenian noble known as Gregory the Illuminator converted the Armenian king and became the patron saint and the official head of the Armenian church.[102] Gregory was born to an

Figure 3.4. Monastery of Geghard, Armenia

[100] *Acts of Thaddeus*, 70.

[101] *The History of the Life and Times of Our Holy Father Gregory the Illuminator*, ed. and trans. S. C. Malan (Oxford: Rivingtons, 1868), 121.

[102] Gregory's mission is thus described: "Wonderful, unsearchable providence of God, in thus preparing for Armenia the Light of her holy Father Gregory!" (*Life and Times of Gregory*, 117).

Figure 3.5. Khor Virap Monastery in the Ararat Province of Armenia with Mount Ararat in the background; the traditional location of the imprisonment of Gregory the Illuminator by King Tiridates III

Armenian Parthian father who was accused of assassinating the Armenian king Khosrov II. Gregory's father was executed and Gregory escaped and was raised by Christians in Cappadocia. After marrying and entering the ascetic life, Gregory returned to Armenia with the goal of converting the deceased king's son, Tiridates III. Tiridates severely persecuted Gregory and attempted to convert Gregory to the Zoroastrian religion of the Armenians. On being told that Gregory's father had assassinated the father and predecessor of Tiridates, the king had Gregory cast into a pit, where he remained for approximately fourteen years. The *Life* vividly displays the ethnic pride of Armenian Christianity and the central role of Gregory: "And there [in the pit] also did he not cease to entreat God in his prayers for the enlightenment of the Armenian nation; and being heard, he was, by the grace of the Holy Ghost, fitted to become the Illuminator of the Armenian race."[103] During the fifth century, a chapel and surrounding monastery called Khor Virap (Armenian for "deep pit") were constructed around the pit in which Gregory was imprisoned and has remained a central pilgrimage site for Armenian Christians to this day.

Because of the persecution of Gregory and the martyrdom of a Roman female missionary to Armenia named Rhipsime, King Tiridates and much of his royal court were stricken with madness as divine retribution, according to the biography of Gregory. Gregory was released from the pit and

---

[103]*Life and Times of Gregory*, 186.

then healed Tiridates of his madness, causing the king to repent and embrace Christianity. Given the prominence of the sun in Armenian Zoroastrianism, it is not surprising that Gregory adapted his presentation of the Gospel: "But ye, now learn to know God your Creator; Him who made the heavens and the earth, the sea and all that in them is, the sun, moon, and the stars, and all other things. He alone is able to make you whole."[104] Similar to the reforms that Eusebius reported Constantine made, Tiridates destroyed pagan temples, supported the building of churches, and installed Gregory as the first bishop of Armenia. The traditional date for the conversion of Tiridates and the beginning of Gregory's thirty-year tenure as patriarch of Armenia is 302, a decade before the Christianization of the Roman Empire.[105] This has resulted in one of the proudest and most unique aspects of the Armenian church: it was the world's first nation to officially adopt Christianity. While it has been suggested that the adoption of Christianity was more politically than religiously motivated,[106] it would be inaccurate to reduce the introduction of Armenian Christianity to political factors alone. However, it is noteworthy that Armenia, while wedged between two larger pagan empires, became the first Christian nation at a time when the notion of a Christian nation would have been inconceivable.

The patriarchal throne in Armenia remained in the lineage of Gregory throughout the fourth century, including Gregory's son Aristakes, who participated in the Council of Nicaea. While Armenian Christians were in agreement with the theological developments in the Roman Empire during the fourth century—notably the councils of Nicaea and Constantinople—expressions of ecclesiastical independence were beginning to emerge. Despite the wish of Roman emperor Valens for the Armenian patriarch to be approved by the Caesarean bishop Basil, the Armenian king appointed a grandson of Gregory the Illuminator named Husik. This marked the first time that an Armenian patriarch was appointed apart from the approval of Roman ecclesiastical authorities.[107]

---

[104]*Life and Times of Gregory*, 224.

[105]*Life and Times of Gregory*, 335.

[106]Agop J. Hacikyan et al., *The Heritage of Armenian Literature*, vol. 1: *From the Oral Tradition to the Golden Age* (Detroit: Wayne State University Press, 2000), 79.

[107]Noel Lenski, *Failure of Empire: Valens and the Roman State in the Fourth Century AD* (Los Angeles: University of California Press, 2003), 133.

In the fifth-century the Armenian church would experience the most significant development in its history second only to the reception of Christianity: the creation of the Armenian alphabet. In the late fourth century, Patriarch Sahak (or Isaac, a descendent of Gregory the Illuminator) assumed leadership of the Armenian church. During this time, Armenia—while still

ruled by the Arsacid dynasty—had become divided into two provinces: Roman on the west and Persian on the east. Greek was the liturgical language of the western provinces and Syriac was used in the east. However, Armenian was the spoken language of the populace, though it did not have a written script. Because the liturgy and reading of the Scriptures was done in either Greek or Syriac, the majority of clergy were foreign born.

Sensing the need for indigenous Armenian leadership and a written language, Catholicos Sahak enlisted the services of an Armenian scholar named Mesrop Mashtots

Figure 3.6. Statue of Mesrop Mashtots in front of the Matenadaran/Mesrop Mashtots Institute of Ancient Manuscripts in Yerevan, Armenia

to create an Armenian alphabet. One of Mesrop's pupils, Koriun, wrote the *Life of Mashtots*, which is the first original book in the Armenian language.[108] Mesrop was born to an Armenian noble family and educated in Greek, Persian, and Syriac literature. Mesrop was also educated in law and military strategy and served the Armenian king Khosrov IV as the *hazarapet*, the highest civil position in Persian-controlled Armenia. Mesrop divested his wealth and entered the monastic life where he engaged in rigorous ascetic practice and performed many miracles. In the midst of his ascetic ministry, Mesrop became concerned about the physical and spiritual condition of his people, desiring to rescue them "from their native traditions and satanic idolatry":

---

[108]For an English translation of this text, see Bedros Norehad, *The Life of Mashtots* (New York: Armenian General Benevolent Union of America, 1964).

And after being occupied with the same [problem] for many days; he rose and came to the Holy Catholicos of Armenia Major whose name was Sahak, and whom he found predisposed and sharing in the same concern. Cordially they came together, and with earnest prayers early every morning [besought] God that all men attain the salvation brought by Christ. And they did this many days. Then as a boon from God the gracious, the council of blessed monks, devoted to the service of the land, gathered to secure letters for the Armenian nation. They conducted much inquiry and exploration, and much toil. Later they disclosed the foremost object of their search to the King of the Armenians whose name was Vramshapouh. The King told them of a man named Daniel, Syrian bishop of noble lineage, who unexpectedly had come into the possession of letters of Armenian alphabet. And when the King told them concerning Daniel's discovery, they prevailed upon him to do what was needful.[109]

Mesrop had a retinue of scribes, some of whom he sent to Urhoy to utilize Syriac literature in the creation of the alphabet, and others of whom he sent to Samosata to study Greek letters. The *Life of Mashtots* reveals the simultaneously religious and national significance of this step in Armenian Christian ethnogenesis: "Thus he experienced many tribulations in order to serve his nation. And God the All-Bountiful finally granted him that good fortune; for with his holy hand he became the father of new and wonderful offsprings—letters of the Armenian language, and then and there quickly designed, named, determined their order and devised the syllabication."[110]

There was a degree of resistance to the creation of the indigenous Armenian alphabet as this was a profound statement of national and ecclesiastical independence. At the beginning of the diffusion of the Armenian alphabet, there was a Roman governor in Western Armenia who began to forbid the instruction of Armenian linguistics. However, Mesrop was successful at petitioning this restriction to the Roman emperor Theodosius II and procuring financial support in Armenian educational programs.[111] Mesrop is credited not only with creating the Armenian alphabet but also providing the first Bible translation in Armenian. The *Life* indicates that he began with the book of Proverbs and that the first words of the Scriptures

---

[109]*Life of Mashtots*, 29.
[110]*Life of Mashtots*, 30.
[111]Vahan M. Kurkjian, *A History of Armenia* (New York: Armenian General Benevolent Union of America, 1958), 111.

ever written in Armenian were *Čanač 'el zimastut'iwn ew zxrat, imanal zbans hančaroy*: "To know wisdom and instruction, to perceive words of understanding" (Prov 1:2). The *Life* compares Mesrop bringing the Armenian language to his nation to Moses bringing the law; however, whereas Moses found his people in sin, the Armenians welcomed the Armenian Bible "as receivers of tidings."[112] Indeed, the *Life* demonstrates the profound sense of cultural pride among Armenian Christians: "At that time our blessed and wonderful land of Armenia became truly worthy of admiration, where by the hands of two colleagues, suddenly, in an instant, Moses, the law-giver, along with the order of the prophets, energetic Paul with the entire phalanx of the apostles, along with Christ's world-sustaining gospel, became Armenian-speaking."[113]

The gospel not only took firm root in the Middle East but even gave rise to written language and national identity. Mesrop's creation of the alphabet ushered in the golden age of Armenian literature including many historical

Figure 3.7. Engraved crosses on the cave church wall at Geghard Monastery in Kotayk Province, Armenia

[112]*Life of Mashtots*, 30.
[113]*Life of Mashtots*, 33.

and theological texts. One of the most prominent fifth-century Armenian theologians, Eznik of Kolb, was a pupil of Mesrop and Catholicos Sahak who aided in the translation of the Bible. Like many of the scholars who aided in the development of the alphabet and the Armenian Bible, Eznik was highly educated in Greek, Syriac, and Persian literature. Of his many writings, his treatise *Against the Sects*, or *On God*, is the most prominent and is one of the finest of classical Armenian literature.[114] In the treatise, Eznik combats the

Figure 3.8. Cave at Geghard Monastery, Armenia

pagan religious movements from both surrounding empires—Hellenistic philosophy among the Romans and Zoroastrianism/Magianism among the Persians. Eznik's *On God* offers a unique window into a particular branch of Zoroastrianism called Zurvanism. Unlike the dominant Mazdaian form of Zoroastrianism, Zurvanists developed a cosmology in which the supreme being Zurvan gave birth to twin beings that brought forth creation and represented good and evil.[115] Eznik presented one of the earliest and most comprehensive refutations of a challenge to the Christian faith unique to the Armenian context:

> Indeed others believe something else about Satan: that God in fact created him evil. So if he was created evil by God, why does the Church persecute demons? If demons were established as avengers of evils, then the Church harms those very ones by means of whom it has been admonished, and she stands in opposition to the will of God because He created them for admonition and she persecutes them. But she does not possess the ability to persecute by herself; but rather she has it from God. It is clear from this that if the Lord first had not blown the Spirit on the twelve (cf. John 20:22) and given

---

[114]Eznik of Kolb, *On God*, ed. Monica J. Blanchard and Robin Darling Young (Louvain: Peeters, 1998).
[115]Mary Boyce, "Some Reflections on Zurvanism," *BSOAS* 19, no. 2 (1957): 305.

authority to the seventy (cf. Matt 10:8; cf. Mark 6:7; cf. Luke 10:17), they would not have been able to expel demons.[116]

Armenian theologians such as Eznik continued to define Christian theology contextualized to the Armenian context throughout the fifth century. While the christological controversies following the Council of Chalcedon (451) separated the Egyptian, Nubian, and Ethiopian churches from the dominant Roman church immediately, the Armenian church, like the Syriac-speaking churches of Mesopotamia and Arabia, did not formally separate from the Chalcedonian Byzantine church until the sixth century. The Armenian Council of Dvin in 506 accepted the conciliatory *Henotikon* of Emperor Zeno because of its denunciation of Nestorianism; however, the Armenians did not accept Chalcedonian Christology. At the second Council of Dvin in 554, the two-nature Christology of Chalcedonian Byzantium was officially rejected and the Armenian church became completely independent of the Roman church. This was likely because, like Syria and Arabia, Armenian Christians were predominately Miaphysite in doctrine and began to be persecuted during the time of Justinian.

An example of this persecution is an Armenian monastic leader named Thomas, who was expelled from his monastery in Armenia by the Byzantine Chalcedonian *praetorium*.[117] Therefore, the Armenian Apostolic Church has remained in the Miaphysite communion with the Coptic, Syrian Orthodox, and Ethiopian Tawahïdo churches since the mid-sixth century. Through succeeding centuries of oppression from Arab, Turk, and Russian powers, Armenian identity has remained almost entirely synonymous with the Armenian Apostolic Church, which was the first national church, provided the nation with its written language, and has retained an independent doctrinal and ecumenical structure for over fifteen hundred years.

GEORGIA

The Caucasus region has been occupied since Paleolithic times and witnessed further civic development in the fourth century BCE. Before and after this time, the region called "Georgia" by the Persians (*gurğān*, "wolves")

---

[116]Eznik of Kolb, *On God*, 124-25. Eznik here is equating Satan with the Zurvanist evil deity Ahrmn, who was thought to be created evil by Zurvan.
[117]John of Ephesus, *Lives of the Eastern Saints*, 296.

was composed of two major geocultural areas: Colchis in the west and Iberia (or Kartli) in the east. Like Armenia, Georgia has been subject to Roman, Persian, Arab, Mongol, Turkish, and Russian rule until its modern independence following the dissolution of the Soviet Union in 1991. Also like in Armenia, the Georgian monarch declared Christianity the national religion in the early fourth century CE.

At the time of the introduction of Christianity, both Armenia and Georgia were split between Roman and Persian rule. In the late third century, a princely dynasty known as the Chosroids rose to power and administered Iberian Georgia under the authority of the newly ascendant Persian Sassanian dynasty. Relatives of the Persian Sassanians, the Georgian Chosroid dynasty was founded by Mirian III as its first king in 284 CE and ruled until the mid-fourth century, at which point he adopted Christianity as the national religion of Georgia. A woman named Nino traveled to Kartli in the early fourth century and has been credited since that time with the conversion of the Georgian people.[118] While the Georgian Orthodox Church holds to its apostolic founding by the New Testament apostle Andrew, the identification of Nino in Georgian chronicles is the earliest historically reliable record of the beginning of Christianity in Georgia.[119] Nino came to Kartli bearing a unique "grapevine" cross which she planted in the ground at Akhalkalaki; it has been an emblem of the Georgian Orthodox Church to this day.[120] The account provided by Rufinus highlights local Georgian culture and the contextualized ministry of Nino: "Now it is said that they have the custom that, if a child falls sick, it is taken around by its mother to each of the houses to see if anyone knows of a proven remedy to apply to the illness."[121] After hearing about the healings performed by Nino, Queen

---

[118]The account provided by Rufinus does not name the woman; the Georgian tradition added the name Nino in the ninth-century Georgian text the *Life of Nino*, itself based on a seventh-century Georgian historical account. Stephen H. Rapp, *Studies in Medieval Georgian Historiography: Early Texts and Eurasian Contexts* (Leuven: Peeters, 2003), 146.

[119]However, there are second- and third-century burial sites indicating an earlier Christian presence in Georgia. Rufinus of Aquileia, *Church History: Books 10 and 11*, ed. Philip R. Amidon (New York: Oxford University Press, 1997), 47n21; a more detailed account is found in the seventh-century *Conversion of Kartli* and the ninth-century *Georgian Chronicles*.

[120]While Georgian sources report that Nino came to Georgia as a missionary, Rufinus claims that she was a prisoner (*Church History*, 20).

[121]Rufinus, *Church History*, 21. In typical fashion, Rufinus describes Georgians as "barbarians" multiple times throughout his account, as he does for all non-Roman people groups.

Nana summoned her to receive healing from a severe sickness. When the queen converted to Christianity in response to her healing, King Mirian III threatened to divorce her as he was persecuting the Christians of his kingdom. After he was struck blind, King Mirian prayed to "Nino's God" and was immediately healed.[122] Mirian believed, was baptized, and accepted Christianity as the official religion of Georgia. Mirian erected Bodbe Monastery (which still houses Nino's relics) and the Svetitskhoveli Cathedral which was the first Christian church built in Georgia. Nino remains one of the most significant figures in Georgian Christianity, and her story was framed in traditional, pre-Christian Georgian narrative structure involving divinized women (called *kadag*) who act as intermediaries between the divine and human realms.[123]

As was the case for other Christian communities in Mesopotamia, Persia, and the Caucasus region, the acceptance of Christianity as the dominant religion had political consequences. Georgian rulers such as Mirian often aided the Sassanian Persian shah in conflicts with the Roman Empire. However, when Georgia began to share the same religion as the Roman Empire, matters became complicated between the Georgian Christian authorities and their Zoroastrian Persian rulers. Indeed, the account of the Christianization of Georgia provided by Rufinus emphasizes Georgia's connection to Rome and Constantine:

> Now after the church had been magnificently built and the people were thirsting even more deeply for God's faith, on the advice of the captive an embassy of the entire people was sent to the emperor Constantine, and what had happened was explained to him. They implored him to send priests who could complete God's work begun among them. He dispatched them with all joy and honor, made far happier by this than if he had annexed to the Roman Empire unknown peoples and kingdoms.[124]

The political implications of the shared religion between Rome and Georgia continued to complicate matters after the time of Mirian III and Constantine.

---

[122]The ninth-century *Life of Nino* embellishes the account provided by Rufinus. *Life of Saint Nino*, ed. David Marshall Lang, in *Lives and Legends of the Georgian Saints* (London: Mowbrays, 1956), 29.

[123]Françoise Thelamon, *Païens et chrétiens au IVe siècle* (Paris: etudes augustiniennes, 1981), 93-119.

[124]Rufinus, *Church History*, 23.

Figure 3.9. Jvari Monastery, built in the late sixth century at Mtskheta, Georgia, at the traditional site of Saint Nino's evangelization of King Mirian III

In the fourth century, Mirian's successor Sauromaces II favored the Roman Empire and therefore was deposed by the Persians and replaced by the pro-Sassanian king Aspacures II in 361. However, Roman emperor Valens restored Sauromaces to control of western Georgia, known as Colchis, while the family of Aspacures ruled the eastern, Iberian region. Persians continued to assert their control over eastern Georgia, notably in their promotion of Zoroastrianism among the predominately Christian population. This contributed to an accentuated need for Georgian Christians to assert their unique identity through the creation of a written language.

After the Christianization of Georgia under Mirian, the Georgian alphabet came into existence in a similar fashion as the Armenian. The impetus for creating a written script for Old Georgian was for the purpose of translating the Bible and composing original theological literature. The Armenian *Life of Mashtots* reports that Mesrop and his team of scholars invented the Albanian and Georgian scripts at the same time that they created the Armenian:

> Again, after the passage of some time, the beloved of Christ thought of taking care of the barbarian regions, and by the grace of God undertook to create an

alphabet for the Georgian language. He wrote, arranged, and put it in order, and taking a few of his pupils, arrived in the regions of Georgia. And he went and presented himself to King Bakour, and the bishop of the land, Moses. He placed his skill at their disposal, advised and urged them, and they consented to do what he requested. And he found a Georgian translator by the name of Jagha, a literate and devout man. The Georgian king then ordered that youths be gathered from various parts and provinces of his realm and brought to the *vardapet*. Taking them he put them through the forge of education, and with spiritual love and energy he removed [from them] the purulent uncleanliness of the worship of spirits and false idols, and he separated and purged them from their native [traditions], and made them lose their recollection to such an extent that they said, "I forgot my people and my father's house." And thus they who had been gathered from among so many distinct and dissimilar tongues, he bound together with one (set of) divine commandments, transforming them into one nation and glorifiers of one God.[125]

The earliest extant Old Georgian inscription comes soon after the time of Mesrop in the early fifth-century Bir el Qutt Inscription. This inscription was written in the early Asomtavruli script of Old Georgian at a Judean monastery in 430. One of the Bir el Qutt inscriptions mentions the famous Georgian theologian Peter (or Murvan) the Iberian, who was the prince of Kartli taken to Constantinople to ensure Georgian loyalty to the Roman Empire. Georgian Christians had a high degree of contact with neighboring ethnic groups as is evidenced by the earliest Georgian inscriptions coming from Palestine and their alphabet being invented by Armenian scribes. However, medieval attribution of the creation of the alphabet to pre-Christian Georgians was an attempt to locate ownership of the alphabet in Georgian sources.[126]

Attempts on the part of Georgian Christians during the Middle Ages to assert independence from Armenia are best understood in light of the schism that transpired between the two at the turn of the seventh century. Along with the Armenian, Egyptian, and Syrian bishops, the Georgian catholicos (later known as "patriarch") initially rejected the Council of Chalcedon. However, tensions began to rise between Armenia and Georgia

---

[125]*Life of Mashots*, 15-16.
[126]Donald Rayfield, *The Literature of Georgia: A History* (New York: Routledge, 2000), 19.

during the sixth century as Armenia began to exercise preeminence in the Caucasus region. Coupled with a desire to gain Byzantine support against the Persian Sassanids, the Georgian church adopted the Chalcedonian confession of the Roman church and split from the Armenians at the Third Council of Dvin in 607.

Political pressure from Persia varied in Georgia. The rulers of Kartli remained primarily loyal to their Persian rulers through the turn of the fifth century. During the reign of Vakhtang I Gorgasali (447–522), however, the Georgians closely allied themselves with the Romans and unsuccessfully revolted against the Persians. Vakhtang I founded the modern Georgian capital of Tbilisi from where the Persians would center their control over eastern Georgia. The Chosroid dynasty lost control after the reign of Vakhtang I and the Sassanians abolished the Georgian monarchy in the late sixth century. Georgian monarchial descendants continued to vie for control of Georgia by appealing to Roman and Persian authorities. Guaram I formed an alliance with the Byzantine emperor Maurice, which resulted in the division of eastern Georgia between Byzantium and the Sassanids. Guaram's son and successor Stephanus I, however, reversed Iberian Georgia's allegiance to Persia, which resulted in the capture of Tbilisi by Roman emperor Heraclius in 627. The reestablishment of Georgian Chosroid rule under the auspices of Byzantine hegemony came only a few years before Georgia was conquered by the Rashidun Caliphate in the mid-seventh century.

The Arab Muslim conquest during the seventh century instigated a process by which Georgian Christians began to assert an autonomous identity distinct from Byzantine Christianity. Although the creation of the alphabet would serve this end to an extent, the fact that the alphabet was created by Armenian scholars lessened the degree of ethnic pride. Likewise, preconquest Georgian hagiography included a majority of foreign saintly figures such as the Armenian noblewoman Shushanik. The influx of monasticism into Georgia in the sixth century brought many foreign cultural influences and many clerics were of foreign origin. After the Arab Muslim conquest, however, the bishops and patriarch were exclusively Georgian, and Georgian hagiography would begin to focus solely on Georgian saints. The need to assert Georgian Christian identity in the midst of the new

Islamic authorities as well as increasing difficulties in communicating with ecclesiastical officials in Constantinople led to this surge in Georgian identity development.[127]

Christians who are members of socially and politically marginalized communities must unapologetically express pride and solidarity with their cultural community. While the extremes of ethnocentrism and nationalism have no place for those in Christ, believers must also be wary of the opposite extreme of leaving no room for biblical expressions of cultural pride. This is especially necessary for Christian cultures that are oppressed and marginalized. Positive self-images that are nurtured internally are vital components to advancing communities that have been historically and systematically marginalized.[128] It is imperative for Christians who come from cultures where Christianity is culturally pervasive to give space for believers who experience cultural alienation from the gospel. Likewise, it is important for subaltern cultures to resist internalized theological racism that cautions them against embracing their own culture. These measures are of greater importance than the fragility, defensiveness, or discomfort they may create for the dominant culture.

I was teaching a course on ancient African church history to a group of Ivorian pastors in Abidjan and showed them how some medieval Nubian monasteries had wall paintings with Africans worshiping Jesus Christ while wearing animal crest masks, a tradition common in many sub-Saharan African cultures. I asked this group how many of them would be open to allowing worship in their church involving crest masks and the vast majority of them said they would never allow this, with only a few saying they would be open to it.

In my context of urban, African-American culture, we deal with similar questions of contextualization. In commemoration of the events that occurred in Ferguson, Missouri, in 2014, the City Ministry Initiative at Covenant Seminary coordinated an event focusing on current justice issues that intentionally brought together church leaders with activists and organizers (all African-American leaders in North St. Louis city and county). One of

---

[127]Rapp, *Medieval Georgian Historiography*, 14.
[128]Beverly Daniel Tatum, *"Why Are All the Black Kids Sitting Together in the Cafeteria?" and Other Conversations About Race* (New York: Basic Books, 1997), 65.

the several points of tension between these two disparate communities that came up was the small but tense issue of young African-American men wearing hats in church. A young, African-American pastor and Christian rapper began speaking in support of urban youth having the freedom to wear hats in church, which greatly displeased many of the older or more traditional African-American leaders. However, this young pastor's church is full of urban, African-American youth and young adults who are following Jesus and lifting their hands in praise to him every week (while wearing hats, many of them even on backward). If a gospel movement is to flourish among cultures that have been historically marginalized in the name of Christianity, it is of paramount importance for indigenous communities to be empowered to develop contextual theology and worship that glorifies Christ and celebrates communal identity.

The focused elevation of Georgian Christian figures helped to solidify this ancient tradition in a time of significant transition. The renewed sense of Georgian independence occurred predominately in the eastern Iberian region while Colchis remained closely affiliated with Constantinople. However, the eastern and western regions of Georgia became more culturally and ecclesiastically related due to Islamic dominance and increasing numbers of citizens of Kartli (Iberia) fleeing persecution and settling in Colchis. By the ninth century, Colchis broke away from Constantinople and came under the authority of the Georgian patriarch centered in Mtskheta. Soon after, in the tenth century, the Bagratid dynasty formed the first united kingdom of Georgia which exercised significant influence in the region until the rise of the Ottoman Empire in the fifteenth century. Soon after the rise of the kingdom of Georgia, the nation entered a golden age that witnessed unprecedented expansion of Georgian borders as well as developments in science, literature, politics, and theology. The Georgian golden age reached its zenith under Georgia's first female ruler, Tamar the Great, who expanded the kingdom to an unprecedented extent.

While Georgia would endure centuries of Arab, Mongol, Turkish, and Russian domination, the unique Christian tradition that developed in the early fourth century would continue to be the most significant component in shaping Georgian identity until the modern period. Centuries before the Western European Renaissance, the formation of the kingdom of Georgia in the eleventh century ushered in three hundred years of philosophical, scientific, artistic, and theological renewal. Contemporary Georgia, where the overwhelming majority identifies with the Georgian Orthodox Church, continues to be defined by the unique Christian tradition that is synonymous with the Georgian identity that began in Late Antiquity.

4

The Beginning of Missions
Along the Silk Road

PERSIA

As in most cases in the first centuries of Christianity, the gospel entered Persia initially through the Jewish community that existed there since the Babylonian exile of the sixth century BCE. The New Testament account indicates the presence of various Persian ethnic groups present at Pentecost, including Parthians, Medes, and Elamites (Acts 2:9). The Elamite and Median empires largely declined in power after the rise of the Achaemenid Empire under Cyrus the Great in 550 BCE, while the Parthian Empire was the ruling dynasty during the earliest years of Christianity in Persia. The Parthian rule of Persia was established by Arsaces I and was the dominant power there from the third century BCE until the rise of the Sassanid dynasty in the mid-third century CE. Before the Sassanians enforced Zoroastrianism as the imperial religion, Christianity entered Persia from the West Syriac regions of the Eastern Roman Empire and was able to thrive in Parthian Persia, which was more religiously heterogeneous with a pantheon of gods from various cultural influences.

The first extrabiblical reference to Persian Christians was in the epitaph of the Cilician evangelist Abercius, who traveled to Persia and found Christians there in the mid-second century CE,[1]

> The citizen of a chosen city, this [monument] made [while] living, that there
> I might have in time a resting-place of my body, [I] being by name Abercius,

---

[1]Cornelia Horn, Samuel N. C. Lieu, and Robert R. Phenix Jr., "Beyond the Eastern Frontier," in *Early Christianity in Contexts: An Exploration Across Cultures and Continents* (Grand Rapids: Baker Academic, 2014), 63.

the disciple of a holy shepherd who feeds flocks of sheep [both] on mountains and on plains, who has great eyes that see everywhere. For this [shepherd] taught me [that the] book [of life] is worthy of belief. And to Rome he sent me to contemplate majesty, and to see a queen golden-robed and golden-sandalled; there also I saw a people bearing a shining mark. And I saw the land of Syria and all [its] cities—Nisibis [I saw] when I passed over Euphrates. But everywhere I had brethren.[2]

Abercius's younger contemporary Bardaisan (Syriac for "son of the Daisan," the principal river of Urhoy) was a prominent early Syriac writer who initiated a version of Christianity that remained popular in Urhoy well into Late Antiquity but eventually was rejected as heretical during the time of Ephrem. Bardaisan was a theologian, astrologist, and poet whose theological cosmology weaved mainstream Christian doctrine together with the Babylonian astrology in which he had been reared. Possibly of Persian origin himself, Bardaisan attests to the presence of Christians in Persia in the famous text attributed to him, *The Book of the Laws of the Countries*. This text describes theological and cultural practices prevalent in various nations while elevating the values of the Christian "race" above them all: "Nor (do) those (Christians) which are in Parthia take two wives; nor those which are in Judea circumcise themselves; nor do our sisters which are amongst the Geli and amongst the Cashani have connexion with strangers; nor do those which are in Persia take their daughters for wives; for those who are in Media fly from their dead, or bury them alive."[3] Given the high degree of international trade between Antioch, Urhoy, and Mesopotamia, in addition to the significant Jewish presence in each place, it is likely that Christianity entered Persia along this route no later than the second century.[4]

---

[2]A third-century epitaph mirrors almost exactly the wording found in the Abercius inscription, attesting to its ancient provenance. Both inscriptions provided source material for the *Life of Abercius* in the fourth century. H. Leclercq, "Inscription of Abercius," in *The Catholic Encyclopedia* (New York: Universal Knowledge Foundation, 1913), 1:41.

[3]Bardaisan, *Book of the Laws of the Countries*, ed. William Cureton (London: Francis and John Rivington, 1855), 33. Geli and Cashani are ancient ethnic groups of the Median territory of the northeastern Persian Empire.

[4]Wilhelm Baum and Dietmar W. Winkler, *The Church of the East: A Concise History* (New York: Routledge, 2003), 8. The same theory is advanced for the beginning of East Syriac Christianity in China in the mid-sixth century (47), while the introduction of Christianity to India seems to have been the result of direct missionary activity in the early fourth century (53).

During the second and third centuries, while Roman Christianity lived under frequent waves of persecution, the East Syriac Christians living in the Persian Parthian Empire experienced a greater degree of peace and autonomy than their fellow Christians to the west. This means that, in the second and third centuries, the areas now known as Greece and Italy were more dangerous for Christians than the areas now known as Iraq, Iran, and Afghanistan! After several Persian victories over Rome, notably Shapur's capturing of Emperor Valerian in 260, many Greek-speaking Christian refugees settled in Persia and formed separate churches from the native, East Syriac-speaking Persian Christians. An inscription from a Persian Magian (Zoroastrian) mobad (priest) named Kartir, boasting on the superiority of Magian religion over other religions, mentions two groups called *naçara* and *kristiyan*. These names refer respectively to Syriac- and Greek-speaking Christians who maintained separate cultural and ecclesiastical communities.[5]

Because the Syriac-speaking community existed along the frontiers straddling the Roman-Persian border, political tension between these two empires was a highly influential factor in the lives of Syriac Christians. After the reforms of Constantine in which Roman Christians were afforded unprecedented autonomy, the Roman emperor sent a letter threatening that Persian Christians would be loyal to Rome (rather than Persia) in the event of war.[6] Indeed, Persian Christians such as Aphrahat expressed vehement criticism of the Persian king in favor of the Roman emperor,[7] "Prosperity has come to the people of God, and a blessing remains for the one [Constantine] through whom this prosperity has come. But disaster looms against the army gathered by the evil and proud [Shapur II] who boasts, and misery waits there for the one through whom this disaster has been stirred up."[8] Statements like this illustrate the view of Constantine as the Roman

---

[5]Sebastian Brock, *Fire from Heaven: Studies in Syriac Theology and Liturgy* (Aldershot, NH: Ashgate, 2006), 71.

[6]Sebastian P. Brock, "Christians in the Sasanian Empire: A Case of Divided Loyalties," in *Religion and National Identity*, Studies in Church History 18, ed. S. Mews (New York: Oxford University Press, 1982), 7.

[7]Brock, "Christians in the Sasanian Empire," 8. Despite the common belief that all Persian Christians held such an attitude, many Christians under Persian rule actually maintained patriotic loyalty to the shah despite religious differences. S. J. McDonough, "A Question of Faith? Persecution and Political Centralization in the Sasanian Empire of Yazdgard II (438–457 CE)," in *Violence in Late Antiquity: Perceptions and Practices*, ed. H. A. Drake (Aldershot, NH: Ashgate, 2006), 78.

[8]Aphrahat, *Demonstrations*, ed. Adam Lehto (Piscataway, NJ: Gorgias, 2010), 148.

Christian patron and the association of *romanitas* with Christianity that began in the fourth century.[9]

Commonly known as "the Persian sage," Aphrahat (from the Persian root meaning "wise") was born in an unidentified part of the Persian Empire in the middle of the third century. His treatise, the *Demonstrations*, is one of the earliest examples of a Christian systematic theology and is the earliest extant orthodox Christian text written in Syriac.[10] The Semitic nature of the treatise is evident in its acrostic structure, and the Greco-Roman traits common to systematic-philosophical treatises are wholly absent from this Persian work. The *Demonstrations* are frequently addressed to a "friend" of Aphrahat and meant to provide encouragement and instruction in the Scriptures and the indigenously Syriac style of asceticism (called the *ihidāye* or "solitary ones") to which both Aphrahat and his "friend" belonged.[11] Aphrahat lived and wrote before, during, and after the Christianization of Rome and therefore experienced the most severe of all Christian persecution in Persia under Shapur II.

While outright criticism of the Persian shah or Zoroastrianism would have certainly at least entailed imprisonment, Aphrahat nonetheless issued veiled criticism of the oppressive Persian government in the above excerpt. He also criticized the dominant Magian worship of the sun and fire as he argued that these natural phenomena are submissive to the will of God:

> O child of Adam . . . your mind gives birth to other gods . . . you make conjectures and speak though you have not seen . . . Speak to me when I ask you: the sun that you see, of what is it made? Is there a soul in it? Does it have knowledge? Does it have discernment? . . . Fire does not reject anything that you give it. It does not abhor that which is evil and despicable. . . . They were made to serve the world from the beginning. . . . All of these things are the servants of heaven and earth, made without souls for the service of the world. . . . Know this, person who does not understand: the will of God carries each of these things, and there is nothing apart from his will.[12]

---

[9]Kyle Smith, *Constantine and the Captive Christians of Persia: Martyrdom and Religious Identity in Late Antiquity* (Oakland: University of California Press, 2016), 13.

[10]While Bardaisan lived before Aphrahat, his *Book of the Laws of the Countries* was actually transcribed by his pupil Phillip (*Demonstrations*, 5n13); likewise, while Ephrem eclipsed Aphrahat in prominence in Syriac theology and history, Aphrahat preceded and influenced Ephrem.

[11]It is likely that Aphrahat intended this treatise for more broad application in the Persian church as he frequently oscillates between addressing "us," "you," and "they" (*Demonstrations*, 13).

[12]Aphrahat, *Demonstrations*, 523.

However, Aphrahat's primary and more blatant target throughout the *Demonstrations* was the neighboring Jewish community. A central theme throughout the treatise is the replacement of "the people" (Israel) with "the peoples" (Gentiles). Aphrahat responds to alleged Jewish critique that if the Christian faith were valid, they would not endure persecution. The concluding encouragement is that Christians who are temporally persecuted will be rewarded in heaven and are superior to the Jews who receive earthly benefit and favor from the Persian government: "This whole discourse that I have written to you above, my friend, concerns the reproach of a Jewish man against our people. But now, as much as I am able, I will prove with respect to the persecuted that they received a good reward. The persecutors, however, have remained in contempt and disgrace."[13] As Jewish oppression increased in Rome under Constantine, many Jews fled the Roman Empire and took up residence in Persia where—from the Christian perspective—Jewish communities were less oppressed than Christians.[14] The shah's preference for Jews, believed by many Persian Christian leaders to be due to the newfound Christian identity of Constantine, led many Christians to convert to Judaism, thus avoiding persecution.

As discussed in chapter one, the association of Christianity with Roman identity significantly complicated the situation for Persian Christians, who began to be held in suspicion by Persian authorities. This dynamic led to the writing of various hagiographical martyr stories that were later known as the *Acts of the Persian Martyrs*. These passion narratives relate accounts of Persian Christians who suffered martyrdom during the fourth and fifth centuries as persecution of Christians became widespread and systematic. A Persian Christian leader named Šim'un was martyred due to his refusal to perform Magian fire worship. However, the real frustration of Shapur II was Šim'un's refusal to impose double taxes on his Christian citizens. In expressing his frustrations with Christians to Šim'un, Shapur called the Persian

---

[13] Aphrahat, *Demonstrations*, 445.

[14] This is despite the fact that sources indicate a high degree of contact between Persian Jews and Christians with Persian society. The Babylonian Talmud, for example, highly influenced the broader Persian social context. Richard E. Payne, *A State of Mixture: Christians, Zoroastrians, and Iranian Political Culture in Late Antiquity* (Oakland: University of California Press, 2015), 15; Shai Secunda, *The Iranian Talmud: Reading the Bavli in Its Sasanian Context* (Philadelphia: University of Pennsylvania Press, 2014), 6.

Christians "servants of Caesar."[15] This reveals the degree to which the Christian faith became compromised for non-Roman Christians because of its association with Roman identity.

The problematic identity politics that resulted for Persian Christians from the Christianization of Rome have deep implications for contemporary matters of race, ethnicity, and Christian identity. Perhaps the greatest challenge for non-Western/non-white people in coming to faith in Christ today is the association of Christianity as a "white/Western religion." In the white/Western world, most people who choose not to be a Christian usually do not do so out of a matter of cultural identity. Usually a Western/white person will reject the claims of the gospel on philosophical or theological grounds. But most white/Western people do not reject Christianity because of it being perceived of as contrary to Western identities (e.g. American, Canadian, European, Australian, etc.). However, this is precisely the obstacle that keeps many non-Westerners from the gospel. I recently taught a course on church history at a Native American seminary where one of the students in the class told me about how his Christian friend, who was also from the Zuni Pueblo, was ostracized from his family and excommunicated from his tribe for becoming a Christian. According to this student, many Zuni people perceive Christianity as the religion of the Manifest Destiny, Indian Removal, mission schools, and other forms of oppression. This dilemma of the white Western cultural captivity of the church is perhaps the greatest missiological challenge facing the church today. Billions of people around the world perceive Christianity as a Western, white religion that is fundamentally at odds with their ethnic and cultural identity. Regardless of the reality that Scripture proclaims the equal acceptability of all cultural groups (Acts 10:34-35), the historical reality of the Western church's complicity in white supremacy has cemented this cultural association with the gospel in the minds of much of humanity. The Western cultural captivity of the church began with the Christianization of Rome under Constantine, and the Persian Christians were the first non-Western Christians to suffer the consequences of this phenomenon. Yet despite the ensuing persecution that transpired for centuries in the

---

[15]Brock, "Christians in the Sassanian Empire," 4. Smith argues these "pro-Roman" glosses were added later (Smith, *Captive Christians*, 12). While this may be the case, the process of identity politics associating Christianity with Roman identity had precedent in the fourth century.

Persian church, this ancient form of Christianity has endured to the present and has continued to espouse a contextualized, indigenous form of worship and theology.

Christian persecution as recorded in the *Acts of the Persian Martyrs* was most severe under the administration of the shahs Shapur II (310–379), Bahrām V (421–439), and Yazdgard II (439–457). In contrast, Yazdgard I (399–420) had a more cordial relationship with the Roman Empire and initially promoted Christianity. Yazdgard I promoted the Synod of Isaac in 410 under the administration of the metropolitan bishop Isaac at the Persian capital Seleucia-Ctesiphon—the first Persian church council with extant records. While Christianity existed in Persia centuries before this council, this event should be seen as the *terminus ante quem* for the establishment of a Persian ecclesiastical hierarchy independent of the Roman church centers of Rome, Constantinople, and Antioch.

While the Persian Christians—and the Assyrian Church of the East today—hold Nestorius to be a "doctor of the church," this community is not "Nestorian," as the Synod of Isaac took place decades before the controversy surrounding Nestorius. The autochthonous nature of the Persian church is also demonstrated in their appropriation and contextualization of the Nicene Creed at the Synod of Isaac:

> We believe in one God, Father, who in his Son made heaven and earth; and in him were established the worlds above and that are below; and in him he effected the resurrection and renovation for all creation. And in his Son, the Only-Begotten who was born from him, that is, however, from the essence of his Father, God from God, Light from Light, true God from true God; he was born and was not made; who is of the same nature as his Father; who for the sake of us human beings who were created through him, and for the sake of our salvation, descended and put on a body and became man, and suffered and rose on the third day, and ascended to heaven and took his seat at the right hand of his Father; and he is coming in order to judge the dead and the living. And we confess the living and Holy Spirit, the living Paraclete who (is) from the Father and the Son; and in one Trinity and in one Essence and in one will.[16]

---

[16]Wilhelm and Baum, *Church of the East*, 16.

The common usage of the plural "we" in the Church of the East (the modern descendants of the ancient Persian church)—as well as in many African and Middle Eastern communities—was a distinction arising from a collectivist culture as opposed to the individualist "I" common in Western Christianity. Likewise, the idea of "putting on a body" was a common Syriac idea developed significantly by Ephrem the Syrian. While the Persian church was clearly orthodox and affirmed the divinity of Christ, this was expressed through their contextual theological framework.

The administration of Isaac brought the Church of the East, centered mostly at that time in Persia, into close allegiance with the shah by declaring the church bishops servants of the shah and establishing a favorable position for this Christian community now centered in Seleucia-Ctesiphon.[17] The councils of Ephesus (449) and Chalcedon (451) are not mentioned in the writing of the contemporary Persian scholar Barhadbshabba, indicating the degree of autonomy of the Persian church and her distance from the ecumenical events of the Roman church.[18] While significant levels of expansion were afforded the Church of the East during the early reign of Yazdgard I, the situation later became reversed.

During the time of Yazdgard I, there were instances of Christian violence against Magian (Zoroastrian) temples, and it has even been suggested that the Persian Christians during this time hoped that the Persian Empire would convert to Christianity like Rome.[19] Yazdgard I began to support the Magian aristocracy against the Christians not out of hostility or retaliation against the Christians but in an effort to stabilize the government and appease Magian leaders who were becoming increasingly frustrated with Christians.[20] As in the case of the earlier Roman Empire, persecution of Christians was rooted in a desire for social and political uniformity, which was also the foundation of the continuing persecutions of Yazdgard's successors Bahrām V and

---

[17]Philip Wood, *The Chronicle of Seert: Christian Historical Imagination in Late Antique Iraq* (New York: Oxford University Press, 2013), 31.

[18]Adam H. Becker, *Fear of God and the Beginning of Wisdom: The School of Nisibis and Christian Scholastic Culture in Late Antique Mesopotamia* (Philadelphia: University of Pennsylvania Press, 2006), 44.

[19]J. Neusner, "Jews in Iran," in *Cambridge History of Iran*, ed. E. Yarshater (New York: Cambridge University Press, 1983), 3/2: 916.

[20]Lucas Van Rompay, "Impetuous Martyrs? The Situation of the Persian Christians in the Last Years of Yazdgard I (419–420)," in *Martyrium in Multidisciplinary Perspective*, ed. M. Lamberigts & P. Van Deun (Leuven: Leuven University Press, 1995), 369.

Yazdgard II.[21] What is of great interest is that the hagiographical evidence suggests that the primary targets for Christian persecution were: (1) social elites attempting to minimize Christian social influence and (2) native Persian Christians, as opposed to the Greek-speaking *kristyane* from the Roman Empire.[22] It is likely that the disproportionate persecution experienced by local Persian Christians over those of foreign origin was rooted in the desire of Persian Magian authorities to extricate Persian identity from Christianity, which they saw as a product of the Roman world.

Continuing conflict and shifting borders between the Roman and Persian empires continued to complicate the situation of Christians straddling the imperial frontier. During Ephrem the Syrian's time in Nisibis, the Persian Empire made three incursions into the city, flooded it, and killed the Roman emperor Julian. After standing above Julian's corpse as it passed through Nisibis, Ephrem attributed the Persian conquest of Nisibis to the pagan practices of the Roman emperor in his *Madrāshe Against Julian*:

> A wonder! By chance the corpse of that accursed one,
> crossing over toward the rampart met me near the city!
> And the Magus took and fastened on a tower
> the standard sent from the east,
> so that this standard-bearer would declare to the onlookers
> that the city was slave to the lords of that standard.
> Refrain: Glory to the One Who wrapped the corpse in shame!
> I wondered, "Who indeed set a time for meeting
> when corpse and standard-bearer both at one moment were present?"
> I knew it was a prearrangement, a miracle of justice
> that when the corpse of the fallen one crossed over,
> the fearful standard went up and was put in place
> to proclaim that the evil of his conjurers had surrendered that city.[23]

The Persian conquest resulted in the exile of Nisibene Christians, including Ephrem.[24] Ephrem served as a theological instructor (*malphono*) in Nisibis

---

[21]J. P. Asmussen, "Christians in Iran," in Yarshater, *Cambridge History of Iran*, 942.

[22]McDonough, "Question of Faith," 74.

[23]Ephrem the Syrian, *Hymns*, trans. Kathleen E. McVey (New York: Paulist, 1989), 244.

[24]Although Ephrem initially found the conditions of Persian Nisibis agreeable and encountered no opposition, he eventually made his way to Urhoy. Arthur Vööbus, *Literary Critical and Historical Studies in Ephrem the Syrian* (Wetteren: Imprimerie Cultura, 1958), 51.

for the local church under the auspices of the various bishops during his career before going to Urhoy. The East Syriac scholar Barhadbshabba, in his *Cause of the Foundation of the Schools*, attributes the beginning of what would eventually be called the School of Nisibis to Ephrem's early teaching career in Nisibis.[25] The School of Nisibis remained a central component of the life and thought of the Church of the East for many centuries. The school developed three primary fields of study—theology, philosophy, and medicine—and is commonly considered the first Christian university and one of the earliest universities in the world.[26] After the exile of many Christians from Nisibis to Urhoy (Edessa), Ephrem took over leadership of the long-established School of Edessa in which his theological writing career flourished, as did the school's influence.

During the fifth century, after the time of Ephrem, the school became known as the "School of the Persians," indicating the significant degree to which this school represented the culture and theological traditions of the exiled Persians who lived in Roman Syrian territory. This School of the Persians developed an academic hierarchy and pedagogical system that was distinct from the earlier School of Edessa and which laid the foundation for what would become the next iteration of the School of Nisibis.[27] The resurrection of the School of Nisibis in the late fifth century was the result of another mass exodus of Persian Christians—this time back to Nisibis from Urhoy. The Syriac Christians of the Persian Empire became independent in 410,[28] and they were declared heretics shortly after the Council of Ephesus (431) because of their close association with the teachings of Theodore of Mopsuestia. The School of the Persians was forced out of Urhoy by Emperor Zeno in 489 because of its allegiance to the teachings of Theodore (as well as to Diodore of Tarsus and Nestorius). Led by the

---

[25]Adam H. Becker, *Sources for the Study of the School of Nisibis* (Liverpool: Liverpool University Press, 2008), 5, 149-50. Becker's edition contains an English translation of the text with an introduction and notes. He demonstrates the manner in which Ephrem's description of God as the teacher became influential among the School of the Persians two centuries later (26); it is likely that these "schools" were ascetic theological study circles which became more formalized in the fifth and sixth centuries; Jeffrey Wickes, "Between Liturgy and School: Reassessing the Performative Context of Ephrem's *Madrāšê*," *JECS* (2018): 43-44.

[26]Dale A. Johnson, *Barhanna Monograph Series*, vol. 2 (New Sinai Press, 2012), 92.

[27]Becker, *Fear of God*, 76.

[28]As opposed to the more common date of 424 (see Baum and Winkler, *Church of the East*, 19).

East Syriac scholar Narsai, it moved to Nisibis and flourished as the School of Nisibis for several centuries.[29]

Narsai is one of the most important Syriac Christian figures, equal in stature among the Syriac tradition to Jacob of Serugh (second only to Ephrem), and his theological and literary aptitude have earned him the title "Harp of the Spirit" among the Church of the East. Narsai set the theological and cultural trajectory for the Church of the East for centuries after his lifetime. One of Narsai's *memra* was on the "three doctors" of the Persian church—namely Theodore of Mopsuestia, Diodore of Tarsus, and Nestorius.[30] While the Church of the East has since the sixth century embraced Nestorius and avoided the term *theotokos* (God-bearer), Theodore of Mopsuestia and Diodore of Tarsus feature much more prominently in the writings of East Syriac Christians. Even Narsai's *Memre on the Three Doctors* displays much greater familiarity with Theodore and Diodore than with Nestorius. Moreover, the ecumenical councils of the Church of the East during the late fifth to early seventh centuries do not even mention Nestorius's name. For these reasons, it is inappropriate and inaccurate to refer to the Church of the East as "Nestorian."[31] While Theodore and Diodore played a significant role in the foundation of Antiochene Christology, it was Narsai who articulated a distinctly East Syriac theological formula that would shape the Persian (and Asian) church for centuries. The christological controversies of the fifth and sixth centuries are typically thought of as existing on a binary Chalcedonian-Miaphysite axis. But the theology of Narsai and the Church of the East nuances and complicates this dichotomy as the Persian Christians articulated a christological formula that fit neither position. In his *memre*, Narsai lays the groundwork of the East Syrian Christology that articulates a two-nature theology but in a different way than the Roman Chalcedonians:

> Let not the hearer suppose by the fact that I have distinguished the natures
> that I am speaking of two *prosopa* which are distant from one another. I am

---

[29]Becker, *Sources*, 5. Becker demonstrates the way the School of Nisibis founded much of its identity and character after its immediate predecessor, the School of the Persians in Urhoy (Becker, *Fear of God*, 74).

[30]Fr. Martin, "Homélie de Narsai sur les trois docteurs nestoriens," *JA* 14 (1899): 446-92; *JA* 15 (1900): 469-525.

[31]Sebastian Brock, "The 'Nestorian' Church: A Lamentable Misnomer," in *Fire from Heaven: Studies in Syriac Theology and Liturgy* (Aldershot, NH: Ashgate, 2006), 8.

talking of one *prosopon*, of the Word and the temple he chose, and I confess
one Son, but I preach in two natures [*kyane*] the venerated and glorious nature
of the Word, the Being [*itutha*] from his Father, and our nature which he took
in accordance with the promises he made. Perfect in his divinity, for he is
equal with his Begetter, and complete in his humanity, with soul and body of
mortal beings. Two that became, in the union, a single love and a single will.[32]

Narsai continued the Antiochene christological tradition rooted in Theodore
of Mopsuestia that represented a concern to maintain the distinction between
the humanity and divinity of Christ. Narsai articulated a distinctly Persian
theology while uplifting the culture of his people. In a *memre* on the nativity,
Narsai focuses on the importance of the Persian people as the first Gentile
group to hear of the birth of Christ.[33] The Christology unique to the Church
of the East was reaffirmed at the Synod of Beth Lapat (484) and was later
clarified through the teachings of Babai the Great (551–628). Babai was born
near Nisibis in the mid-sixth century and was educated at the School of Nisibis.
When Henana of Adiabene assumed leadership of the school and began to
emphasize the unity of Christ's natures, Babai left the school and entered a
monastery in the mountains near Nisibis. Babai participated in a monastic
reform in the Persian church, which included returning to the practice of
celibacy. Earlier monastic communities removed the vow of celibacy due to
persecution from Zoroastrians who abhorred the practice. Babai later
served as an interim catholicos of the Church of the East during the early
seventh century due to the political unrest resulting from wars between
Persia and Rome as well as interventions in church affairs from the Persian
government. During this time, Babai greatly influenced the life and theology
of the Church of the East. Babai produced many biblical commentaries, monastic hagiographies, and theological writings.

   As mentioned above, the Christology that became normative for the
Church of the East was articulated most clearly in Babai's most famous
writing, the *Book of Union*.[34] Babai speaks of the natures of Christ using the
Syriac word *kyane* while also speaking of two corresponding *qnome*. In East

---

[32]Sebastian Brock, "The Christology of the Church of the East," in *Fire from Heaven*, 170-71.
[33]Scott W. Sunquist, *Explorations in Asian Christianity: History, Theology and Mission* (Downers
   Grove, IL: InterVarsity Press, 2017), 288.
[34]Babai the Great, *Book of Union*, ed. A. Vaschalde (Louvain: Secretariat du SCO, 1953).

Syriac thought, a *qnoma* does not necessarily exist apart from a corresponding *kyane*. The *kyana* is an abstract, individual existence while a *qnoma* is the individual instance of a specific *kyana*.[35] Although Syriac writers often translated *hypostasis* using *qnoma*, the Syriac concept of *qnoma* has a wider range of interpretive possibilities than the Greek *hypostasis*. Therefore, the word *qnoma* should not be translated as "person" in the sense intended by the Greek *hypostasis*. For Babai and the Church of the East, each *kyana*—along with its *qnome*—is united in one *parsopa* (from the Greek *prosōpon*). The deployment of *qnome* in the *Book of Union* clearly demonstrates the incongruity of this term with both *hypostasis* and *prosōpon* and highlights its uniquely East Syriac usage: "And he will take conjointly in his nature [*qnoma*] the name of his humanity in a unity of personhood (*parsopayita*). For He said, 'And the Word became flesh and dwelt among us.' For it was flesh that He took and made a dwelling in it. And it was in one of the natures (*qnome*) of our humanity."[36] The christological formula developed by Narsai and Babai became normative for the Church of the East just before the Islamic conquest forever changed this ancient Christian community.

After the fall of the Persian Empire and the capture of its imperial city, Seleucia-Ctesiphon, the catholicos of the Church of the East, Isho'yahb II (Syriac for "Jesus gives"), recentered the Church of the East further north at Karka de Beth Slokh and strengthened the Persian church during this tumultuous time. Despite the massive political and cultural shifts during the seventh century, the Church of the East continued to expand with metropolitan bishops and dioceses placed in Afghanistan and Uzbekistan, and the earliest Christian mission to China under Catholicos Isho'yahb II. While the Western world was entering into its "Dark Ages," the Islamic Golden Age was beginning during the eighth century with dramatic advances in science, art, and literary production. After the fall of the Umayyad Caliphate centered in Damascus, the Abbasid Caliphate rose to prominence and established its capital in Baghdad in the mid-eighth century. The Islamic Golden Age is exemplified best by the *Bayt al-Hikma* ("House of Wisdom") founded by Caliph al-Ma'mun in Baghdad in the early ninth-century, which served as an academic powerhouse in the medieval world for teaching mathematics,

---

[35]Brock, "Christology," 173; Baum and Winkler, *Church of the East*, 39.
[36]Babai, *Book of Union*, 126.

astronomy, medicine, geography, and philosophy. Many Jews, Christians, Zoroastrians, and others studied in Baghdad. Syriac-speaking Christians became cultural mediators between the Greek-speaking Roman Empire and the Arabic Muslim world in which they lived. As Syriac-speaking Christian theologians, philosophers, and doctors began to learn Arabic, they led the way in a massive translation movement where Greek philosophy came into Arabic via Syriac. One of the most prominent examples was the Syrian Miaphysite Yahya ibn Adi (893–974), who studied medicine and philosophy in Baghdad and translated Plato's *Laws* and Aristotle's *Sophistical Refutations* and *Topics*.[37] The translation work of ibn Adi followed that of another philosopher-scientist based in Baghdad and member of the Church of the East, Hunayn ibn Ishaq (809–873). Like, ibn Adi, Hunayn ibn Ishaq translated Plato and Aristotle into Arabic from Greek through Syriac and was known among Muslim scholars as "the Sheikh of the translators."[38] Yet despite the success and influence of Syriac Christians under Abbasid rule, persecution of Christians also increased after Umayyad times. Abbasid caliphs had to approve the election of the catholicos of the Church of the East, who acted as the representative for the Christian community.

Timothy of Baghdad (patriarchate 780–823) enacted many reforms that galvanized and expanded the reach of the Church of the East. Timothy, a native of the Assyrian province of Adiabene, was born in the early eighth century and became the metropolitan bishop of his province before rising to the rank of catholicos after a dubious and suspicious election process. Perhaps his most famous text is his recording of an interfaith dialogue that took place between himself and the Abbasid caliph al-Mahdi. In his apology of the Christian faith (quoted in chapter one above), Timothy responds to typical Muslim questions of the Christian faith posed by al-Mahdi in a tone that displays great respect for the Muslim faith. In response to al-Mahdi's inquiry as to the prophetic status of Muhammad from a Christian perspective, Timothy writes:

> Further, all the prophets drove men away from bad works, and brought them
> nearer to good works, and since Muhammad drove his people away from bad

---

[37]Sidney H. Griffith, *The Beginnings of Christian Theology in Arabic: Muslim-Christian Encounters in the Early Islamic Period* (Aldershot, NH: Ashgate, 2002), 8.

[38]G. Osman, "'The Sheikh of the Translators': The Translation Methodology of Hunayn ibn Ishaq," *Translation and Interpreting Studies* 7, no. 2 (2012): 161-75.

works and brought them nearer to the good ones, he walked, therefore in the path of the prophets. Again, all the prophets separated men from idolatry and polytheism, and attached them to God and to His cult, and since Muhammad separated his people from idolatry and polytheism, and attached them to the cult and the knowledge of one God, beside whom there is no other God, it is obvious that he walked in the path of the prophets. Finally Muhammad taught about God, His Word and His Spirit, and since all the prophets had prophesied about God, His Word and His Spirit, Muhammad walked, therefore, in the path of all the prophets.[39]

Timothy's tone throughout the dialogue highlights the cordiality that often existed in interfaith dialogue in the highly cosmopolitan Baghdad. The strategic phrasing of "God, His Word and His Spirit"—a defense of the Trinity using Muslim terminology—as well as echoing wording from the Shahada ("there is no other God") demonstrates the ingenuity and graciousness with which East Syriac Christians such as Timothy missionally engaged their Muslim rulers. Timothy's recording of the dialogue in Syriac is likely meant to serve as a manual for Christians on how to engage their Muslim rulers.

One of the most significant aspects of Timothy's patriarchate was his missionary effort to expand the Church of the East throughout Central, East, and South Asia. It was largely through Timothy's keen interest in establishing metropolitan bishops throughout Asia that the Church of the East became the largest geographical Christian community in the medieval world. Timothy fortified and added to the metropolitan bishoprics of Syria, Armenia, Azerbaijan, and Iran. Timothy also looked east and strengthened the Christian leadership of Merv (Turkmenistan), as well as established metropolitans among the Turks of Central Asia, Tibet, and China. Timothy also granted autonomy for the Christian communities of India who, up to that time, had existed as part of the Diocese of Fars (Iran). The Church of the East would become fragmented due to Western Christian intervention in the sixteenth-century and geographically reduced to the area surrounding modern Iraq due to intense waves of persecution by Mongol and Turkic empires. However, in the medieval period the Church of the East experienced some of the greatest missionary success and expansion of any

---

[39]Timothy of Baghdad, *Apology of Patriarch Timothy of Baghdad before the Caliph Mahdi*, ed. Alphonse Mingana (Piscataway, NJ: Gorgias, 2009), 61.

Christian community in history, starting in Persian territory and extending all the way to the Pacific and Indian oceans.

INDIA

The origins of Christianity in India have been connected with the missionary career of the apostle Judas Thomas for almost the entirety of Christian history. The tradition that Thomas landed at the island of Malankara—the namesake of the Malankara Orthodox Syrian Church—corroborates the commonly held belief that ancient Indian Christianity was introduced through maritime routes shared between India, Arabia, and Egypt.[40] The *Acts of Thomas* is an apocryphal Syriac text that tells the story of the apostle's sojourn in India and the beginning of Christianity in India.[41] This text has been completely dismissed by many scholars but utterly embraced as historically accurate by many Christian communities. There are many points at which the *Acts* both agrees with and contradicts external historical records. Like many other ancient texts, the *Acts* is often considered a "historical fiction" that embellishes events that are rooted in historical reality.[42] The text claims that Thomas was chosen by lot to evangelize India: "And India fell by lot and division to Judas Thomas the Apostle. And he was not willing to go, saying: 'I have not strength enough for this, because I am weak. And I am a Hebrew: how can I teach the Indians?'"[43] The *Acts* then claims that Thomas encountered a Jewish Indian flute girl, which fits with the theory that Christianity first grew in India among the Jewish Indian community that increased after the destruction of Jerusalem in 70.[44]

---

[40]George Menachery, *The Nazranies* (Trichur: South Asia Research Assistance Services, 1998), 509; Robert Eric Frykenberg, *Christianity in India: From Beginnings to the Present* (New York: Oxford University Press, 2008), 92. Alternative tradition places his arrival on other points on the Malabar coast.

[41]*Acts of Thomas*, ed. A. F. J. Klijn (Leiden: Brill, 2003), 1. The Syriac versions bear unique features such as a poetic composition known as the *Hymn of the Pearl*; M. R. James, *The Apocryphal New Testament* (Oxford: Clarendon, 1924), 1.

[42]James F. McGrath, "History and Fiction in the Acts of Thomas: The State of the Question," *JSP* 17, no. 4 (2008): 306.

[43]*Acts of Thomas*, 17.

[44]Frykenberg, *Christianity in India*, 103. There is the possibility of earlier Jewish presence in India preceding the fall of Jerusalem; George Mark Moraes, *A History of Christianity in India: From Early Times to St. Francis Xavier: AD 52-1542* (Bombay: P. C. Manaktala, 1964), 39; A. Mathias Mundadan, *History of Christianity in India*, vol. 1: *From the Beginning up to the Middle of the Sixteenth Century (up to 1542)* (Bangalore: Theological Publications in India, 1984), 19.

The *Acts* reports that Jesus sold Thomas as a slave to an Indian merchant, who brought the apostle to serve as a carpenter for the Indo-Parthian king Gundaphorus, or Gaspar, whom some consider to be one of the magi who visited the baby Jesus.[45] While the tradition connecting Thomas to India is ultimately uncertain, it is noteworthy that numismatic evidence (i.e., coins) corroborates the existence and reign of an Indian monarch named Gundaphorus. Gundaphorus and his brother Gad, who is also mentioned in the *Acts*, ruled over a vast Indo-Parthian region on both sides of the Indus River between the years 19 and 55.[46] According to the *Acts*, Thomas agreed to use his carpentry skills to build Gundaphorus a palace but was later imprisoned and sentenced to death. Instead of building the palace, Thomas used the funds to help the poor, drawing the anger of the king. But Gundaphorus received a vision from his recently deceased brother imploring him to accept the faith of Thomas, resulting in the conversion of the king: "I beg of you, as a man who begs of a minister of God, that you would pray for me, and beg for me from the God whom you worship, that he would forgive me what I have done you; and that he would make me worthy to enter into the palace which you have built for me; and that I may become a worshipper of this God whom you preach."[47] Thomas then baptized the members of the imperial court, taught the populace the value of celibacy, and administered the Eucharist.[48] After performing many miracles and leading much of the population to the Christian faith, Thomas traveled south, where he attracted the ire of the king and his court: "Karish says to him: 'King Mazdai, I have a new fact to tell you, and a new calamity, which Sifur has brought to India.

---

[45]F. H. Mountney, *The Three Kings of Cologne* (Leominster: Gracewing, 2003), 31. Inscriptional and numismatic evidence places the reign of Gundaphorus during the first half of the first century CE (Moraes, *History of Christianity in India*, 23).

[46]Frykenberg, *Christianity in India*, 98. The claim that Thomas came to Northern India has led to further doubts regarding the historicity of the Thomas tradition, given that most historical and traditional claims place him arriving in the Southern Malabar coast. Some claim that the fall of the Parthian dynasty of Gundaphorus necessitated Thomas's move south (McGrath, "History and Fiction," 303).

[47]*Acts of Thomas*, 69. The emphasis in the *Acts* on celibacy, an overall denigration of the physical world, and a keen focus on special knowledge available through Christ are some of the principle characteristics of the *Acts* that have resulted in its association with Gnosticism (86). The *Acts* also understands Judas Thomas to be the twin brother of Jesus (108).

[48]Some scholars believe that the late nineteenth-century discovery of ancient crosses bearing depictions of royal figures with Christian iconography supports the tradition that Thomas converted royalty in India (Mundadan, *History of Christianity in India*, 34).

A Hebrew, a conjuror, is sitting in his house and never goes out from beside him; and many go in to him, and he teaches them the new God and gives them new laws, which have never been heard of by us."[49]

The Bardaisanite character of the *Acts* is evident in the significant emphasis placed on chastity and the denigration of corporeality and sexuality.[50] Thomas converted many high-ranking officials to Christianity including Vizan, the son of king Mazdai. However, the brand of Christianity advocated by the author of the *Acts* describes conversion to Christianity entailing a vow of celibacy—even for married couples. It is this radical lifestyle commitment, as well as the charge of sorcery, that resulted in Thomas's execution by King Mazdai. After the martyrdom of Thomas, one of Mazdai's sons became possessed, prompting the king to place his faith in Jesus and using the relics of Thomas to heal the prince. King Mazdai then declared his Christian faith and prayed for forgiveness from Sifur, the priest and successor of Thomas.[51] The *Acts* leaves the reader with the perception that the apostolic ministry of Thomas resulted in a significant Christian presence in various regions of India at every social level.[52] Gregory of Tours reported that the Christians of Urhoy had received from a traveler named Theodore the relics of Thomas, which had been originally placed in a shrine in Mylapore.[53] The identification of Calamina as the location of Thomas's martyrdom first appears in the seventh century in Pseudo-Sophronius and is later reiterated by Isidore of Seville.[54]

Eusebius, along with other Roman church historians of the fourth and fifth century who followed his lead, dismissed the *Acts of Thomas* as "heretical"

---

[49]*Acts of Thomas*, 177.

[50]Most scholars have associated the *Acts* with the Bardaisanite brand of Gnosticism, which was prevalent in the Syrian Christian milieu and in which the *Hymn of the Pearl* and the *Acts* were composed. The authorship of the *Hymn on the Pearl* has been commonly assumed to be the Syriac heresiarch Bardaisan. Johan Ferreira, *The Hymn of the Pearl: The Syriac and Greek Texts with Introduction, Translations, and Notes* (Sydney: St. Paul's Publications, 2002), 31. It should be noted, however, that the themes present in the *Acts* and the *Hymn*—namely the imagery of the pearl and robe—are also present in the writings of the anti-Bardaisanite Ephrem the Syrian.

[51]*Acts of Thomas*, 251.

[52]The *Acts* is also unique in its relatively complete narrative unity in comparison to other apocryphal texts, which come to modern editors as piecemeal collections of excerpts. Christine M. Thomas, *The Acts of Peter, Gospel Literature, and the Ancient Novel: Rewriting the Past* (New York: Oxford University Press, 2003), 81.

[53]Moraes, *History of Christianity in India*, 51.

[54]Mundadan, *History of Christianity in India*, 56.

and "absurd," and warned that it should not "even be reckoned among the spurious books."[55] For this reason, the majority of fourth-century Roman historians attribute early Christian missions in India to Bartholomew, while they claim that Thomas went to Parthia (Persia).[56] However, the matter becomes even more geographically complicated in the writings of the Roman historians, who typically divide India into various sections which may refer to the subcontinent as well as the Arabian Peninsula, Iran, Ethiopia, or Nubia. These various regions were often confused or conflated in Hellenistic literature as a result of Greco-Roman racialization and the subsequent association of these regions with "dark" skin. In the unique case of Rufinus's *Church History*, India is reimagined in terms of "Hither" and "Further":

> In the division of the earth which the apostles made by lot for the preaching of God's word, when the different provinces fell to one or the other of them, Parthia, it is said, went by lot to Thomas, to Matthew fell Ethiopia, and Hither India, which adjoins it, went to Bartholomew. Between this country and Parthia, but far inland, lies Further India. Inhabited by many peoples with many different languages, it so distant that the plow of the apostolic preaching had made no furrow in it, but in Constantine's time it received the first seeds of faith.[57]

While the geographical complications raised here must be discussed elsewhere, it is important to note the common Roman historical association of Thomas with Parthia and Bartholomew with "Hither India." Hellenistic historiography commonly conceived of India in two portions, "India maior" and "India minor";[58] however, the terminology of "Hither" and "Further" India is unique to Rufinus.[59] The Arian historian Philostorgius uses similar language in describing the missionary work of Theophilus the Indian, whom Emperor Constantius sent to "the interior of India," a clear reference to

---

[55]Eusebius, *Ecclesiastical History*, 101.

[56]Eusebius, *Ecclesiastical History*, 80. Moffett points out that Indian church history has always dismissed or downplayed the role of Bartholomew as described by Eusebius in order to highlight the importance of Thomas. Yet despite the confusion in the ancient sources, it is significant that the sizable Jewish community of the Malabar coast as well as the numerous claims of apostolic presence in India indicate a very early date for Indian Christianity (Moffett, *Christianity in Asia*, 25).

[57]Rufinus, *Church History*, 18. Rufinus's account corroborates the later Indian Christian tradition that a group of Christians arrived at the Malabar coast in the fourth century, as will be discussed further below.

[58]*Expositio totius mundi et gentium*, ed. Jean Rogué (Paris: Les Éditions du Cerf, 1966), 152-53.

[59]Albrecht Dihle, *Umstrittene Daten: Untersuchungen zum Auftreten der Griechen am Roten Meer* (Köln: Westdeutscher, 1965), 41.

Southern Arabia, given Philostorgius's connection of this region with the Himyarites and Sabeans.[60] Despite the complications arising from Roman historians, contemporary Christian figures closer to the Syriac provenance of traditions surrounding Thomas in India corroborate this ancient tradition. Ephrem the Syrian followed the association of Thomas and India as presented in the *Acts* and was followed in this by many prominent fourth- and fifth-century theologians such as Basil of Caesarea and Jerome.[61] The *Breviary of the Church of Antioch*, attributed to Ephrem, states:

> Blessed are thou, Thomas, the Twin, in thy deeds. Twin is thy spiritual power;
> nor one thy power, nor one thy name: But many and signal are they; re-
> nowned is thy name among the Apostles. From my lowly state thee I haste
> to sing. Blessed art thou, like unto the solar ray from the great orb; thy
> grateful dawn India's painful darkness doth dispel. Thou the great lap, one
> among the Twelve, with oil from the Cross replenished, India's dark night
> floodest with light.[62]

Ephrem mentioned Thomas's sojourn to India and the removal of his relics to Urhoy in several of his writings.[63] However, the Roman historian Jerome—relying heavily on the account provided by Eusebius—claimed that the Alexandrian theologian Pantaenus traveled to India to "preach Christ to the Brahmans and philosophers there."[64] The earliest internal account reporting the Thomas tradition was the early seventeenth-century *Thomma Parvam* ("Song of Thomas"), which reported that Thomas's mission resulted in over seventeen thousand converts evenly spread across the various castes.[65] Some of these early Indian narratives of the Christian tradition provide conflicting accounts that are disputed among contemporary Thomas Christian communities. There are also many modern Brahman-caste families who bear ancient stone crosses and claim succession from the original Thomasine converts.[66] During the persecution of Christians in Persia under Shapur II

---

[60]Philostorgius, *Church History*, ed. Edward Walford (London: Henry G. Bohn, 1955), 22.

[61]Baum and Winkler, *Church of the East*, 52.

[62]Cyril Bruce Firth, *An Introduction to Indian Church History* (Madras: Christian Literature Society, 1961), 6.

[63]Scott F. Johnson, *Literary Territories: Cartographical Thinking in Late Antiquity* (New York: Oxford University Press, 2016), 112.

[64]Moffett, *Christianity in Asia*, 36.

[65]Frykenberg, *Christianity in India*, 100.

[66]Placid J. Popidara, *The Thomas Christians* (Madras: Darton, Longman, and Todd, 1970).

in the mid-fourth century, Persian Christian migrants began to resettle along the Malabar coast and were welcomed by the governmental authorities of Kerala. Ancient immigration songs, such as the *Valiyapalli*, report a group of seventy-two Persian Christian families led by a wealthy Jewish Christian merchant named Thomman Kinnān ("Thomas of Cana") and a bishop named Uraha Mar Yausef who arrived in India in the mid-340s:

> For great devotion he started
> With delight from the country of Uz [Babylon]
> On that day Kinay Thomma
> With seventy-two families[67]

There are extant copies of copper plates from this period that served as receipts for the land and royal privileges afforded these Persian Jewish-Christian migrants, who enjoyed such privileges due to their claim of descent from King David.[68] Only a few years after the arrival of Thomman Kinnān and his group, the missionary Theophilus the Indian—a native of the Maldive Islands—traveled from Arabia to India and reported the existence of Christian communities there. The events surrounding Theophilus the Indian's arrival are recorded in Philostorgius's *Church History*, providing an interesting account of the nature of Indian Christianity during the fourth century:

> Theophilus, then, having settled the various matters with the Himyarites as far as was possible in each case, as opportunity allowed, and having consecrated the churches and decorated them as best he could, sailed off to the island of Diva, which, as has been said, was his homeland. From there he went on to the rest of the Indian country, where he corrected much that was not being done by them in a lawful way. They would, for instance, listen to the gospel readings while seated, and they did other things not permitted by divine law. When, however, he had amended each of these matters with a view to their reverence and love of God, he confirmed the church's teaching. For, says our heretic, they had not need of instruction to correct their worship, since they had held to the doctrine of "other in substance" unfailingly from the beginning.[69]

---

[67]Jacob Kollaparambil, *The Babylonian Origin of the Southists Among the St. Thomas Christians* (Rome: Pont. Institutum Studiorum Orientalium, 1992), 23.

[68]T. K. Joseph, *Malabar Christians and their Ancient Documents* (Trivandrum: Popular Press, 1929), 3-7.

[69]Philostorgius, *Church History*, 42. "Says our heretic": The original version of Philostorgius's work is lost; the surviving manuscript is an epitome by the Constantinopolitan patriarch Photius.

The account of Philostorgius provides an Arian gloss to the history of Christianity in India that presupposes this particular strand of Christianity as that which was communicated originally by the apostle Bartholomew, whose very connection to India is a confusion rooted in Eusebius. Despite the report found in Philostorgius, there is no evidence that the Christians of fourth-century India were Arian in persuasion, as most available evidence connects the early Thomas Christians to the Persian church centered in Seleucia-Ctesiphon. The account of Philostorgius claims that Theophilus "corrected" the Indian liturgical practice of sitting during the reading of the Gospels, an unlikely claim that yet reveals indigenous liturgical practices unique to earliest Indian Christianity.[70]

In the mid-sixth century, an Egyptian monk named Cosmas Indicopleustes ("Indian traveler") recorded one of the most expansive journeys at that time, nearly a millennium before the journeys of Marco Polo. In his *Christian Topography*, Cosmas provides eyewitness accounts of the Christian communities of Ethiopia, Arabia, Persia, India, and Sri Lanka:

> Even in Taprobane [Sri Lanka], an island in Further India, where the Indian sea is, there is a Church of Christians, with clergy and a body of believers, but I know not whether there be any Christians in the parts beyond it. In the country called Male [the Malabar coast], where the pepper grow, there is also a church, and at another place called Calliana there is moreover a bishop, who is appointed from Persia.[71]

Cosmas later describes in significant detail his voyages throughout Sri Lanka, as well as the nation's political, social, and ecological dynamics. Cosmas relays the story of an Egyptian businessman named Sopatrus who enjoyed significant influence and privileges at the benevolence of the Sri Lankan king. However, it is his description of the Christian situation in Sri Lanka that provides a glimpse into early South Asian Christianity:

> This is a large oceanic island lying in the Indian sea. By the Indians is it called Sielediba, but by the Greeks Taprobane. . . . The island has also a church of Persian Christians who have settled there, and a Presbyter who is appointed from Persia, and a Deacon and a complete ecclesiastical ritual. But the natives

---

[70]Joseph A. Jungmann, *The Mass of the Roman Rite* (New York: Benziger, 1951), 1:448-49; Frykenberg, *Christianity in India*, 110.

[71]Cosmas Indicopleustes, *Christian Topography*, ed. J. W. McCrindle (New York: Cambridge University Press, 2010), 118-19.

and their kings are heathens [*allofuloi*]. In this island they have many temples and one, which stands on an eminence, there is a hyacinth as large as a great pine-cone, fiery red, and when seen flashing from a distance, especially if the sun's rays are playing round it, a matchless sight. The island being, as it is, in a central position, is much frequented by ships from all parts of India and from Persia and Ethiopia, and it likewise sends out many of its own. And from the remotest countries.[72]

Cosmas's reinforcement of the long-held connection between Indian and Persian Christianity clarifies the theological orientation of early South Asian Christians, who would likely have been unfamiliar with Arianism. Despite Cosmas's observation that the natives were "heathen" while the majority of Christians in this region were Persian (known as *Tarisapalli*), this period witnessed an increased consolidation of the Christian tradition with local Malabar culture and society. In some cases, Christian communities operated contrary to the hierarchy of *jati* (caste) by being inclusive across socioeconomic and ethnic stratification. The Islamic conquest of Persia resulted in increased numbers of Persian Christian migrants to the Malabar region, where they continued to enjoy social capital. Communication between the catholicos of Seleucia-Ctesiphon and the bishops of India became complicated during the beginning of the Arab Muslim conquest but was later improved by Timothy of Baghdad in the ninth century.[73]

Figure 4.1. Nasrani cross with Persian inscription, Kadamattom Church, Kerala, India

---

[72]Cosmas Indicopleustes, *Christian Topography*, 365.
[73]Firth, *Indian Church History*, 27.

The wall of Islamic hegemony that cut India off from the Persian and Roman worlds resulted in the churches of India developing a more distinct identity. Even so-called polluting or untouchable (Āvarna) members of society were allowed into Christian communities. Yet Indian Christians did embrace elements of Indian cultural values. Thomas Christians were predominately divided between the descendants of the converts of Thomman

Figure 4.2. Icon from St. Thomas Cathedral in Palai, Kerala state, India, sixteenth century

Kinān—known as the Southists, or *Tekkumbhāgar*—and the Northists, or *Vatakkumbhāgar*, who claimed to be the descendants of the converts of the apostle Thomas. Many Thomas Christians existed in the middle Kshatriya Vaishya castes. In particular, many Southists were of the Nayar—a caste of barbers local to the Kerala region— and maintained many traditions including recognizing Hindu holidays and observing ritual purity by avoiding certain foods and dead bodies (*pulakuli*).[74] Contextualization of Indian Christianity is vividly captured in this tradition's proliferation of unique crosses typically accompanied by a dove, adorned on sides with petals and emerging from a lotus flower—the symbol of enlightenment in Buddhist iconography.[75] These beautiful and contextual crosses, often called Nasrani crosses, are a fantastic example of how the gospel adapted to local culture and extant religious imagery. A little after this time, the Celtic crosses of northwestern Europe began to emerge and are commonly thought to have deployed a similar fusion of Christian and traditional religious imagery. However, the Celtic cross has been promulgated throughout the Western world to a much higher degree than the Nasrani crosses of India. Because

---

[74]Frykenberg, *Christianity in India*, 115.
[75]Moraes, *History of Christianity in India*, 78.

of the prevalence of the white, Western captivity of Christianity throughout South Asia, it is necessary to place special emphasis on early examples of Indian Christian contextualization efforts in order to encourage such work to continue in the modern church.

The cultural uniqueness and social autonomy of Thomas Christians along the Malabar coast reached a zenith during the semiautonomous Christian kingdom whose center was Udayamperur. The existence of an autonomous Christian kingdom in the Kerala region is attested in the chronicle of the fifteenth-century Italian historian Poggi Bracciolini: "There arrived another person from Upper India, towards the north. He says that there is a kingdom twenty days' journey from Cathay, of which the king and all the inhabitants are Christians, but heretics, being said to be Nestorians."[76] The label "Nestorian" used by Bracciolini indicates that East Syriac continued to be the liturgical language for the majority of Indian Christians, a situation that persists into the present for many of the ancient Thomas Christian communities. Even after the arrival of Portuguese Jesuits in the late fifteenth century, this autonomous and indigenous Christian society continued to flourish. While Western missionary and political interventions have resulted in the fragmentation and division of various Indian Christian communities, the majority of them root their Christian origin in the uniquely Indian tradition initiated by the apostle Thomas. Despite the debatable issues surrounding the beginnings of Christianity in India, it is clear that Christianity came into the subcontinent very early due to the missionary work of East Syriac Persian Christians. While the perception of Christianity as a Western religion is prominent in India this side of European colonialism, it is necessary for modern Christians to familiarize themselves with the early, non-Western Christian origins of the Indian church and to support indigenous mission efforts to contextualize the gospel in the various cultures of the subcontinent.

CENTRAL ASIA

One of the earliest and most detailed references to Christianity in Central Asia came in 549 in the biography of Mar Aba who was catholicos of the Church of the East during the mid-sixth century. The *History of Mar Aba* reports that

---

[76]Moraes, *History of Christianity in India*, 68.

the catholicos consecrated a bishop for the already strong Christian community in the region of the White Huns, northeast of Persian territory:

> And after little time passed, the king of the Hephthalites [*haptrāye*] sent a priest to the King of Kings, and many Christian Hephthalites wrote letters to the Saint [Mar Aba] so that he would send a priest that would be commissioned from there by the King of Kings as a bishop for the entire Hephthalite kingdom. After the priest had come before the King, and he learned of the affair for which he was sent, the King of Kings wondered at what he heard concerning this, and marveled at the great power of Jesus. The Christian Hephthalites also considered the Lordly One [Mar Aba] as their chief and regent, and he said to him that he should go and adorn the church according to custom, and should go into his church and house and collect the bishops according to custom, and ordain the man sent by the king of the Hephthalites. . . . The following morning the church was adorned with a multitude of believers; the Saint appointed the Hephthalite priest as bishop for the land of the Hephthalites [*beyt haptrāye*], and in the people of the Lord joy grew over the provision by divine providence.[77]

The late antique kingdom known to the Greeks as *Hephthalites*, to Arabs, Persians, and Armenians as *Haytal*, and to Indians as *Hunas* (or Huns), was a Central Asian ethnic group that organized a powerful kingdom and established independence from Persia in the early fifth century. Until the decline of this civilization in the sixth century, the Hephthalites were the dominant political and social force in Central Asia. Before the coming of Christianity to Hephthalite territory in the mid-sixth century, the religious landscape was predominately Zoroastrian and hostile toward Buddhism.[78] In his *Wars*, Roman historian Procopius claimed that the Hephthalites were of the same stock as the Huns but lived far from other Huns, just northeast of Persian territory. The name "White Huns" comes from Procopius's reference to their skin complexion: "They are the only ones among the Huns who have white

---

[77] *History of Mar Aba*, ed. Paul Bedjan, in *Histoire de Mar Jabalaha et de trois autres patriarches, d'un prête et de deux laïques, nestoriens* (Leipzig: Otto Harrasssowitz, 1895), 266-69. "Adorn the church according to custom": the "custom" or "culture" (*'yde*) with which one of the earliest Central Asian churches was to be built likely refers to traditions common to the Persian Christian culture, indicating a degree of cultural assimilation at the beginning of Central Asian missions.

[78] B. A. Litvinsky, *History of Civilizations of Central Asia*, vol. 3: *The Crossroads of Civilizations: AD 250 to 750* (Delhi: Motilal Banarsidass, 1996), 147.

bodies and countenances which are not ugly."[79] Procopius also claimed that the Hephthalites were not nomadic like other Hunnic groups but had a centralized monarchy centered in a city called Gorgo. That the *History of Mar Aba* reports an already established Christian community indicates that Christianity entered Central Asia from Persia sooner than the mid-sixth century. During the period of the *History of Mar Aba*, the Hephthalites controlled the oasis town of Merv in modern Turkmenistan. Merv was the launching pad of East Syriac Christianity from Persia into Central Asia and produced one of the most significant Central Asian Christian writers, Ishodad. While Ishodad of Merv eventually served as an East Syriac bishop in the interior of Persian territory in Hdatta, he represents perhaps the most prominent Christian writer of Central Asian background.[80] Ishodad wrote various biblical commentaries in Syriac and drew on both Miaphysite West Syriac as well as Antiochene Greek exegetical traditions and was the first prominent East Syriac theologian since the time of Narsai and Babai the Great.

One of the most significant discoveries for Central Asian Christianity is the Shūï-pang monastery discovered in Bulayiq, a city in the modern northwest Xinjiang province of China. The majority of manuscripts found at Bulayiq are from no earlier than the ninth century; however, the monastery itself is thought to have been founded earlier, perhaps in the early fifth century.[81] It is also unknown exactly when the monastery closed, but there is clear evidence of activity as late as the thirteenth century.[82] Bulayiq was located in the Turfan oasis, a region that served both as a center of Silk Road commerce and East Syriac missionary activity. Many of the manuscripts at this monastery were East Syriac Christian texts. Discovered in the early

---

[79] Anthony Kaldellis, *Ethnography After Antiquity: Foreign Lands and Peoples in Byzantine Literature* (Philadelphia: University of Pennsylvania Press, 2013), 17.

[80] Clemens Leonhard, *Ishodad of Merw's Exegesis of the Psalms 119 and 139–147: A Study of His Interpretation in the Light of the Syriac Translation of Theodore of Mopsuestia's Commentary* (Louvain: Peeters, 2001), 11; Margaret Dunlop Gibson, *The Commentaries of Isho 'dad of Merv, Bishop of Hedatha (c. 850 AD) in Syriac and English* (New York: Cambridge University Press, 1911), vii.

[81] Kenneth J. Thomas, *A Restless Search: A History of Persian Translations of the Bible* (Atlanta: Nida Institute for Biblical Scholarship, 2015), 40. Mark Dickens has suggested that Christianity may have reached Bulayiq due to the exodus of Christians from China because of the anti-Christian (as well as anti-Manichean, anti-Zoroastrian, and anti-Buddhist) persecutions in ninth-century Tang China. "Scribal Practices in the Turfan Christian Community," *JCSSS* 13 (2013): 4.

[82] Erica C. D. Hunter, "Syriac, Sogdian and Old Uyghur Manuscripts from Bulayïq," in *The History Behind the Languages: Essays of Turfan Forum on Old Languages of the Silk Road*, ed. Academia Turfanica (Shanghai: Shanghai guji chubanshe, 2012), 88.

twentieth century, the Bulayiq monastery provides invaluable insight into Central Asian Christianity as the library of the monastery contained hundreds of manuscripts written primarily in Syriac, Uyghur (a Central Asian language still spoken by the ethnic group of the same name in northwestern China), and Sogdian (a language and people group that existed in modern Uzbekistan and Tajikistan and were active merchants along the Silk Road for the entire first millennium after Christ).

First mentioned in Persian documents from the sixth century BCE, the Sogdians established a commercial trade that lasted over fifteen hundred years and were among the most active merchants across the Silk Road due to their central location amidst Persia, China, and India.[83] Given the condition of maritime winds, the land route through Sogdian territory was often the fastest route across the Eurasian steppe.[84] Because Syriac was the dominant language of the Persian Church of the East, a missiological problem arose as Christianity entered into new areas in Central Asia. The biography of the seventh-century East Syriac monastic saint John of Dailam reports ethnic and linguistic tension between Syriac-speaking and Persian-speaking Christians in central Persia and disagreement over which language would be used during liturgy.[85] John of Dailam's response to this dilemma as reported in his biography was to create culturally distinct monasteries for the Syriac and Persian Christians:

> Now the Persian and Syrian brethren quarreled with each other over the services: the Persians said, "We should all recite the services in our language, seeing that we live in Persian territory"; while the Syrian said, "Our father is a Syrian, and so we should recite the services in our language, on account of the founder of the monastery; furthermore we do not know how to recite the services in Persian." When Mar Yohannan [John] saw the quarrel that had arisen, he pacified the brethren and prayed to God with deep feeling. Thereupon he was told in a revelation from God: "Build them another monastery the other side of the river, opposite this one, resembling it in every

---

[83]Étienne de la Vaissière, *Sogdian Traders: A History* (Leiden: Brill, 2005), 13.

[84]Susan Whitfield, *Life along the Silk Road*, 2nd ed. (Oakland: University of California Press, 2015), 12.

[85]Chiara Barbati, *The Christian Sogdian Gospel Lectionary E5 in Context* (Vienna: Verlag der Österreichischen Akademie der Wissenschaften, 2016), 21; Nicholas Sims-Williams, *The Life of Serapion and Other Christian Sogdian Texts from the Manuscripts E25 and E26* (Turnhout: Brepols, 2015), 57.

respect. Let the Persians live in one, and the Syrians in the other." So he built another monastery just like the first, and the Syrian brethren lived there. Thus the quarrel between the brethren was resolved.[86]

This excerpt illustrates the significant degree to which Syriac functioned as the dominant liturgical language and how this created cultural struggles especially with Persian Christians. However, Sogdian was used for liturgy and theology more often because the Sogdian language had an expansive mercantile presence along the Silk Road. In fact, Central Asian missionaries strategically deployed the Sogdian language in evangelization due to the vast geographical presence of the language.[87] The Sogdian region was centered in Samarkand, which served as a major center of Central Asian Christianity beginning no later than the eighth century.[88] Samarkand, as well as Kashgar further east, established East Syriac archbishoprics by the mid-seventh century.[89] The missionary expansion of the Church of the East centered in Persia throughout Central Asia at the turn of the ninth century was in large part due to the administration of Patriarch Timothy I, who took an active interest in establishing churches and bishoprics across the Asian continent.[90] It was during the same time that the Bulayiq manuscripts were being written that Christianity was making significant inroads in Tibet. East Syriac inscriptions and crosses near the Tibetan town of Lhasa date to the mid-ninth century, which was also the time of the missionary journey of a Sodgian monk named Nösh-farn to the Tibetan khan.[91]

Another church was founded at the turn of the tenth century further north in the Turfan oasis in the ancient Uighur capital of Kocho (Kaochang). One of the frescos of this church depicts a Sogdian priest holding a liturgical chalice administering the sacraments for Turkic and Chinese

---

[86]*Life of John of Dailam*, ed. Sebastian P. Brock, *Parole de l'Orient* 10 (1981–1982): 150–51. The East Syriac version of the *Life* reported that the Syriac-speaking Christians received a bigger monastery than the Persians (172).

[87]Chiara Barbati, "Syriac into Middle Iranian: A Translation Studies Approach to Sogdian and Pahlavi Manuscripts Within the Church of the East," in *Translation Techniques in the Ancient and Oriental Cultures*, ed. Artemij Keidan (Berlin: De Gruyter, 2015), 445.

[88]The biography of the ninth-century Byzantine missionary Constantine the Philosopher attests to the presence of Christians among the Sougds—or Sogdians (De la Vaissière, *Sogdian Traders*, 245).

[89]Richard Foltz, *Religions of the Silk Road: Premodern Patterns of Globalization*, 2nd ed. (New York: Palgrave Macmillan, 1999), 65.

[90]Barbati, *Gospel Lectionary*, 17.

[91]Wilhelm and Baum, *Church of the East*, 50.

congregants.[92] The dominant picture of Central Asian Christianity that emerges from textual and material evidence is that Sogdian and Persian Christians constituted much of the church leadership, while Turkic and other ethnic groups—considered to be of a lower social strata—composed the laity.[93] This may in part be why it was the heretical Manicheans that came to dominate the Uighur Empire during this same time period. The Uyghurs occupied much of the northern steppe area and, with the support of the Chinese Tang dynasty in the mid-eighth century, consolidated their power across much of northern Central Asia to form the Uyghur kingdom (or khaganate). The Uyghur khaganate is unique in being the only recorded nation to adopt Manichaeism as the state religion. Likely in an attempt to distance themselves from their Chinese Tang allies, the Uyghur khaghan Mo-yu accepted Manichaeism as the national religion after being proselytized by Sogdian Manichean merchants. Tensions between the Uyghur Khaganate and the Tang administration—much of which centered on a heightened sense of Uyghur independence, much to the chagrin of Tang officials[94]—left the Uyghurs defenseless against their quick defeat by neighboring Turkic Kirghiz a century later.[95]

Initiated by the Persian figure Mani in the mid-third century, Manichaeism purported to be a synthesis and culmination of various religious teachings—Buddhism, Zoroastrianism, Taoism, and Christianity—and holds its founder to be the reincarnation of Zoroaster, Buddha, Lao-tzu, Jesus, and the Paraclete. Grounded in a specific form of dualism, light and dark are thought to be trapped in the cosmos and must be separated through a specific eating ritual performed by the "elect" for the salvation of the "hearers."[96] Manicheans were

---

[92]H. J. Klimkeit, "Manichaeism and Nestorian Christianity," in *History of Civilizations of Central Asia*, vol. 4: *The Age of Achievement: AD 750 to the End of the Fifteenth Century, Part Two: The Achievements*, ed. C. E. Bosworth and M. S. Asimov (Delhi: Motilal Banarsidass, 2003), 73.

[93]Ian Gillman and Hans-Joachim Klimkeit, *Christians in Asia before 1500* (New York: Routledge, 1999), 225.

[94]Uighur Manichaeism likely had a decidedly national flavor given its marked influence by Uighur Shamanism/Tengrism. Lyndon A. Arden-Wong, "Some Thoughts on Manichaean Architecture and Its Applications in the Eastern Uighur Khaganate," in *Between Rome and China: History, Religions and Material Culture of the Silk Road*, ed. Samuel N. C. Lieu and Gunner B. Mikkelsen (Turnhout: Brepols, 2016), 225.

[95]Samuel N. C. Lieu, *Manichaeism in the Later Roman Empire and Medieval China: A Historical Survey* (Manchester: Manchester University Press, 1985), 196.

[96]Jason David BeDuhn, *The Manichaean Body: In Discipline and Ritual* (Baltimore: Johns Hopkins University Press, 2000), 22.

Figure 4.3. Wall painting depicting a Church of the East priest from Persia ministering in a church with Central Asian congregants, from Khocho in the Turfan Oasis (modern Xinjiang, China), eighth century

severely persecuted by Christians, Muslims, and Zoroastrians in all parts of the world—especially in the Roman Empire. Even Mani himself was imprisoned and died under the Persian shah Bahram I. However, across Central and East Asia, Manichaeism flourished with relative ease alongside its East Syriac Christian neighbors. Buddhist, Taoist, Zoroastrian, Mongol, and Muslim authorities—as well as European travelers like Marco Polo—often conflated these two religions as they appeared throughout Central Asia. This was in part because Manicheans would often claim to be Christian. East Syriac Christians, however, disassociated themselves from Manicheans and denounced them as heretics.[97] One such example comes from a fragmentary

---

[97]Samuel N. C. Lieu, *Manichaeism in Central Asia and China* (Leiden: Brill, 1998), 187. Manicheans were often confused for Buddhists as well due to its more highly Sinicized nature in comparison to East Syriac Christianity.

Sogdian text that critiques local Sogdian Manicheans for the alleged belief in the eternality of Satan: "If it should be as we Christians say, that the eternal God created the angels; and souls too, (as) spiritual (beings), nevertheless he did not create and fashion (them) from his own nature but by his grace and mercy; moreover they did not become capable—neither angels nor souls—of completely attaining the eternity of God."[98]

The religious power dynamics in Central Asia shifted when Islam began to make significant inroads through the Persian Samanid Empire centered in Bukhara (modern Uzbekistan). During the ninth and tenth centuries, the Samanids brought Islamic theology into the Persian language and consolidated power across modern Afghanistan, Pakistan, and Uzbekistan.[99] In 893, the Samanid emir Isma'il ibn Ahmed conquered much of Central Asia including the Turkic town of Talas in modern Kazakhstan. Talas had an East Syriac church that Isma'il converted into a mosque.[100] The Samanids were zealous for the conversion of Persian, Turkic, and broader Central Asian society to Islam. The Islamicization of Central Asia was advanced by the defeat of the Byzantine Empire by the Islamic Turkic Empire of the Seljuks at the Battle of Manzikert in 1071.

The rise of Seljuk hegemony throughout Anatolia initiated the Islamicization of Turkish society and intensified the expansion of Islam along the Silk Road. The conquest and conversion of the Sogdians—the principle people and language around which both Silk Road trade and Central Asian Christian missions centered—at the turn of the eleventh century resulted simultaneously in the decrease of Christian missions and the decline of the Sogdian language, as it was supplanted by Persian.[101] This is likely due to the fact that, while adaptation to the local Sogdian context was present, much of Sogdian Christianity was dependent on the dominant Syriac culture to

---

[98]Sims-Williams, *Life of Serapion*, 27. Sims-Williams also points out that the argumentation here is based on the false assumption that Manicheans hold all eternal beings to be good (33). While it is likely that the text misconstrues Manichean doctrine, what is of note is the degree to which Sogdian Christians distinguished themselves from Manicheans and contended for Christian orthodoxy.

[99]Robert L Canfield, *Turko-Persia in Historical Perspective* (New York: Cambridge University Press, 2002), 12.

[100]René Grousset, *The Empire of the Steppes: A History of Central Asia* (New Brunswick, NJ: Rutgers University Press, 1970), 142.

[101]Baum and Winkler, *Church of the East*, 76.

the west, "the language of prestige."[102] However, Christianity did not completely disappear as it was during this time that the Turkic Öngüt tribe of modern northern China converted to Christianity.[103] The religious landscape of Central Asia continued to be altered when a significant challenge to Islamic dominance appeared in the form of one of the most powerful and expansive empires in world history.

The Mongolian opposition to Islamic hegemony in Central Asia arose first through the khan Yeh-lü Ta-shih and the Kara-Khitai Khaganate in 1130. A native of northern China, Yeh-lü Ta-shih led the remnants of the Liao dynasty (907–1125) westward after the rise of the Jin dynasty (1115–1234) to establish the Kara-Khitai Empire at the border of what is now Xinjiang, Kyrgyzstan, and Tajikistan. Due to their Sinitic ancestry, the Liao rulers of the Kara-Khitai Empire were Buddhist and Confucian in religious orientation and were hostile to Islamic Persian and Turkic empires to the west. This allowed Christians to begin to flourish again in Central Asian territory. While Mongolian civilization was predominately Buddhist, Confucian, or Tengrian,[104] Christians experienced tolerance and support. The heightened autonomy experienced by Christians would continue when the rulers of Kara-Khitai were overthrown and replaced by the most significant Mongolian ruler in history—Genghis Khan.

---

[102]Barbati, *Gospel Lectionary*, 92. In her study on the Gospel lectionary found at the Bulayiq monastery, Barbati demonstrates the linguistic adaptation of the original Syriac text into Sogdian in the late tenth century. While much of its translation involved significant degrees of inculturation, Sogdian translators made significant efforts to stick closely to the Syriac originals due to the sense among Sogdian Christians that the Syriac people were the "donors" of Christianity. Hunter likens the role of Syriac across Asia to that of Latin throughout medieval and the early modern Christian West ("Syriac, Sogdian and Old Uyghur," 82).

[103]Tjalling H. F. Halbertsma, *Early Christian Remains of Inner Mongolia: Discovery, Reconstruction and Appropriation*, 2nd ed. (Leiden: Brill, 2015), 37.

[104]*Tenger* refers to the "sky" or Eternal Heaven common to Turkic and Mongol cosmology (Halbertsma, *Early Christian Remains*, 36); it is the highest deity in many early Central Asian shamanistic religions. The term *Tengrism* is not used to describe a specific religion but is deployed in modern religious scholarship to denote the specific form of shamanism prevalent in much of medieval Central Asia. Halbertsma claims that the continued use of *Tenger* among Turkic and Mongol Christian tribes demonstrates the syncretistic nature of Central Asian Christianity. This assessment is unwarranted, however; the practice should rather be seen as an example of contextualization, much like the English adoption of the pagan Anglo-Saxon concept of heaven. Frederick Metcalfe, *The Englishman and the Scandinavian: Or, a Comparison of Anglo-Saxon and Old Norse Literature* (London: Trübner & Co., 1880), 484.

Temüjin (or Genghis Khan) rose to prominence in the early thirteenth century, consolidated various nomadic Central Asian peoples, and launched a violent invasion of much of the Eurasian steppe that resulted in the largest contiguous empire in human history. The increased presence of Christians during the Mongolian Empire was immense. The famous visit of the Franciscan friar William of Rubruck to Möngke Khan—the fourth Great Khan and grandson to Genghis Khan—is believed to have been an attempt by King Louis IX to build an alliance against the Islamic Ayyubid dynasty.[105] The French monarch supposed Möngke Khan to be a Christian, and Rubruck confirmed the existence of Christians in the court of the khan. Möngke had an East Syriac wife and his brother, the prince Ariq-bögä, was reported by Rubruck to be a Christian. Since the formulation of the Mongol Empire under Genghis Khan, intermarriage between Mongol rulers and East Syriac Christians was commonplace. Most khans remained Tengrian while they placed value on Christian spouses and revered them as fitting parents.

The *Secret History of the Mongols*, the earliest and most important extant Mongolian-language text, describes in great detail the conquests of Genghis Khan. It is telling that the *Secret History* makes no mention of Buddhism or Christianity but focuses solely on the role of Genghis Khan as supreme ruler ordained by Heaven and Earth. Among many of Genghis Khan's progeny who married Christians was his son Tolui. Yet, despite his marriage to a Christian, Tolui is described as engaging in Tengrian "sorcery."[106] The *Secret History* describes the Christian spouse of Tolui, Sorkaktani, and other Christian royal spouses as helpful wives and mothers. It is likely the perception of them as ideal in-laws that attracted Mongol rulers to Christian spouses while Christian theology likely made little to no impact on Mongol imperial religion. Yet the presence of Christians in the Mongol imperial court resulted in unprecedented freedom for Central Asian Christians as a result of the Pax Mongolica. Beginning with the children of Genghis Khan, every khan of the Mongol Empire for the next century had either a Christian

---

[105]Frances Wood, *The Silk Road: Two Thousand Years in the Heart of Asia* (Berkeley: University of California Press, 2002), 118. Wood confuses Möngke with his predecessor and cousin Güyük.
[106]*The Secret History of the Mongols*, ed. Fráncis Woodman Cleaves (Cambridge, MA: Harvard University Press, 1982), 213.

mother, wife, or both.[107] Prince Tolui's wife Sorkaktani was a member of the Keraite tribe, a Turco-Mongol nation that had accepted East Syriac Christianity two centuries before the rise of Genghis Khan.

The West Syriac (Miaphysite) historian Bar Hebraeus recounted the conversion of the Keraites (whom he refers to as *Kayreth* of the inner *Turkaye* region) during the mid-tenth century in his *Ecclesiastical Chronicle*. According to Bar Hebraeus, the Keraite khan received a vision of a Christian saint who guided him out of the wilderness after he got lost. The khan then requested to meet with the council of Christian merchants who regularly traveled to the Keraite region, who informed him of the importance of baptism and fasting. This account further attests to the significance of Silk Road merchants in the growth of early Central Asian Christianity. Christianity was predominant for the Mongol-Yuan-era Keraites, as most of them attested in history were Christians, and many of whom served in the Mongol imperial court.[108] The khan requested that he and the reported two thousand Keraite Christians be baptized but expressed concern about fasting as the Keraites relied only on milk and meat. The East Syriac patriarch allowed the Keraites to drink milk during fasting "provided that foods which were suitable for seasons of fasting were not, as they said, found in that country."[109] The patriarch also sent elders and deacons to the Keraites and instructed them to teach the Keraites "Christian customs" (*'ede dkrestyane*). The vagueness of this statement raises curiosity as to the degree to which these *'ede* ("customs") were cultural or spiritual in nature—especially given that this word in Syriac typically refers to cultural "habits."[110] However, what is clear in the report provided by Bar Hebraeus is the degree to which Central Asian Christians experienced cultural subjugation to the East Syriac Christianity centered in Persia. This is evidenced in the liturgical regulations imposed from Persia on the Keraite khan, despite his expressed concern at the difficulty of Persian Christian traditions for the local Keraite culture.

While the Syriac language and its theological tradition have been largely unknown and often marginalized in the Western Christian world, it is a

---

[107]Jack Weatherford, *Genghis Khan and the Quest for God: How the World's Greatest Conqueror Gave Us Religious Freedom* (New York: Viking, 2016), 103.

[108]Li Tang, *East Syriac Christianity in Mongol-Yuan China* (Wiesbaden: Harrassowitz, 2011), 28.

[109]Bar Hebraeus, *Ecclesiastical Chronicle*, 398.

[110]Jessie Payne Smith, *A Compendious Syriac Dictionary* (Oxford: Clarendon, 1903), 403.

sobering reality that as it spread throughout Central Asia, Syriac-speaking Christians enacted their own form of cultural captivity. Available evidence indicates that Syriac was seen as the best language in which to worship, while Turkic, Mongolian, Persian, Sogdian, and other languages were seen as subservient. This is a reminder to ethnic minority groups in the modern world to be cautious of similar micro-oppressions that all people groups can commit. To use an example from modern times, when the autonomous Ethiopian church (based in South Africa) was being established in the late nineteenth century by South African pastors who were disenchanted with the paternalistic oversight of the Church of England, their initial desire was to merge with the African Methodist Episcopal Church—the oldest African-American denomination. However, the Ethiopian church eventually joined the Anglican Church of South Africa as many leaders felt that the African-American leadership was just as unfavorable as the earlier British authorities.[111] As marginalized groups move into intercultural church partnerships, it is important not to revisit the same kind of cultural imperialism on others as has been practiced by the dominant culture.

Even though theological deference to the Syriac language and culture was prevalent in medieval Central Asian Christianity, there were yet many Christians of various cultures, especially among the Keraites. Many Christians of the Mongol court and populace were of the Keraite group. The famous European legend of Prester John—an East Syriac king among Islamic rulers—was often thought to be a Keraite member of the Mongol court.[112] William of Rubruck reported Prince Ariq-bögä supervising Christian liturgy and "extending his hand to us, making the sign of the cross in the manner of the bishops."[113] Various European travelers to Mongol territory during the thirteenth and fourteenth centuries provide eyewitness accounts of Mongol Christianity. The Venetian merchant traveler Marco Polo testified to the existence of East Syriac churches in the city of Kashgar (in the modern Xinjiang province of northwest China) in his *Book of the Marvels of the World*: "There are in the country many Nestorian Christians, who have churches of their own. The people of the country have a peculiar

---

[111]William David Spencer, *Dread Jesus* (London: SPCK, 1999), 11.
[112]Grousset, *Empire of the Steppes*, 191.
[113]*Secret History of the Mongols*, 281.

language, and the territory extends for five days' journey."[114] The account of Marco Polo is consistent with that of Rubruck, who claimed that the dominant faith of the Mongols was East Syriac Christianity. Throughout his account, Rubruck demeans the unique customs of Mongol Christians and only displays interest where similarities can be found with Western Roman Christian tradition:

> Holy Thursday and Easter were nigh, and I did not have our vestments, and I was considering the manner of doing of the Nestorians [J: I was observing the way the Nestorians consecrated], and was greatly worried about what I should do, whether I should receive the sacrament from them, whether I should say mass in their vestments, with their chalice and on their altar, or whether I should wholly abstain from the sacrament. Then came a great number of Christians, Hungarians, Alans, Ruthenians, Georgians, Hermenians, all of whom had not seen the sacrament since their capture, for the Nestorians would not admit them into their church, so they said, unless they were re-baptized by them. However (the Nestorians) had not told us anything of all this; on the contrary, they confessed that the Roman Church was the head of all churches, and that they should receive their patriarch from the Pope, if the roads were open. And they offered us freely their sacrament, and made us stand in the entry of the choir to see their way of doing, and, on Easter eve (11th April), beside the font to see their mode of baptizing. They said that they had some of the ointment with which Mary Magdalen anointed the feet of the Lord, and they always pour in oil to the amount they take out, and they knead it into their bread. For all the Eastern (Christians) put grease into their bread instead of yeast, or else butter or sheep's tail fat or oil. They also say that they have some of the flour with which was made the bread that the Lord consecrated, and they put back in it as much as they take out; and they have a room beside the choir, and an oven where they bake the bread, which they must consecrate with great devotion.[115]

From the account found in Rubruck, it is clear that the East Syriac church in Mongol territory developed undisturbed from Western influence and practiced indigenous expressions of theology and liturgy. The nomadic cultural

---

[114]Marco Polo, *Book of the Marvels of the World*, ed. Henry Yule (New York: Cambridge University Press, 2010), 1:169.
[115]William of Rubruck, *The Journey of William of Rubruck to the Eastern Parts of the World, 1253–55*, ed. William Woodville Rockhill (London: Hakluyt Society, 1900), 213-14.

background to Central Asian culture created a special affinity for the wandering Hebrews of the Old Testament. Jesus was portrayed as a powerful shaman, and the consumption laws regarding meat and alcohol during communion were appealing to Mongols. This was in contrast to Buddhist or Muslim prohibitions regarding these practices. The symbol of the cross fit into Mongol cosmology as representing the four directions of the world.[116]

With the acceptance of Christianity by Ariq-böga, son of Tolui, the Mongol Empire had its first Christian emperor in the line of Genghis Khan. After the death of his brother and Khan Möngke, Ariq-böga attempted, unsuccessfully, to claim authority over the Mongol Empire, which ultimately fell to his brother Kublai Khan. While the extent of Mongol authority reached its high point under Kublai Khan, the beginning of Mongol disunity began at the contention between Kublai and his brothers at the time of his ascension. Mongol territory was eventually conquered by the emperor of the Chinese Ming dynasty, Zhu Yuanzhang, in 1368. Only two years later, central Mongol territory was conquered by the newly ascendant Islamic Timurid Empire led by the Turco-Mongol Timur Lenk (or Tamerlane). After consolidating power across Central Asia, Tamerlane proceeded to enact one of the greatest persecutions of Christians in the history of the Church of the East.[117] Christians across Central Asia were slaughtered in mass numbers, which ended Christianity there. The Christian tradition across the Central Asian steppe lasted almost a millennium and was rooted in nations and languages often unheard of in Western circles, attesting to the strength and diversity of the gospel movement across various Asian contexts.

CHINA

As with other regions across Asia in Late Antiquity, Christianity first entered China through the missionary efforts of East Syriac travelers along the Silk Road. This occurred during the Tang dynasty (618–907), commonly considered the "Golden Age" of Chinese history, technology, and culture. The beginning of the Tang dynasty entailed the reopening of Silk Road commerce to China that had previously been closed due to military conflicts

---

[116]Weatherford, *Genghis Khan*, 29.

[117]Aptin Khanbaghi, *The Fire, the Star and the Cross: Minority Religions in Medieval and Early Modern Iran* (New York: Tauris, 2006), 89.

between China and East Turkestan (modern Xinjiang).[118] The gospel message first reached the Tang capital of Chang'an (Xi'an) during the reign of the dynasty's second emperor, Taizong, who was one of the most influential and successful emperors in Tang and in all of Chinese history. As an expert statesman and scholar, Taizong expanded China's borders, established Xi'an as the world's most populous city at the time, and was actively engaged in religious and philosophical discourse. Soon after the reign of Taizong, the Big Wild Goose Pagoda, which housed sutras (religious writings) and was one of the largest libraries in the world, was built. While the founder of the Tang Dynasty and Taizong's father, Gaozu, repressed foreign religions such as Buddhism, Taizong displayed great interest in foreign religious teachings. A central belief undergirding much of Tang political values was that cultural pluralism and interreligious dialogue strengthened the Chinese Empire.[119] Therefore, when a Persian East Syriac Christian named Alopen arrived at the imperial court in Xi'an in 635, he was welcomed.

The history and missionary activity of Alopen in China is recorded in the most significant witness for ancient Chinese Christian history—the Xi'an Stele, also called the Nestorian Stele. This magnificent work of limestone—standing over nine feet tall—was created in 781 and tells of the beginning of Christianity in China, primarily in the Chinese language with some Syriac autographs and footnotes.[120] The Syriac identifies a certain priest from Turkestan named King-Tsing as the architect of the tablet.[121] In the year 845, Tang emperor Wuzong began severely persecuting foreign religions in an attempt to promote Chinese identity and religious movements (Confucianism/Taoism). While Buddhists were the primary target of this persecution, Manicheans, Zoroastrians, and East Syriac Christians also suffered. It is likely this persecution caused the stele to be buried, and it remained hidden until local workers discovered it around the year 1625.

---

[118]Li Tang, *A Study of the History of Nestorian Christianity in China and Its Literature in Chinese* (Frankfurt: Peter Lang, 2001), 78.

[119]Xu Longfei, *Die nestorianische Stele in Xi'an: Begegnung von Christentum und chinesischer Kultur* (Bonn: Borengässer, 2004), 29.

[120]Stone monuments were common in Tang China as extremely expensive ways that families, villages, and religious communities could narrate their history and propagate their commemoration; Johan Ferreira, *Early Chinese Christianity: The Tang Christian Monument and Other Documents* (Strathfield: St. Paul's Publications, 2014), 140. The Christian stele is now in a museum in Xi'an with many other steles from the same region.

[121]King-Tsing, *The Nestorian Tablet*, in *The Sacred Books and Early Literature of the East*, ed. A. Wylie (London: Parke, Austin, and Lipscomb, 1917), 12:382.

The stele begins with a summary description of core biblical doctrines including the Trinity, creation, sin, affirmation of both Old and New Testament canonicity, and the life and ministry of Jesus. Support for orthodox Christian theology is clear while other religious communities are critiqued:

> Three hundred and sixty-five sects followed each other in continuous track, inventing every species of doctrinal complexity; while some pointed to material objects as the source of their faith, others reduced all to vacancy, even to the annihilation of the two primeval principles, some south to call down blessings by prayers and supplications, while others by an assumption of excellence held themselves up as superior to their fellows.[122]

While orthodox Christian theology was upheld and referred to as *jingjiao* ("illustrious religion"), it was still contextualized in dialogue with the various religions that were prevalent in medieval China (Taoism, Buddhism, Confucianism). In fact, the term *jing* ("great," "illustrious") had significant currency in classical Chinese literature and philosophy as it indicated the supremacy of a particular *jao* ("way," i.e., religion). In this regard, earliest

Figure 4.4. Top of the Tang Christian Monument (Nestorian Stele) in the Beilin Museum in Xi'an, China

---

[122]King-Tsing, *Nestorian Tablet*, 382.

Christians went to greater lengths to contextualize their message for local Chinese culture. By contrast, Manicheans simply referred to their Persian leader Mani in reference to their religion.

The situation changed when Chinese imperial documents began to refer to *jingjiao* as the *daqin jiao* ("Roman religion"). Moving from the deeply contextualized *jingjiao* to the "Roman religion" even caused a distaste for this name among many Chinese Buddhists.[123] Many of the Chinese scholars who examined the tablet after its seventeenth-century discovery had difficulty associating the *jingjiao* religion described in it with the contemporary European

Figure 4.5. Copy of the top of the Tang Christian Monument, showing the common Church of the East cross emerging from the lotus flower

Christianity introduced by seventeenth-century Jesuits like Matteo Ricci.[124] The cross is described as a "means for determining the four cardinal points" and God is accredited with the creation of the "two principles of nature," "three constant principles," and "the extent of the eight boundaries."[125] Indeed, the top of the stele presents a cross emerging from a lotus flower—a common symbol representing life in Buddhist imagery.

As the Church of the East spread into India, Central Asia, and China, the image of the cross emerging from a lotus flower was very common. In Buddhism, the lotus represents nirvana (Enlightenment), as it is rooted in the mud but emerges to form a beautiful flower. This symbol also indicates divinity and Buddhahood. The appropriation of this symbol by Asian

---

[123]Zhang Xiaogui, "Why Did Chinese Nestorians Name Their Religion Jingjao?" in *Winds of Jingjiao: Studies on Syriac Christianity in China and Central Asia*, ed. Li Tang and Dietmar W. Winkler (Vienna: Lit Verlag, 2016), 300.

[124]Michael Keevak, *The Story of a Stele: China's Nestorian Monument and Its Reception in the West, 1625-1916* (Hong Kong: Hong Kong University Press, 2008), 11.

[125]King-Tsing, *Nestorian Tablet*, 382.

Christians is a masterful contextualization of the human and divine natures of Christ. While the cross atop the lotus flower was common in China as well, the Taoist context of China also led to Christians creating crosses on top of clouds. Because of the emphasis on heaven, the sky and clouds in Taoism iconography functioned in a similar fashion as an indication of divinity. Ancient Chinese crosses would often be drawn on top of clouds and sometimes even on a combination of lotus flowers and clouds.[126]

Alopen is reported to have arrived from "Daqin"[127] at the court of Taizong in 635 bearing sacred books: "The Emperor sent his Prime Minister, Duke Fang Hiuen-ling; who, carrying the official staff to the west border, conducted his guest into the interior; the sacred books were translated in the imperial library, the sovereign investigated the subject in his private apartments; when becoming deeply impressed with the rectitude and truth of the religion, he gave special orders for its dissemination."[128] Alopen's act of seeking alliance and permission from the imperial court allowed Christianity to thrive in Tang China and demonstrated contextualization to local culture with regard to the value placed on imperial authority.[129] Taizong hailed Christian theology as "purely excellent and natural" and "advantageous to mankind," calling for the promotion of Christianity throughout China and the construction of a "Syrian church" in the capital city of Xi'an.[130]

---

[126]Xiaojing Yan, "The Confluence of East and West in Nestorian Arts in China," in *Hidden Treasures and Intercultural Encounters: Studies on East Syriac Christianity in China and Central Asia*, ed. Dietmar W. Winkler and Li Tang (Wien: Lit Verlag, 2009), 387. The position of the cross above the lotus—and sometimes above dragons in Chinese Christian graves—indicates the supremacy of Christianity over the Buddhist and Taoist concepts to which Chinese Christians adapted the teachings of Scripture. The theology of the stele should be thought of as contextualization rather than "synthesis." Christoph Baumer, *Frühes Christentum zwischen Euphrat und Jangtse: Eine Zeitreise entlang der Seidenstraße zur Kirche des Ostens* (Stuttgart: Urachhaus, 2005), 222.

[127]The Chinese name for the Roman Empire. It is likely that the Chinese tendency to refer to Christianity as originating from the Roman Empire was part of a growing alliance between China and Byzantium in the eighth century. However, the Syriac of the Tang Monument displays less *romanitas* as the Syriac-speaking writers would have been aware of Chinese Christianity's Persian origins. Samuel N. C. Lieu, "The 'Romanitas' of the Xi'an Inscription," in *From the Oxus River to the Chinese Shores: Studies on East Syriac Christianity in China and Central Asia*, ed. Li Tang and Dietmar W. Winkler (Vienna: Lit Verlag, 2013), 130.

[128]King-Tsing, *Nestorian Tablet*, 384.

[129]Ferreira, *Early Chinese Christianity*, 354.

[130]King-Tsing, *Nestorian Tablet*, 385.

It is interesting that, from the Chinese perspective in the Far East, Christianity was seen as a "Syrian" religion.[131]

The stele reports the beginning of persecution of Christians by Buddhists at the turn of the eighth century resulting in the desecration of churches and liturgical objects. Competition between the two religions comes forth clearly from the stele as the superiority of Christianity is writ boldly: "Even among the most pure and self-denying of the Buddhists, such excellence was never heard of."[132] Tang emperors were reported to be supportive of Christians as reparations were made for the damage done to Christian property. Liturgical items were even provided by the emperors, and churches were reported to be in existence in every major city in China. Alopen was elevated to the highest position over the Chinese church and enjoyed a place at the imperial court. Tang sources also corroborate the presence of Christians during this period. The Xi'an stele reproduced an imperial edict from 638 allowing the diffusion of *jingjao* ("Christianity") throughout China. While the original edict is lost, it was reproduced in a collection of Tang imperial edicts called the *Tang hui yao* in 961.[133] It was during this time that a particular temple near Xi'an is supposed to have come under Christian usage.[134]

During or shortly after the ministry of Alopen another significant development in Chinese Christianity occurred. At the turn of the twentieth century, a Taoist priest named Wang Yuanlu stumbled on a sealed-off library cut into the mountains of Dunhuang—an ancient oasis town along the Silk Road. Dunhuang was settled in the late second century BCE under the Han dynasty and served as a vital commercial, military, and cultural outpost

---

[131]This changed, however, when in the late eighth century Tang emperor Xuanzong decreed that *jingjao* ("Christianity")—which had been known as a Persian religion—should now be known as a Roman (*Da Qin*) religion since it entered Persia from the Roman Empire (Tang, *Nestorian Christianity*, 93). The perception of Christianity as a Persian religion did not entirely fade, as the collection of Tang imperial documents written in the tenth century, *Tang hui yao*, still refers to Alopen as a Persian (Bosi) monk. Nicolas Standaert, *Handbook of Christianity in China*, vol. 1: *635–1800* (Leiden: Brill, 2001), 18.

[132]King-Tsing, *Nestorian Tablet*, 389.

[133]Standaert, *Handbook of Christianity in China*, 8.

[134]Martin Palmer, *The Jesus Sutras: Rediscovering the Lost Scrolls of Taoist Christianity* (New York: Ballantine, 2001), 39. Palmer's claim led to significant reconstruction of the pagoda and the surrounding area. A replica of the Christian stele was placed outside the pagoda as Palmer theorized the pagoda to be the site of its composition, a claim that has been challenged by more recent scholarship (Keevak, *Story of a Stele*, 136).

Figure 4.6. Mogao Caves at Dunhuang in the Gansu Province, China

Figure 4.7. Fragmentary silk painting discovered in the library cave at the Mogao Caves, from the Tang Dynasty, ninth century; depicting a Christian, perhaps Jesus

throughout various Chinese dynasties as a crucial junction point between East and West. During the fourth century CE, a confederation of over a thousand monastic caves, known as the Mogao Caves, were constructed along the mountainside. The predominately Buddhist Mogao Caves were largely untouched by the religious persecutions of Wuzong during the ninth century. The massive evidence unearthed in Dunhuang spanning Buddhist, Taoist, Confucian, Manichean, and Christian traditions suggests a significant degree of peaceful coexistence in the region. The Mogao Caves began to decline after the disintegration of the Tang dynasty and the conversion of many Central Asian people groups to Islam by the end of the tenth century. However, the Mogao Caves continued to be a pilgrimage site into modern times. Wang Yuanlu functioned as a Taoist priest at the Mogao Caves and worked to clear away sand and otherwise conserve the monastic settlements. One day Yuanlu stumbled on a door that had gone unnoticed leading to the library wherein thousands of religious manuscripts—as well as numerous statues, textiles, and icons—were stored, including the Buddhist *Diamond Sutra*, the oldest extant printed book in the world. It is likely that the library had been sealed to protect the manuscripts from raiding nomads or Islamic conquerors or simply because the space had reached its capacity.[135]

While the majority of the Dunhuang texts were Buddhist, among the other religious writings represented in its corpus were several East Syriac Christian texts written in Chinese. Together with the stele, these documents constitute the Corpus Christianorum Sinicum, or Chinese Christian literature. The authorship of these texts has often been attributed to Alopen; they offer a fascinating articulation of Christian theology in Taoist, Confucianist, and Buddhist terminology and ideology. The titles of the four principle Christian Dunhuang texts—alternatively referred to as *Jesus Sutras* or Alopen's *Documents*—include: *I-shen-lun* ("Discourses on Monotheism"), *I-t'ien-lun-ti-I* ("Discourse on the Oneness of the Ruler of the Universe"), *Shih-tsun-pu-shih-lun-ti-san* ("The Lord of the Universe's Discourse on Almsgiving") and *Hsü-t'ing Mi-shih-so-ching* ("Jesus Messiah Sutra").[136] The

---

[135]This was the view of one of the earliest European explores to Dunhuang; M. Aurel Stein, *Ruins of Desert Cathay: Personal Narrative of Explorations in Central Asia and Westernmost China* (New York: Cambridge University Press, 2014), 2:63.

[136]P. Y. Saeki, *The Nestorian Documents and Relics in China* (Tokyo: Maruzen, 1951), 113.

opening words of the *Hsü-t'ing Mi-shih-so-ching* display the synthesis of Christian theology deploying Buddhist and Taoist terminology: "All the Buddhas as well as Kinnaras and the Superintending-devas and Arhâns can see the Lord of Heaven."[137] Throughout the Dunhuang Christian texts, the Holy Spirit is referred to as the "Cool Wind" and Jesus as the "Real Buddha."[138]

Figure 4.8. Interior of the Mogao cave library discovered by Wang Yuanlu in 1900

A summary and expansion on the Ten Commandments is contextualized for a Tang audience, and the *Hsü-t'ing Mi-shih-so-ching* provides a uniquely Chinese Christian response that both critiques Chinese emperor worship as well as the Buddhist anti-emperor-worship movement: "If people should fear the Lord of Heaven, they ought to stand in awe of the Sacred Superior [i.e., the Ruler] also. The previous state of existence of the Sacred Superior and His opulence and happiness all have been assigned and appointed by the Lord of Heaven."[139] A unique description of the nativity is also provided in the Dunhuang texts:

> Seeing such was their manner of living, the Lord of Heaven took great pity on them and admonished them to do good deeds, and not to trust to (the old teaching). The Lord of Heaven, therefore, made "the Cool Wind" [the Holy Spirit] to enter a virgin named Mo-yen [Mary]. Hereupon, the "Cool Wind" entered the body of Mo-yen in accordance with the instruction of the Lord of Heaven. Suddenly Mo-yen became pregnant. . . . After her conception, Mo-yen gave birth to a son named I-shu [Jesus], whose father was the above-mentioned "Cool Wind." . . . And when I-shu Mi-shih-ho [Jesus the Messiah] was born, all the people of the world saw bright signs in heaven and earth.[140]

The Dunhuang texts adapted Christian theology to the Chinese context in which emperor veneration and family allegiance were tantamount. These

---

[137]*Hsü-t'ing Mi-shih-so-ching*, ed. P. Y. Saeki. In *The Nestorian Documents and Relics in China* (Tokyo: Maruzen, 1951), 127.
[138]*Hsü-t'ing Mi-shih-so-ching*, 130.
[139]*Hsü-t'ing Mi-shih-so-ching*, 133.
[140]*Hsü-t'ing Mi-shih-so-ching*, 140-41.

ancient Christian texts retain the biblical doctrine of the supremacy of God's rule while also highlighting respect for the emperor and one's parents. Likewise, the Dunhuang texts display no interest in the christological controversies that occupied the attention of the Roman and Persian churches but focused primarily on the teachings of Jesus in the Gospels.[141] The Christian *Sutra on Mysterious Rest and Joy* displays striking adaptation of Taoist and Buddhist philosophy. The author of this sutra imagines Jesus to speak the following instructions to Simon Peter:

> In order to cultivate the superior way, first eliminate movement and desire. If you have no movement and no desire, you will not seek and you will not act. If you have no seeking and no action, you will be able to be clear and pure. If you can be clear and pure, you will be able to understand and be enlightened. If you can understand and be enlightened, then you will comprehensively illuminate all surroundings. To comprehensively illuminate all surroundings is the cause for rest and joy.[142]

Tang-era China greatly prized Taoism as the primary religion of China. However, Taoism of this period was, in turn, greatly influenced by Mahayana Buddhism. The common philosophical values of nonaction and nondesire leading to enlightenment were core principles of Taoist and Buddhist religious life.

During his short reign in the mid-ninth century, Tang emperor Wuzong began a campaign of persecution primarily targeting Buddhism. Because of their tax-exempt status and significant expenses incurred due to military campaigns, Wuzong began to demand taxes of Buddhist monks and nuns as well as force them into lay life. Even though Buddhism had been regarded in China as one of the "three religions," Confucianism and Taoism enjoyed primacy in Chinese society.[143] Buddhism (as well as Manichaeism, Zoroastrianism, and East Syriac Christianity) was disfavored because of its foreign

---

[141]Tang, *Nestorian Christianity*, 139. While Tang critiques the use of the Chinese word *Fo*—typically used to describe one who has achieved Enlightenment and become a Buddha—in reference to God in the Dunhuang texts, his ultimate conclusion is that Tang Christianity should not be thought of as syncretistic (142); see also Ferreira, *Early Chinese Christianity*, 352.

[142]Stephen Eskildsen, "Parallel Themes in Chinese Nestorianism and Medieval Daoist Religion," in *Jingjiao: The Church of the East in China and Central Asia*, ed. Roman Malek (Sankt Augustin: Institut Monumenta Serica, 2006), 61.

[143]Tang, *Nestorian Christianity*, 80.

status, while Taoist and Confucian values were upheld. The destruction of thousands of Buddhist temples and Christian churches resulted in a diminishment of both religions in China from which they never fully recovered. By the tenth century, Christianity had become all but extinct in China. The late tenth-century Muslim historian Ibn al-Nadim in his *Kitāb al-Firhrist* notes the perspective of an Arabian Christian missionary to China:

> I asked him for some information concerning his travels, and he answered that Christianity had become extinct in China. The Christians who had been in that country had perished in different ways, the church that had been built for them had been destroyed and there remained not one single Christian in China. The monk, not having found any one whom he could aid by his ministry, had returned more quickly than he went.[144]

While a dwindling Christian presence in the tenth to twelfth centuries is plausible, Chinese Christianity experienced a resurgence in the thirteenth century with the conquest of the Mongols.

Much like the neighboring Central Asian communities to the West, the Chinese church underwent a renewal due to the religious tolerance of the Mongolian Empire established by Genghis Khan. With the rise of this empire came a second wave of Christian presence that preceded European missions. During the Mongol Yuan dynasty of the thirteenth and fourteenth centuries, Chinese imperial documents referred to Christians, regardless of creed, as *Yelikewen*.[145] The increased presence of Christians across Asia during this period resulted in unprecedented contact between East and West. In the mid-thirteenth century, the first European missions arrived in China. However, the Franciscan missions to Yuan China were not as successful as the reemergent East Syriac church.[146] Perhaps the most significant witness of late medieval Christianity in China is the history regarding the thirteenth-century diplomat, explorer, and monk named Rabban (Syriac for "Master") bar Sawma (Syriac for "Son of Fasting").[147]

---

[144]Évariste Régis Huc, *Christianity in China, Tartary and Thibet* (London: Longman, Brown, Greek, Longmans, and Roberts, 1857), 101.

[145]Standaert, *Handbook of Christianity*, 44.

[146]Standaert, *Handbook of Christianity*, 46.

[147]The biography of Rabban Sawma indicates that his parents fasted due to their barrenness and gave him this name in celebration of their heir at his birth. *History of Mar Yahballaha*, ed. E. A. Wallis Budge, in *The Monks of Kublai Khan Emperor of China: Medieval Travels from China Through Central Asia to Persia and Beyond* (New York: Tauris, 2014), 125.

A Chinese native of Beijing, Rabban Sawma traveled from his homeland as far west as France at the behest of the Mongolian khan Arghun and the East Syriac patriarch Mar Yahballaha III during the 1280s. While Marco Polo is likely the best-known traveler during this period, Rabban Sawma completed his journey before Marco Polo and provides a rarer perspective of the West looking from the East.[148] Rabban Sawma recorded his unique observations of his travels through East Asia, Central Asia, Persia, the Middle East, and Europe in a Syriac text typically named the *History of Yahballaha III*. The *History* recounts the travels of Rabban Sawma as well as the life of his student Rabban Mark, who later became the East Syrian patriarch and took the name Mar Yahballaha III.

Born in an educated Christian family, Rabban Sawma disappointed his parents greatly when he sold his possessions and gave the proceeds to the poor, renounced his plans of betrothal, and entered the monastic life.[149] Rabban Mark was a native of the central Shanxi province of China and came under the monastic apprenticeship of Rabban Sawma. The two men desired to visit the holy sites of Jerusalem, and they set out on a journey in which they attested to the presence of Christians in various Central Asian communities, including Western Xia, Hotan, and Kashgar. Rabban Sawma and Mark visited the East Syrian patriarch Mar Denha I in the Persian province of Adhôrbîjân (modern Azerbaijan). The patriarch Denha commissioned the two monks to obtain *pukdânê*—a Syriac term for documents confirming the patriarch's ecclesiastical rank—from the Mongol emperor Hulagu Khan. After Rabban Sawma and Rabban Mark successfully obtained the *pukdânê* from Hulagu Khan, they visited the holy sites of Baghdad, Seleucia-Ctesiphon, Beth Garmai, Nisibis, Armenia, and Georgia. Though the author of the *History* is unknown, it is clear that the intention was to exhibit the prominence and extent of the Church of the East.[150]

After being inhibited from visiting Jerusalem due to high crime rates along the roads, Rabban Mark received the title Yahballaha and was named the Metropolitan bishop of *Katî* (northern China). The two men remained

---

[148]For this reason, Rabban Sawma has been called the "Nestorian Marco Polo from Asia" (Baumer, *Frühes Christentum*, 230).
[149]*History of Mar Yahballaha*, 127.
[150]Halbertsma, *Early Christian Remains*, 25.

in northern China, where they endured a season of persecution from the Muslim khan Ahmad[151] until the ascension of Arghun Khan in 1284. Arghun desired to form an alliance with Western Christian rulers, which resulted in Rabban Sawma's next expedition:

> For his [Yahballaha's] affection for the house of King Arghon was very warm, because Arghon loved the Christians with this whole heart. And Arghon intended to go into the countries of Palestine and Syria and to subjugate them and take possession of them, but he said to himself, "If the Western Kings, who are Christians will not help me I shall not able to fulfil my desire." Thereupon he asked the Catholicus to give him a wise man, "one who is suitable and is capable of undertaking an embassy, that we may send him to those kings." And when the Catholicus saw that there was no man who knew the language [Greek] except Rabban Sawma, and knowing that he was fully capable of this, he commanded him to go [on the embassy].[152]

Rabban Sawma then arrived in *Bêth Rômâyê* ("territory of the Romans") and then was welcomed in Constantinople by Byzantine emperor Andronicus II. After visiting various relics and holy sites in Constantinople, Rabban Sawma departed for the territory of the *Prôgâyê* ("Franks").

Rabban Sawma arrived in Naples and then journeyed to Rome, where he was welcomed in the Church of Peter and Paul in the Vatican. There he had a lengthy theological conversation with the Roman cardinals in which his ecclesiastical and doctrinal background was investigated. Rabban Sawma identified Thomas, Addai, and Mari as the apostolic founders of the Church of the East, which had subsequently spread "into the countries of the Mongols, and Turks, and Chinese."[153] Many Mongol rulers were reported to be baptized Christians who "demanded" that the Western Christian rulers aid the Mongols in recapturing Palestine.[154]

The cardinals then asked Rabban Sawma to explain the doctrinal confession of the Church of the East, and the Chinese monk provided the following explanation:

---

[151]The *History* refers to Muslims as *Hâgârâyê* ("Hagareans," or children of Hagar; *History of Mar Yahballaha*, 158).

[152]*History of Mar Yahballaha*, 165-66.

[153]*History of Mar Yahballaha*, 174.

[154]*History of Mar Yahballaha*, 174.

> I believe in One God, hidden, everlasting, without beginning and without end, Father, and Son, and Holy Spirit: Three Persons, coequal and indivisible; among whom there is none who is first, or last, or young, or old: in Nature they are One, in Persons they are three: the Father is the Begetter, the Son is the Begotten, and the Spirit proceedeth. In the last time one of the Persons of the Royal Trinity, namely the Son, put on the perfect man, Jesus Christ, from Mary the holy virgin; and was united to Him Personally [*parsôpâîth*], and in Him saved (or redeemed) the world. In His Divinity He is eternally of the Father; in His humanity He was born [a Being] in time of Mary; the union is inseparable and indivisible forever; the union is without mingling, and without mixture, and without compaction. The Son of this union is perfect God and perfect man, two Natures [*kêyânîn*], and two Persons [*kênômîn*]— one parsôpâ [*prosōpon*].[155]

Despite the fact that Christology had been the most significant theological variance between the Church of the East and both the Chalcedonian and Miaphysite formulas, the Roman cardinals responded to Rabban Sawma's confession by pressing more deeply not into Christology but the more recent theological issue between the Roman West and Byzantine East—namely, the question of the procession of the Holy Spirit. However, when asked the position on whether the procession of the Holy Spirit comes from the Father or the Son—a question which had occupied the theological attention of the Western Christian world at this time—Rabban Sawma displays autonomy by recentering the conversation on procession in the context of the East Syriac concept of *kyanē* (natures). Rabban Sawma respectfully pushes back against the idea that the Father and the Son are the cause of the Spirit because it is incongruous with the East Syriac doctrine of their fundamental unity in *kyanē* and *qnomē*: "It is not right that to something which is one, two, or three, or four causes should be [assigned]; on the contrary I do not think that this resembleth our Confession of Faith."[156] While Rabban Sawma indicates the incompatibility of the two confessions, Western Christians expressed unity between the churches at various times in the text. When Rabban Sawma later traveled to England and France, both kings enthusiastically agreed to the alliance against the Muslims, and the king of England

---

[155]*History of Mar Yahballaha*, 175.
[156]*History of Mar Yahballaha*, 177.

proclaimed that "there are not two Confessions of Faith, but only one Confession of Faith, namely, that which confesseth Jesus Christ."[157] Likewise, when Rabban Sawma met the Roman pope and agreed to celebrate the Eucharist at the Vatican in the East Syriac tradition, the Roman populace exclaimed that "the language is different, but the use is the same."[158] Rabban Sawma's agency is further demonstrated as he suggested that the theological interlocution—by which the Roman cardinals were impressed—come to an end and the officials give him access to the holy sites and relics in Rome. This text depicts the autonomy and expansive presence that the East Syriac church experienced in East Asia during the reign of the Mongols.

Christianity began to decline in Central and East Asia at the beginning of the fourteenth century due to Islamic persecution. The *History* points to this as Mar Yahballaha endures persecution and imprisonment at the hands of Islamic officials under the rule of Öljeitü Khan, who, though baptized a Christian, eventually converted to Islam. Interestingly, the text displays little direct critique of the emperor but instead attributes the difficulties of the Christians to other leaders in the Mongolian government who were hostile to Christianity. The *History* deploys a rhetorical strategy casting the East Syriac patriarch Yahballaha as a "lover of the Mongolian kingdom" in contrast to the Muslim opponents instigating Christian persecution whom the text refers to as *yâjâyê* ("enemies") of the Mongolian kingdom.[159] However, the anti-Christian campaigns under Tamerlane soon after the time of Yahballaha resulted in the decimation of Christian communities in China.[160]

The East Syriac and Franciscan missionaries who had been working in China since the mid-thirteenth century began to disappear. Christians experienced difficulty gaining a foothold in China in the first place largely due to economic inferiority compared to Buddhists.[161] After the dissolution of Mongol control of China and the rise of the Ming dynasty in the mid-fourteenth century, religions considered to be contrary to Chinese identity

---

[157]*History of Mar Yahballaha*, 187.

[158]*History of Mar Yahballaha*, 190.

[159]*History of Mar Yahballaha*, 265.

[160]Baumer, *Frühes Christentum*, 234. The fourteenth century is also the end of the production of material evidence for Chinese Christianity. Philip G. Rott, "Christian Crosses from Central Asia," in Malek, *Jingjao*, 398.

[161]Ge Chengyong, "The Live Style of Nestorian Preachers and their Cultural Influence on China During the Tang Dynasty," in Malek, *Jingjiao*, 174.

—namely Islam and, more so, Christianity—were expelled from China. By the time of the arrival of Western Jesuit missionaries such as Francis Xavier to China in the mid-sixteenth century, the nearly millennium-old Christian tradition that had developed in China by East Syriac missionaries had faded away.[162]

---

[162]The earliest Jesuit missionaries to China during the fifteenth-century reported the remnants of what Chinese citizens referred to as *shizi huihui* ("*Huihui* of the cross"—*huihui* being the traditional term for Muslim) (Standaert, *Handbook of Christianity*, 97). Earliest Western perceptions of the Tang Monument ranged from alleging it to be a forgery to calling it a witness to early Roman Chalcedonianism, both sides of which ignore the East Syriac theology of earliest Chinese Christianity. Glen L. Thompson, "How *Jingjiao* Became Nestorian: Western Perceptions and Eastern Realities," in Tang and Winkler, *From the Oxus River*, 430.

Conclusion

Following Jesus the Way He Made Us

The origins of early Christianity in the non-Western world have far-reaching missiological, historical, and theological implications. Contemporary Christians in the non-Western world must be familiar with and engage the contextualization efforts of ancient African, Middle Eastern, and Asian Christians. As this historical survey has demonstrated, the perseverance and demise of ancient African, Middle Eastern, and Asian Christianity is significantly related to the degree of ownership and autonomy experienced in church growth. There emerge two crucial principles from this brief survey: the missiological primacy of contextualized theology and autochthonous leadership. As seen in the examples of musical, theological poetry in Syriac; monolithic churches in Lalibela; and Chinese crosses atop clouds and lotus flowers, earliest Christianity in Asia and Africa was deeply contextualized by indigenous Christian leaders. These two elements essential for church growth among specific communities should be thought of as the two wings of effective missional practice.

THE URGENCY OF CONTEXTUALIZATION

All theology is contextual; it is impossible to interpret the Scriptures or speak about God apart from one's historical-cultural context. Yet the common assumption is that theological and ministerial production emerging from the dominant white culture should be seen as normative, free from the situatedness of cultural specificity. The common phrase "ethnic food" typically refers to food emerging from cultures not including the dominant white, American one. In like manner, nonwhite churches are called "ethnic churches," and theology produced by nonwhite communities is identified with ethnic/racial monikers (black theology, mujerista theology, womanist theology, etc.). Theology emanating from white men, however, is simply theology. Perceived to be unencumbered by the limited applicability of minority theology, it is the normative standard by which Christian orthodoxy is measured.

The tendency for Western culture to act as the barometer of Christian orthodoxy is a trend that reaches back to the Romanization of Christianity. It is important to recognize and lament the reality of the Western, white cultural captivity of Christianity and for the people of God to take responsibility for the genocide wrought on countless millions in the name of (Western) Christianity. It is equally incumbent to recall that the Christian faith did not have its beginnings—nor the totality of its history—embedded in white supremacy. In this way, the Western epistemological framework is not unavoidable in approaching the Christian tradition.[1] This point is crucial, as contemporary non-Western non-Christians can easily dismiss the rapid growth of Christianity in the non-Western world as simply a function of Western colonialism and US American globalization. For this reason, it is important for church historians and missiologists to responsibly recount the cultural roots of Christianity. David Bosch erroneously refers to the first centuries of Christianity as a transition "from a Jewish into a Greco-Roman religion." Bosch's historiography is as dangerous as it is incomplete. The argument that Christianity is essentially a Roman religion that was advanced by Neo-Platonist apologists and established by Constantine is common among new religious movements in the African-American community that are decadently critical of Christianity. Bosch's conception of late antique Christianity as a "Hellenistic Paradigm of Missions" ignores the expansive early Persian Christian missionary activity that operated free of the Hellenistic world.[2] Cognizance of Christianity's deep African and Asian roots dispels the common sense of the indebtedness of Christianity to the Western world. Rather, early African and Asian Christianity provides an entry point

---

[1] William A. Dryness and Oscar García-Johnson, *Theology Without Borders: An Introduction to Global Conversations* (Grand Rapids: Baker Academic, 2015), 15.

[2] David J. Bosch, *Transforming Mission: Paradigm Shifts in Theology of Mission* (Maryknoll, NY: Orbis, 2002), 190.

free from Western dominance for a contemporary non-Western convert to Christianity.[3] Even a brief survey of non-Western Christianity renders the assumption of Christianity being a Western religion untenable.

In the same way, familiarity with the variegated articulations of Christian orthodoxy demonstrates the theological elasticity of the church's God-talk. The Scriptures testify to the tension between universal truth and cultural relativism in which the church must bear faithful witness. Upon realizing that God equally embraced Gentiles on the basis of grace through faith apart from adherence to Jewish customs, the apostle Peter proclaimed: "I now realize how true it is that God does not show favoritism but accepts from every nation the one who fears him and does what is right" (Acts 10:34-35). Along with Paul and Barnabas, Peter quickly had the opportunity to apply this lesson at the Jerusalem Council where the apostles persuaded the council to remove circumcision—and general adherence to Jewish customs— as a prerequisite for membership in the Christian church: "It is my judgment, therefore, that we should not make it difficult for the Gentiles who are turning to God" (Acts 15:19). The letter sent to Gentile believers expressed the council's intention to adhere to the desire of the Holy Spirit to place no further "burden" on their fellow Christians (Acts 15:28). The missiological implications of the Jerusalem Council decision are difficult to over-emphasize. The realization that God has not bound his plan of restoration to the Jewish culture is why Lamin Sanneh has described the language of Christianity as translation.[4] For Sanneh, the function of translating the Christian message to local language and cultural system "gives the gospel a multifaceted pluralist character while preventing the imposition of a uniform, monolithic template."[5]

The value of cultural translation is contrasted with the damaging mis-sional practice Sanneh calls "diffusion"—the process of presenting the gospel message while imposing foreign, extrabiblical, cultural frameworks. Sanneh's work finds echoes in Andrew Walls, who speaks of an "indigenizing principle" in Christian mission: "Since God has accepted him as he is, the

---

[3]Sebastian Brock, *The Luminous Eye: The Spiritual World Vision of Saint Ephrem* (Kalamzoo, MI: Cistercian Publications, 1985), 15.

[4]Lamin Sanneh, *Translating the Message: The Missionary Impact on Culture*, 2nd ed. (Maryknoll, NY: Orbis, 2009), 56.

[5]Sanneh, *Translating the Message*, 37.

Christian mind will continue to be influenced by what was in it before. . . .
All churches are culture churches—including our own."[6] Walls goes on to
explain that the indigenizing principle is held in tension with the "pilgrim
principle," which "whispers to [the Christian] that he has no abiding city
and warns him that to be faithful to Christ will put him out of step with his
society."[7] Walls has helpfully summarized the missiological work of contextualization as a two-sided process by which Christian communities
around the world must both embrace and transform their cultural systems.
Central to the thesis of Walls and Sanneh is the biblical presentation of the
gospel expanding beyond Jewish cultural confinements to include Gentile
individuals and cultural frameworks. The missiological model advanced by
Walls and Sanneh has received some pushback in the work of Willie Jennings, who argues that Sanneh's focus on translation "nationalizes theological formation."[8] For Jennings, the conceptualization of Walls and
Sanneh is too narrow in that it fails to account for the "multiple levels of
translation" where "worlds overlap and in that overlap they are altered ir-
revocably, hybridized, and cross-pollinated."[9] Jennings perceives the his-
toriographic imagination of Walls and Sanneh as supersessionist in its
seeming denial of the centrality of Israel in God's story of salvation:

> When did we leave Israel's world? Language creates a kind of mystification in
> Sanneh's and Walls's work in which translation points to the world-constituting
> realities of language. Yet language is inside the world it constitutes. The worlds
> of Christian language are inside Israel's house. Israel's house is a space where
> people are joined in worship and where ways of life come into the communion
> of the common, of eating, sleeping and living together. And through language
> Israel's house indeed covers the entire world. Through Christian faith, new
> languages and the people who speak them are drawn into that house.[10]

Jennings's critique is rooted in a laudable—though somewhat misguided—
attempt to critique the real problem in Western theological discourse of

---

[6]Andrew Walls, *The Missionary Movement in Christian History: Studies in the Transmission of Faith* (Maryknoll, NY: Orbis, 2002), 8.
[7]Walls, *Missionary Movement*, 8.
[8]Willie James Jennings, *The Christian Imagination: Theology and the Origins of Race* (New Haven, CT: Yale University Press, 2010), 157.
[9]Jennings, *Christian Imagination*, 159.
[10]Jennings, *Christian Imagination*, 160.

resisting theological conceptualizations of identity. Jennings traces the social, political, and theological oppression embodied in the European triangular colonial enterprise to a theological imagination in which Jesus and the church have supplanted Israel as the "original constituting relation": "This boundary-less desire is to 'bring the sheep entrusted to him by God into the single divine fold,' presenting a totalizing vision that activates a thoroughgoing antiessentialist rendering of peoples. Through this rendering all peoples become simply sheep bound under paternal-ecclesial care."[11] Jennings's concern that theological supersessionism has led to the problem of white supremacy and European colonial domination is reflected in the work of J. Kameron Carter, who also sees the disassociation of Christianity from its Jewish roots as pivotal in the theological formulation of racialized thinking. For Carter, "the loss of a Jewish-inflected account—and thus a covenantal, nonracial account—of Christian identity cleared the way for whiteness to function as a replacement doctrine of creation. Hence, the world was re-created from the colonial conquests from the late fifteenth century forward in the image of white dominance."[12]

While Carter has accurately identified the effect of white theological dominance, the cause is mistakenly attributed to Gnosticism. For him it is the Gnostic tendency to denigrate the corporeal world in favor of the pneumatic, or spiritual, world that provided the foundation for the problematic exegetical practice in modern racial discourse that sustains the theological supremacy of whiteness.[13] The problem with this historical and intellectual trajectory is that Gnosticism was a heterodox movement that was eventually suppressed by the dominant church beginning in the fourth century. It is deeply problematic, therefore, to posit a continuity of thought between ancient Gnosticism and modern and postmodern white supremacist ideology. Moreover, what Jennings and Carter call "supersessionism"—and what I would prefer to more directly label as Christian anti-Semitism—was in no way unique to the Gnostics. Most of the church fathers who were considered orthodox after the fourth century expressed vehemently anti-Semitic claims and held that the "nation" of the church had supplanted the nation of Israel. The theological

---

[11]Jennings, *Christian Imagination*, 26-27.
[12]J. Kameron Carter, *Race: A Theological Account* (New York: Oxford University Press, 2008), 35.
[13]Carter, *Race*, 20.

imagination that would become dominant and informative for modern European colonists was rooted not in the schismatic Gnostics, whose influence greatly waned toward the end of Late Antiquity, but rather in the writings of the most revered church fathers. Ephrem the Syrian and John Chrysostom exemplify a decided attempt to disassociate the church from Judaism through expressions of deplorable hatred toward Jews.[14] Rather, the dominant expression of Christianity that came to power in the fourth century through the reforms of Constantine more closely reflects the contemporary theological construction of racial hierarchy. As was traced in chapter one of this book, the steady assimilation of Western Christendom to Greco-Roman norms coupled with the marginalization of non-Western expressions of Christianity gave rise to the concept of Christianity as an inherently Western religion.

Christians operating in the Roman Empire began to adopt many aspects of Greco-Roman culture including Roman racialized concepts of the "other" and cultural superiority.[15] During and after the Romanization of Christianity in the fourth century, church fathers began to adopt Roman concepts of race as blackness began to represent spiritual depravity and whiteness was held as normative and pure.[16] These cultural assumptions came from Roman culture and not from Gnosticism. Interestingly, racialized concepts from Roman culture were much more prevalent in Greek and Latin literature but are not present in Christian texts composed in African languages (i.e., Coptic, Old Nubian, Ge'ez). This is but one reason why the historical significance of early, non-Western Christianity complicates much of contemporary historiography and vernacular discourse on the origins of Christianity. As the survey of early African, Asian, and Middle Eastern Christianity demonstrates, the gospel spread in every direction from the very beginning and "indigenized" according to the local custom.

Carter and Jennings are helpful in pointing to the problematic nature of white normativity and the poverty of theological language of identity in contemporary discourse. However, the methodology of Walls and Sanneh

---

[14]Robert Michael, *A History of Catholic Antisemitism: The Dark Side of the Church* (London: Palgrave Macmillan, 2011), 24

[15]Benjamin Isaac, *The Invention of Racism in Classical Antiquity* (Princeton, NJ: Princeton University Press, 2004), 1.

[16]Gay Byron, *Symbolic Blackness and Ethnic Difference in Early Christian Literature* (New York: Routledge, 2002), 124-25.

proves more useful in dismantling white theological supremacy. Most white theologians are aware that Christianity was birthed in a Middle Eastern, Palestinian Jewish context. Yet this knowledge has not engendered a heightened degree of self-awareness and sense of how identity shapes theological discourse. However, emphasizing cultural particularity and its role in translating the message of Scripture helps to decentralize whiteness as normative and empowers non-Western believers to remove the shackles of Westernized Christianity toward the contextualized embrace of the image of God in every people group.

The cultural burdens placed on believers for centuries have grieved the Holy Spirit. The Western, white cultural captivity of the church is the single greatest obstacle for people coming to faith in Christ. While the gospel has indeed spread at unprecedented rates over the last century, it is often a Westernized expression of Christianity that fails to adopt local cultural norms and empower indigenous leadership. This dynamic only exacerbates the perception of Christianity as a Western religion. Christian organizations and denominations must not allow nearsighted enthusiasm engendered by increasing numbers of converts to derail the task of supporting indigenous, contextualized church growth. The brief historical survey provided above should serve as a reminder that a Christian tradition that fails to deeply root itself in local culture—while sometimes successful for centuries—runs the risk of fading away due to the perception of "foreignness." The ancient Christian traditions that were present in Nubia and North Africa for centuries ultimately did not survive the process of Islamicization, and it is likely not a coincidence that these ancient churches never gained a strong rootedness in local language, art, and culture. Likewise, Christianity was expelled from China twice primarily for cultural rather than theological reasons, and the perception of Christianity as a foreign, imported movement remains a dominant perception across contemporary China despite vast numbers of recent converts. If it is the desire of the church to exist deeply rooted for the long term among all nations, tribes, and tongues, it is necessary for the gospel to be stripped of any geocultural association and contextualized to particular milieu.[17]

---

[17]Some excellent examples include Cheryl Bear-Barnetson, *Introduction to First Nations Ministry* (Cleveland, TN: Cherohala, 2013); Kwame Bediako, *Christianity in Africa: The Renewal of a*

The Primacy of Indigenous Leadership

The first major schism in the Christian tradition divided the early church along geo-cultural lines due to conflicting christological formulas. The two centuries following Chalcedon entailed concerted effort to replace Miaphysite leadership in Egypt, Syria, and Arabia with Chalcedonian leadership—usually foreign bishops. Much of the breakdown between the mainstream Roman Empire and its East African and Middle Eastern provinces was the result of refusing to accept contextualized theology at variance with the dominant church and undermining the validity of local leadership. In the same way, one of the principal reasons medieval Chinese Christianity did not survive was that, despite significant efforts at contextualization, the majority of church leaders were foreigners from Persia and Sogdiana.[18] These examples point to the missiological primacy of partnering with indigenous leadership.

Foreigners and outsiders are not as well equipped as indigenous leaders with the cultural insight to guide the contextualization process. Outsiders should rather support and follow the leadership of locals who are rooted in biblical orthodoxy. Missions strategies often take their cues from Paul, who spent much of his time establishing and overseeing churches throughout the Roman world. In the first century, Christianity was a new movement and most of the believers were Jewish. It was necessary, therefore, that missionaries such as Paul be the first to bring the gospel message into a particular country or region and establish local leaders. There are several

Non-Western Religion (Maryknoll, NY: Orbis, 1995); Orlando Crespo, Being Latino in Christ: Finding Wholeness in Your Ethnic Identity (Downers Grove, IL: InterVarsity Press, 2003); Gospel of Luke and Ephesians: First Nations Version (Maricopa, AZ: Great Thunder, 2016); Justo L. González, Mañana: Christian Theology from a Hispanic Perspective (Nashville: Abingdon, 1990); Daniel I. Kikawa, Perpetuated in Righteousness: The Journey of the Hawaiian People from Eden (Kalana I Hauola) to the Present Time (Kea'au: Aloha Ke Akua, 1994); Fred Lynch, The Epic: The Coming (Hutchins, TX: Godstyle Productions, 2003); M. Sydney Park, Soong-Chan Rah, and Al Tizon, Honoring the Generations: Learning with Asian North American Congregations (Valley Forge, PA: Judson, 2012); Daniel A. Rodriguez, A Future for the Latino Church: Models for Multilingual, Multigenerational Hispanic Congregations (Downers Grove, IL: InterVarsity Press, 2011); The Sacred Road Book: North American Edition: New Testament Contemporary English Version (New York: American Bible Society, 1995); Efrem Smith and Phil Jackson, The Hip-Hop Church: Connecting with the Movement Shaping Our Culture (Downers Grove, IL: InterVarsity Press, 2005); Chan Kei Thong, Faith of Our Fathers: God in Ancient China (Shanghai: China Publishing Group, 2006); Terry M. Wildman, Sign Language: A Look at the Historic and Prophetic Landscape of America (Maricopa, AZ: Great Thunder, 2011);
[18]Tang, Mongol-Yuan China, 146.

points to consider about how Paul's missionary endeavors are interpreted and applied in contemporary missionary practice. First, the nature of the Christian faith in the twenty-first century is nothing close to the reality of the church in the first century. First-century missionaries lived in a world where the majority of the human race had literally never heard of Jesus or the gospel message. Today Christians find themselves in a world where the problem is not that the lost have not heard of Jesus; rather, not only have they heard of Jesus, but they are also familiar with the atrocities wrought by his followers in his name for the last seventeen hundred years. The twenty-first-century church is one that has indigenous Christian leaders present in all one hundred and ninety-five nations. In our mission strategies, we must stop operating as if we live in the first century and overlooking the abundant resources that exist in indigenous Christian leadership around the world. Second, Paul was both a Jew and a citizen of the Roman Empire and, therefore, can be considered an indigenous leader in the Jewish-Gentile Christian dynamic in which he ministered. Paul can indeed become a Jew to the Jews and a Gentile to the Gentiles (see 1 Cor 9:20) because his cultural hybridity enabled him to do so. Third, Paul submitted to indigenous leadership when it was present. When Paul arrived in Jerusalem, instead of coming as a leader, he submitted to the local leadership of James regarding Jewish Christians obeying Mosaic law. James and the Jerusalem Christian leadership told Paul to "do what we tell you" (Acts 21:23) and to pay for the Jewish brothers to fulfill their temple purification rites. The text reports that "the next day" (Acts 21:26) Paul obeyed the local leaders who wanted to use this as a public declaration that Paul was not encouraging Jewish believers to disregard the temple traditions. Rather than attempting to create indigenous leaders in our own image or bring them to "our table," outsiders should follow Paul's example and submit to the wisdom and directives of indigenous leaders in gospel efforts in their communities.

Missiological conversations regarding the growth of indigenous churches over the last two centuries have primarily fallen into two schools of thought: indigenization and indigeneity. A paradigm of indigenization entails the foreign missionary building a church community that is then handed off to indigenous leaders who have been trained and equipped by the missionary. The analogy often deployed in this paradigm is that which conceives of the

missionary as the "scaffolding" that is eventually taken off when the
"building" of indigenous leaders is completed.[19] The prominence of the indigenization paradigm during the nineteenth-century significantly shifted
toward indigeneity in the twentieth century. An increasing number of missiologists of the twentieth and twenty-first centuries have advocated the
paradigm of indigeneity where foreign missionaries do not plant churches
at all but provide support for indigenous leaders to plant their own churches.[20]

While I would agree that this latter model is more effective, I would like
to add a caveat and recommend *strategic indigeneity*. This means that in
addition to understanding outside missionaries' primary function as providing support for indigenous leaders, I propose that outsiders should enter
a community only if they have been invited and if strategic components are
in place that make their presence viable and not counterproductive.

MISSIONS AS CULTURAL SANCTIFICATION

Jesus' closing words as recorded in Matthew's Gospel have rightfully served
as one of the foundational passages in world missions: "Therefore go and
make disciples of all nations, baptizing them in the name of the Father and
of the Son and of the Holy Spirit, and teaching them to obey everything I
have commanded you. And surely I am with you always, to the very end of
the age" (Mt 28:19-20). However, the emphasis has inordinately been placed
on the word *go* in US evangelicalism. The word *go* appears in the past tense
in a participle form and could be translated as "having gone." It does not
appear in the imperative mood, as it is usually translated and quoted, and
therefore should be seen as a subordinate clause providing context to Jesus'
primary directive. What does appear in the imperative is Jesus' command
to "make disciples." While mission has been commonly reduced to the act
of going somewhere, the biblical text explains that God's ultimate concern
is that his chosen people are making disciples wherever they find themselves.
The object of discipleship in Matthew 28 is the *ethnē* ("nations," "peoples,"
"races"). Just as the English derivative *ethnicity* has an expansive field of reference, so too did the ancient concept of *ethnē*. Translation of the *ethnē* as

---

[19]Robert Clark, *The Missions of the Church Missionary Society and the Church of England Zenana
   Missionary Society in the Punjab and Sindh* (London: Church Missionary Society, 1904), 24.
[20]Soong-Chan Rah, "Rethinking Incarnational Ministry," *CCDATJ* 1 (2013): 31.

"nations" could be misleading, as the modern concept of the nation-state was likely not what the biblical text nor the ancient world envisioned. The Roman Empire—as well as other ancient empires—was composed of diverse *ethnē*, many of whom were present at Pentecost. Another way of defining ethnicity in antiquity and in its modern usage is as the changing boundary that ascribes in-group and out-group status and provides a shared system of symbols and meanings. Simply put, ethnicity is how human beings identify themselves and their reference point for their behavior and values.

Another way of looking at the Great Commission in Matthew 28 is as Jesus' call for believers in all times and places to disciple their ethnic identities and value systems. If ethnicity is more than just a group of people but also shared systems of beliefs governing social interaction, then the call of Jesus is not simply to make disciples of people but also of ethnic and cultural systems. It is our cultural, racial, and ethnic identities themselves that must be discipled and formed into the image of God. The mission of Christ's church in this world is one of cultural sanctification. Lamin Sanneh describes the language of Christianity as one of translation. Rather than implanting the gospel wrapped in outside cultural trappings, it is translated by taking on the vernacular idiom and cultural framework. As mentioned above, Andrew Walls describes the interaction between the gospel and cultural systems in two principles: indigenizing and pilgrim. The gospel simultaneously indigenizes itself to the local culture and reminds the church that she is a pilgrim in this world and must be out of step with culture where it conflicts with the call of following Jesus. This two-sided process of the gospel both embracing and transforming culture is the process of cultural sanctification.

The process of cultural sanctification is incumbent on all members of the Body of Christ.[21] Walls's analogy of the theater is apt for describing the necessity of cultural sanctification. The theater stage of the gospel is the universal truth, which the audience of the church views from our respective seats. The limited and specific view from our seats represents our cultural perspective, which we all have. However, in the intermission we have the opportunity to get out of our seats and see from other perspectives. Soong-Chan Rah

---

[21]Walls, *Missionary Movement*, 8.

similarly uses the analogy of a baseball game. When we're watching a baseball game, our experience is enhanced by seeing the game from the perspective of the multitude of cameras placed throughout and above the stadium. And yet, while our perspective is enhanced by learning from others, we can never fully enter into and understand the perspective of other cultural experiences. Neither should this be the goal. As each group works out our cultural sanctification with fear and trembling, the purpose of crosscultural partnership is not for us to become part of a different people group but to become better versions of ourselves. Vibrant missional partnership encourages us to more fully transform our cultural systems into the image of God, for which he has destined every nation, tribe, and tongue.

Timeline

Approximate dates of select events by region

Europe	Africa	Middle East	Asia
	Late second century Foundation of the Catechetical School of Alexandria		**Mid-second century** Abercius inscription mentions Persian Christians
200 CE			
	Anthony the Great of Egypt born		
	Councils of Carthage under Cyprian		
Constantine born	Cyprian of Carthage martyred under Emperor Valerian		Acts of Thomas reports the apostle's journey to India
300 CE			
The Great Persecution under Diocletian		Armenia adopts Christianity as the state religion	
313 Edict of Milan	Donatism rejected at Council of Arles		Persecutions recorded in *Acts of the Persian Martyrs* begin under Shapur II
325 Council of Nicaea		Georgia adopts Christianity as the state religion	Aphrahat begins writing *Demonstrations*
	Frumentius ordained first patriarch of Ethiopian Church under King Ezana	Biography of a monk named Jonah mentions a monastery in Qatar	Persian Christians led by Thomman Kinnān arrive in India
		Ephrem the Syrian flees to Urhoy after Persian conquest of Nisibis	
381 Council of Constantinople	Shenoute becomes leader of the White Monastery in Upper Egypt	Arab queen Mania defeats Roman forces, demands the Nicene Moses be named bishop for her people	
391 Theodosius I establishes Christianity as state religion of the Roman Empire	Augustine ordained bishop of Hippo		

Europe	Africa	Middle East	Asia
400 CE			
		Mesrop Mashtots creates Armenian alphabet and translates first Armenian Bible	
410 Rome destroyed by Visigoths	Murder of Hypatia in Alexandria	Abraham of Cyrrhus travels from Syria to Lebanon as a missionary	Synod of Isaac at Seleucia-Ctesiphon, Persian Capital where Nicene Creed was adopted and modified
	Possible date of earliest Ethiopian Garima Gospel manuscript		
431 Council of Ephesus	Silko Inscription points to Christianity in Nubia		
449 Council of Ephesus II ("Council of Robbers")			
Tome of Leo			
451 Council of Chalcedon	Patriarch Dioscorus of Alexandria exiled; Chalcedonian theology imposed on Egypt	Juvenal appointed Patriarch of Jerusalem; revolts follow	
	Timothy Aelurus writes *Against Chalcedon*		
476 Emperor Romulus Augustulus deposed by Ostrogoth Odoacer			Synod of Beth Lapat reaffirms Christology of Church of the East
			East Syriac School of the Persians moves to Nisibis under Narsai
500 CE			
	Saint Yared, legendary creator of Ethiopian liturgical style, born	Under Dhu Nuwas, Jewish kingdom of the Himyarites (Yemen) persecutes Christians	
		506 First Council of Dvin, Armenia	
		518 Justin I expels Miaphysite clergy, deposes Severus, Bishop of Antioch	
527–565 Reign of Justinian and Theodora	Justinian reconquers North Africa from the Vandals		Christianity enters Hephthalite territory in Central Asia from Persia

Europe	Africa	Middle East	Asia
	Nubian court embraces Miaphysite Christianity		Cosmas Indicopleustes describes Christian communities in India and Sri Lanka in *Christian Topography*
553 Council of Constantinople II		**554** Armenian Church breaks from Roman Church at Second Council of Dvin	
589 *Filioque* added to Nicene-Constantinopolitan Creed			
600 CE			
		607 Georgian Church splits from Armenian Church at Third Council of Dvin	Babai the Great becomes abbot of Mt. Isla monastery near Nisibis
	Persian conquest of Arabia, Syria, Palestine, and Egypt		
	Coptic Patriarch Benjamin of Alexandria deposed by Byzantine Emperor Heraclius		East Syriac missionary Alopen arrives in Xi'an, China
		636 Muslim capture of Jerusalem	Catholicos Isho'yahb II re-centers Church of the East at Karka de Beth Slokh after Arab conquest
	640–642 Muslim conquest of Egypt		
	Initiation of the *baqt* treaty between Nubian and Islamic forces	Isaac the Syrian ordained bishop of Ninevah	
680–681 Third Council of Constantinople		John Maron becomes first Maronite Patriarch	
700 CE			
	702 Muslim commander defeats Numidian Queen Dihya		
732 Franks defeat Muslims at Poitiers, Gaul			Death of John of Dailam, founder of monasteries in central Persia
			Timothy of Baghdad becomes Catholicos of Church of the East
		Syrian Theodore Abu Qurrah becomes bishop of Harran	Xi'an "Nestorian" Stele created, recording the beginnings of Christianity in China

Europe	Africa	Middle East	Asia
800–1000 CE			
800 Charlemagne crowned emperor by Pope Leo III			
			Persian Samanid emir Isma'il ibn Ahmed conquers much of Central Asia
962 Otto I establishes Holy Roman Empire	Coptic *Apocalypse of Samuel of Kalamun*		Turco-Mongol Keraites accept East Syriac Christianity
1000–1500 CE			
		Bagratid dynasty forms united Kingdom of Georgia	
1054 East-West Schism			**1071** Islamic Turkic Seljuk Empire defeats Byzantine Empire at Battle of Manzikert
1096 Pope Urban II calls for First Crusade	Construction of Lalibela		Genghis Khan gains control of Mongolian peoples
Early thirteenth century Sack of Constantinople		**Mid-thirteenth century** Bar Hebraeus serves as Maphrian of the Syrian Orthodox Church	Franciscan friar William of Rubruck travels to Mongol Empire
	Early fourteenth century Abba Estifanos begins reform movement in Ethiopia		Rabban Sawma travels west from Beijing, meets with Roman cardinals
			Mid-fourteenth century Christianity expelled from China under Ming Dynasty
	Early fifteenth century Giyorgis of Sagla writes the *Mashafa Mestir*		
Mid-fifteenth century *Dum Diversas, Romanus Pontifex*, and *Inter Caetera* issued	Zar'a Ya'qob reigns in Ethiopia, writes *Mashafa Berhan*		

Image Credits

Figure 2.9. The coins of Ebana, Aksumite gold, Classical Numismatic Group, Inc. / Wikimedia Commons

Figure 3.1. Church of Saint Jacob, photo from Livius.org / Creative Commons

Figure 3.2. Jubail Church, Saudi Arabia, photo by Harold Brockwell / Wikimedia Commons

Figure 3.3. Jubail, historical ruins, Barry Iverson / Alamy Stock Photo

Figure 3.4. Monastery of Geghard, Armenia, used courtesy of Jesse Arlen

Figure 3.5. Khor Virap Monastery, photo by Diego Delso, delso.photo, CC-BY-SA License / Wikimedia Commons

Figure 3.6. Mashtots statue, photo by Rita Willaert / Wikimedia Commons

Figure 3.7. Engraved crosses on the cave church wall at Geghard Monastery in Kotayk Province, Armenia, used courtesy of Jesse Arlen

Figure 3.8. Cave at Monastery of Geghard, Armenia, used courtesy of Jesse Arlen

Figure 3.9. Jvari Monastery, photo by Alexxx1979 / Wikimedia Commons

Figure 4.1. Nasrani cross, Kadamattom Church, Ernakulam dt. Kerala, India, photo by Jogytmathew / Wikimedia Commons

Figure 4.2. Icon from St. Thomas Cathedral, used courtesy of Blake Hartung

Figure 4.3. Wall painting, unknown artist of the T'ang Dynasty, Nestorian Temple, Palm Sunday / Wikimedia Commons

Figure 4.4. Top of Nestorian Stele in the Beilin Museum in Xi'an, China, David Castor / Wikimedia Commons

Figure 4.5. Top of Tang Christian Monument / Wikimedia Commons

Figure 4.6. Mogao Caves, photo by Zhangzhugang / Wikimedia Commons

Figure 4.7. Fragment of silk painting, Mogao Caves, Wikimedia Commons

Figure 4.8. Interior of library, Mogao Caves, photo by Aurel Stein, 1907, from "Secrets of the Cave II," *Early Tibet* (blog) / Wikimedia Commons

All other photos are by the author.

Index of People

Index of Places

Scripture Index

MISSIOLOGICAL ENGAGEMENTS

Series Editors: Scott W. Sunquist,
Amos Yong, and John R. Franke

Missiological Engagements: Church, Theology, and Culture in Global Contexts charts interdisciplinary and innovative trajectories in the history, theology, and practice of Christian mission at the beginning of the third millennium.

Among its guiding questions are the following: What are the major opportunities and challenges for Christian mission in the twenty-first century? How does the missionary impulse of the gospel reframe theology and hermeneutics within a global and intercultural context? What kind of missiological thinking ought to be retrieved and reappropriated for a dynamic global Christianity? What innovations in the theology and practice of mission are needed for a renewed and revitalized Christian witness in a postmodern, postcolonial, postsecular, and post-Christian world?

Books in the series, both monographs and edited collections, will feature contributions by leading thinkers representing evangelical, Protestant, Roman Catholic, and Orthodox traditions, who work within or across the range of biblical, historical, theological, and social-scientific disciplines. Authors and editors will include the full spectrum from younger and emerging researchers to established and renowned scholars, from the Euro-American West and the Majority World, whose missiological scholarship will bridge church, academy, and society.

Missiological Engagements reflects cutting-edge trends, research, and innovations in the field that will be of relevance to theorists and practitioners in churches, academic domains, mission organizations, and NGOs, among other arenas.